W9-CEI-961

More praise for
The Hiring and Firing Question and Answer Book:

"Anyone who serves in a supervisory role and is involved in the process of hiring and firing should read this book. In today's litigious society, the area of employee relations has become laden with legalities, making it highly important for managers to be armed with the knowledge and tools to effectively handle these responsibilities. This book presents answers to key questions in an easy-to-follow format, including valuable 'how to' examples and useful sample documents, and is a must for every manager's library."
    —Laura Verucchi Perkins, Vice President and Treasurer,
        Flin Industries, Inc.

"Once again Paul Falcone has provided the HR professional and the line manager with another 'must have' resource that's easy to use and on target. He offers the key answers to critical hiring and firing questions and explains the why in excellent 'Tell Me More' sections."
    —Peter M. Shapiro, Vice President, Human Resources,
        Electro Rent Corporation

"*The Hiring and Firing Question and Answer Book* is both highly readable and usable, providing substantial content and accessibility to pertinent information. Falcone offers the reader not only answers but alternatives, along with thoughtful rationale for doing what he suggests. The book is a great reference a reader can turn to for immediate answers, but its longer range effect on the reader is the development of a rich understanding of complexity and context in arriving at appropriate solutions. I recommend this to anyone who must deal with recruitment and termination issues."
    —Patricia Hunt, Ph.D., Director, Leadership, Management, and
        Communication Programs, UCLA Extension

"Paul has an amazing ability to take a difficult subject and explain it in a way that is understandable for a junior manager and still educational for a more experienced manager."
    —Patricia Trytten, Human Resources Consultant,
        Toyota Motor Sales, USA

THE

HIRING

AND

FIRING

QUESTION AND ANSWER BOOK

THE

HIRING

AND

FIRING

QUESTION AND ANSWER BOOK

Paul Falcone

AMACOM
American Management Association
New York • Atlanta • Chicago • Kansas City • San Francisco • Washington, D.C.
Brussels • Mexico City • Tokyo • Toronto

Special discounts on bulk quantities of AMACOM books are available to corporations, professional associations, and other organizations. For details, contact Special Sales Department, AMACOM, a division of American Management Association, 1601 Broadway, New York, NY 10019.
Tel.: 212-903-8316. Fax: 212-903-8083.
Web site: www.amacombooks.org

This publication is designed to provide accurate and authoritative information in regard to the subject matter covered. It is sold with the understanding that the publisher is not engaged in rendering legal, accounting, or other professional service. If legal advice or other expert assistance is required, the services of a competent professional person should be sought.

Library of Congress Cataloging-in-Publication Data

Falcone, Paul.
    The hiring and firing question and answer book / Paul Falcone.
        p.   cm.
    Includes index.
    ISBN 0-8144-0640-8—ISBN 0-8144-7110-2 (pbk.)
    1. Employees—Recruiting.   2. Employees—Dismissal of.   I. Title.

HF5549.5.R44 F35 2001
658.3'11—dc21
                                                        2001034087

Printing number

10   9   8   7   6   5   4   3   2   1

For **Janet**—
my wife, my best friend, and the love of my life

Contents

Chapter 5: Making the Final Selection .114

Part II: Firing

Chapter 6: Common Questions About the
Performance Management and Termination Process 141

Chapter 7: Progressive Discipline 165

Chapter 8: Terminations for Cause and Summary Offenses 196

Chapter 9: Reductions-in-Force (RIFs) and Layoffs 212

Acknowledgments

Writing a manuscript as broad as *The Hiring and Firing Question and Answer Book* takes the effort and dedication of many professionals in the various disciplines of human resources management. Attorneys, headhunters, background investigation specialists, Internet recruitment consultants, and academicians have all helped this book make its way through the editing process.

I would especially like to thank my fellow UCLA Extension instructors in the School of Business and Management: Dick Kaumeyer, principal of The Kaumeyer Consulting Group, in West Hills, California; Larry Comp, principal of Humanomics, Inc., in Granada Hills; Heather Hand, vice president of global human resources with Sunrise Medical in Carlsbad; Denise Jackson, HR professional extraordinaire; and Karen Fritz, director of human resources with the Los Angeles office of Gibson, Dunn & Crutcher LLP.

Thank you as well to my dear friends and colleagues Roger Sommer, SPHR, vice president of client relations with The McGuire Group/OI Partners, Torrance; Delonna Kaiser, human resources consultant; Frederic R. Horowitz, impartial arbitrator and mediator, Santa Monica; and Manny Avramidis, American Management Association, for all your help with selected portions of this text.

Special thanks go to my friends and gurus in the virtual recruitment world: Laura Jean Whitcomb, director of marketing communications at Advanced Internet Recruitment Strategies (AIRS), Hanover, New Hampshire, and Christopher Defoe, recruitment automation practice lead for the Hunter Group, Burlington, Massachusetts.

Most important, to my dear friend and the inspiration for this book, AMACOM's executive editor, Adrienne Hickey. Thank you, Adrienne, for your encouragement and friendship! How fortunate I am to call you my friend. Thank you as well to Christina McLaughlin, AMACOM's development editor, for your detailed and systematic approach to organizing this manuscript into a cohesive book.

You've all been wonderful mentors and friends, and I couldn't have created this book without you!

Portions reprinted with the permission of *HR Magazine* are published by the Society for Human Resource Management (www. shrm.org), Alexandria, Virginia.

Introduction

Hiring and firing issues raise more questions among managers and human resources professionals than just about any other tasks in their portfolios. Both functions are critical to the well-being of their organizations, which cannot thrive without skilled, motivated, and productive people. Other reasons for the many questions that arise about hiring and firing include:

- Both processes are fraught with potential legal problems.
- Both often involve not only hiring and firing per se but also a whole range of employee relations issues.
- Both require specific skills and knowledge that many managers do not possess, or even recognize as important.

These skills and knowledge are particularly important in a labor market that is predicted to remain tight through 2010. Whatever the fluctuations in the economy, the fact is that over the past three decades, the U.S. birth rate has dropped by 24 percent. As members of the baby boom generation retire, a much smaller number of "baby bust" workers will be ready to take their place. Simply put, employers have no choice but to become more creative in hiring *and retaining* talent and more adept at handling terminations and employee relations.

There are a lot of questions that need to be answered regarding the new-hire process. Questions about interviewing techniques, tests, background checks, classified ad recruitment, affirmative action plans and diversity outreach, and the proliferation of the Internet as a brand-spanking–new recruitment tool with untapped potential make the process a little difficult to navigate at times. And of course there are always those shadows of potential liability in the form of negligent hiring and retention claims that lurk in the back of our corporate minds should we stray too far from accepted hiring norms and practices.

In spite of these questions, hiring is fun. People put on their Sunday best and convince us that they're wonderful and that they deserve to join our company. Interviewing is like putting together pieces of a puzzle, and many of us agree that meeting new people— even in the somewhat artificial interviewing environment—still has its positive side because people are interesting. Checking references is instructive because you get to see how well you did in your interview: Were your gut feelings and instincts about the candidate on the money? Did your first impression stand up to a prior supervisor's scrutiny, or were you shocked to find that you had really missed the mark? And job offers—well, there's nothing more exciting than inviting someone to join your team.

Many aspects of employee relations, on the other hand, are not fun, such as firing or initiating disciplinary actions. It is crucial that managers know how to motivate employees, structure progressive disciplinary actions, and create written records regarding terminations for cause and layoffs. Firing is a traumatic experience for everyone involved. However, no book on employment and termination—whether written by an HR practitioner or by an employment lawyer—should make readers afraid to put their socks on in the morning. In other words, there is rarely a need to be so bogged down in "analysis paralysis" that we fail to reach a reasonable conclusion regarding how we should treat our workers. Nor should we be afraid to initiate termination or disciplinary action should we feel such action is necessary.

The purpose of this book is to give managers not only the tools they need to address serious problems but also the tools to address workplace issues before they develop into serious problems. The premises we've used are simple:

- Everyone wants to make a positive difference at work.
- People want to be treated with dignity and respect.
- People will respond in kind: They will assume responsibility for their actions when they are treated as adults and held accountable for their performance.

Remember, employees become disheartened for one of two reasons: They perceive either (1) a lack of communication with their supervisors and peers or (2) a lack of recognition or appreciation for their efforts. Employee relations problems come in a thousand different faces, but almost all issues can be boiled down to one of these two fundamental areas. It's up to us to ferret out which of these two issues is at stake in any given situation and to solve the problem proactively. The easiest way to find out is simply to ask.

Some people at certain times in their lives actually function in more of a destructive than constructive mode. They thrive on chaos and look for negative outcomes in both their personal and their work lives. As a result, they sometimes see themselves only as victims and refuse to assume any responsibility for their actions.

Although about 98 percent of workers will respond to heightened expectations once those expectations are brought to their attention, 2 percent of the population at any given time will be looking for lawsuits to fund their retirements. These peoples' actions account for long and drawn-out legal battles and sometimes rise even to the level of workplace violence.

There are times when it becomes necessary to consider ending employment as swiftly as possible. When this becomes the case, it becomes even more important to:

- Treat the employee in question with respect and dignity.
- Allow the individual to make choices and have some say in the outcome of the management intervention.

This book is written for those of us in the trenches who spend a good portion of our time hiring the best candidates for our job openings and attempting to repair the bruised egos and hurt feelings that are inevitable in any employment relationship. Recruitment and employee relations go hand in hand. In essence, if you don't hire right from the beginning, you'll be condemned to lengthy employee-relations problems with your staff over the long haul.

That's where this book comes in handy. From years of experience and interviews, I've selected the questions that seem to plague line and staff managers, hiring supervisors, human resource professionals, and recruiters. Written in an easy-to-use question and answer format, *The Hiring and Firing Question and Answer Book* gives you quick answers to these key questions, as well as more detailed discussions in the "Tell-Me-More" sections. It frames the conceptual issues before us and then proposes practical solutions, as every "how to" book should. In other words, it explains not only *what* you're supposed to do but *how* you're supposed to do it. The book also includes appendixes with sample policies, letters, and tools to help you initiate creative and effective hiring and firing practices. Check the resources section for more information about the resources cited throughout the book. Many of the legal and HR terms are defined in the glossary.

Employment law is a little more complicated than most U.S. employers realize. Usually a company's HR department is responsible for ensuring compliance. In companies without HR professionals, it becomes the job of a manager or administrative personnel. Laws are important to keep in mind, but they must also be kept in perspective. I'm not a lawyer, and I don't pretend to offer legal advice. What I have attempted to accomplish throughout this book is to provide fellow employers with the tools and vocabulary necessary to treat employees with respect and dignity and to act in compliance with key employment laws related to hiring and firing. Professional outside counsel should be sought when specific situations warrant appropriate legal analysis.

When you're confident that you're selecting the best candidates for your team, from both a technical and an interpersonal standpoint, you're simultaneously creating an environment in which your existing employees can motivate themselves. Handling difficult situations like firing and disciplining employees in a fair and humane fashion will also increase your effectiveness as an employer. Managers will be able to delegate more, and the team will work more efficiently and effectively. I hope this book becomes one small tool in your arsenal, that it helps you accomplish your goals, and that it multiplies your career progression opportunities. More important, I hope it helps you to have fun at work as you build, accomplish, and achieve on your own and through the people you supervise.

Part I
Hiring

Chapter 1

Common Questions About the Hiring Process

1. What are the key employment laws related to hiring?

The proliferation of worker protection laws over the past forty years has severely limited employers' discretion in their dealings with individual workers. To see how far we've come in the past half century, all we need to do is think back to the 1930s, when company foremen chose hungry and unemployed workers off lines outside the facility gate for a day's work. One mistake and the worker was fired—only to be replaced by the next poor soul waiting in line.

Flash ahead to the 1960s: Thirty-three Black sanitation workers were fired for seeking union representation, bringing Martin Luther King, Jr., to Memphis to meet his untimely death. Even today, labor laws are still changing to meet the needs of particular employee groups: doctors and engineers contemplate union representation to improve working conditions, wages, and benefits. The Americans with Disabilities Act continues to be refined and clarified, allowing greater benefits to American workers through stricter interpretation of its standards.

The blistering pace of technology unleashes new tools like cell phones and the Internet, which were supposed to make life easier for all of us. Instead, they just accelerated our expectations for work turnaround. Techno-stress led to workers comp stress claims and unparalleled incidents of workplace violence. The breakdown of the modern nuclear family led to the passage of the Family and Medical Leave Act (FMLA), a labor standard and leave law that mandated that employers allow employees time to take care of family medical emergencies. And on top of all this, legislators increased penalties

7

against employers by including punitive damages that could render an organization bankrupt for failing to meet any of a multitude of laws enacted to protect individuals.

Although we employers may see ourselves as the victims of the law of unintended consequences and a judiciary run amok with overly aggressive plaintiff attorneys looking for unlawful motives in even our most benevolent actions, we could all agree that we wouldn't want to go back. The twentieth century was one of stunning progress for American workers. The pace of change in our laws continues faster than ever. The key, however, remains in our finding a balance between companies' prerogatives and employees' rights.

Tell Me More

For the most part, the laws that govern our companies are fair and practical. Of course, all it takes to file a lawsuit in many venues is a typewriter and a $100 application fee. Still, we need to understand the umbrella of laws that govern the workplace, not only to avoid or minimize lawsuits but also to be perceived as fair employers who look to increase profits and productivity while respecting our workers' needs for privacy, respect, and satisfaction.

The easiest way to classify the laws that follow is according to company size. The larger your company, the more the laws that govern it. You'll find more information about these particular laws throughout the text. For now, this section will serve as a primer and overview. Remember that the legislature's intent in passing these laws was to protect American workers from company abuses; however, plaintiff attorneys will use these same statutes *against* your company as proof that you violated the law. As a result, special consideration should be given to any employee who falls within the protections of the following laws:

Company Size	Laws and Other Employment Provisions That Govern Your Company	General Guidelines
One or more employees	Federal and state wage and hour laws	When state and federal laws conflict, generally the law that is more generous to the employee must be followed. Federal wage and hour law is regulated by the Fair Labor

Company Size	Laws and Other Employment Provisions That Govern Your Company	General Guidelines
		Standards Act (FLSA) and is enforced by the U.S. Department of Labor's Wage and Hour Division.
	Equal Pay Act of 1963	The Equal Pay Act requires all employers covered by the FLSA to provide equal pay for equal work, regardless of sex.
	Sexual harassment prohibitions	Employers must take all reasonable steps to prevent harassment from occurring. Harassment on the basis of sex generally includes sexual harassment, gender harassment, and harassment based on pregnancy, childbirth, or related medical condition.
	Unemployment and disability insurance	With few exceptions, federal and state unemployment insurance laws cover all employers.
	Immigration Reform and Control Act (IRCA)—Employment Verification	Form I-9 must be completed for every employee hired after November 6, 1986, in order to verify eligibility to work in the United States
	Child labor laws	Employers generally must acquire a work permit before employing a minor.
	Time-off provisions	All states require employers to provide time off for certain activities like jury duty, voting, emergency duty as a volunteer firefighter, and military service.
	Posting and notice requirements	All employers are required to display certain posters relat-

Company Size	*Laws and Other Employment Provisions That Govern Your Company*	*General Guidelines*
		ing to harassment/discrimination, safety and health, unemployment and disability insurance, and state and federal minimum wage requirements. Other notices may include information sheets regarding sexual harassment and workers' compensation claims.
	Occupational Safety and Health Administration (OSHA)	All employers must comply with both federal and state health and safety laws.
	Uniformed Services Employment and Re-Employment Rights Act (USERRA) of 1994	Congress provides additional benefits and job protection for individuals returning to civilian employment after serving in the military (including those with military-related disabilities).
Fifteen or more employees	Title VII of the Civil Rights Act of 1964	Title VII stipulates that employers may not discriminate on the basis of race, color, religion, sex, or national origin. The Civil Rights Act of 1991 amended Title VII to include the right to jury trials and punitive damages.
	Pregnancy Discrimination Act of 1978	Broadens the definition of sex discrimination under Title VII to include pregnancy, childbirth, or related medical conditions. Prohibits employers from discriminating against pregnant women in employment benefits if they are capable of performing their job duties.

Company Size	Laws and Other Employment Provisions That Govern Your Company	General Guidelines
	Americans with Disabilities Act (ADA)	The ADA requires that companies accommodate qualified individuals with disabilities. Note that this law covers not only employees but also extends to job applicants.
Twenty or more employees	Consolidated Omnibus Budget Reconciliation Act of 1985 (COBRA) and Health Insurance Portability and Accountability Act (HIPAA) of 1996	Any employer with a group insurance plan who has twenty or more employees must extend COBRA rights to continued benefits under the plan to all qualified beneficiaries. COBRA allows employees who might otherwise lose their health coverage to continue coverage through their ex-employer's group plan at their own expense. HIPAA requires employers to provide terminating employees with a notice advising them of the availability of continued health insurance coverage.
	Age Discrimination in Employment Act of 1967 (ADEA)	Prohibits discrimination in employment against persons forty years of age or older. Exceptions are permitted where age is a bona fide occupational qualification. All public sector employers are covered regardless of the number of employees. For private sector employers to be covered, however, they must employ twenty or more employees for each working day in each of twenty or

Company Size	*Laws and Other Employment Provisions That Govern Your Company*	*General Guidelines*
		more calendar weeks in the current or preceding year.
Fifty or more employees	Family and Medical Leave Act (FMLA)	Companies are required to provide unpaid leaves of absence to a maximum of twelve weeks and to guarantee employees the right to return to their jobs if they need to tend to their own or a family member's serious health condition or to bond with a newborn child.
	Affirmative Action Plans (AAP)	Federal and state contractors with fifty employees and $50,000 or more in government contracts must develop a written affirmative action plan.
100 or more employees	Worker Adjustment and Retraining Notification Act (WARN)	Companies must provide sixty days' notice before laying off or terminating fifty or more employees

2. What's the most effective recruitment method?

If it were only that easy to decide! As nice as it would be to pull down a book like this and find the magic answer to this complicated question, the real solution lies in your company's particular hiring history. First, you need to determine both the cost-per-hire and the "source cost." Then you can determine which recruiting method is the most cost-effective for your company and your industry.

The Employment Management Association (EMA) also gives us some guidelines. Its *Cost-per-Hire and Staffing Metrics Survey* has been conducted annually since 1983 and gives the best insights into the most cost-effective recruitment practices.

Before we explore some of the figures shared in a recent EMA survey, understand that, due to limited sample size, the figures shared should not be considered statistically valid. Instead, the true value of the report lies in its multiyear trends analysis and averages. Those averages will help you predict market trends and plan appropriate recruiting strategies. As a result, the only valid metrics to track the most cost-effective recruitment methods lie in your own company's historical results.

Tell Me More

The cost-per-hire (CPH) is a simple calculation: total costs associated with the recruitment process divided by the number of full-time hires in a given period of time (typically a month). For example, if all recruitment-related expenses for a particular month totaled $10,000 and you hired eight FTEs (full-time equivalents) as a result, your CPH for that month would equal $1,250 ($10,000 divided by 8).

Most HR practitioners who track cost-per-hire differentiate between exempt and nonexempt recruitment costs. According to EMA's 2000 survey, the average cost-per-hire looks like this:

	Direct CPH	Factored CPH*
Exempt hires	$6,034	$10,057
Nonexempt hires	$361	$1,203
Total hires	$1,943	$3,886

*The Factored Cost-per-Hire includes recurring costs associated with overhead, recruiters' salaries and benefits, and management interview time. The Direct CPH, in comparison, looks only at variable "hard expenses" such as advertisement fees, search costs, and internal referral fees.

Of course, this is an average of all industries for all jobs in all sectors of the nation. Regional differences, manufacturing versus service hires, and the various recruitment sources available will dramatically impact your company's particular results.

The costs in the following table would normally be included in the CPH calculation. The cost by source is an important piece of information to consider when evaluating the success of your recruiting programs. In addition, the "source cost analysis" measures the effectiveness of each particular method. The table on the following page shows how EMA's survey ranked its members' results according to source effectiveness in 1999.

Source	Percent of Total Hires (a.k.a. Source Cost Analysis)	Average Cost-per-Hire (CPH) from Each Source
Advertising	28.9%	$1,589
Employee referrals	21.8%	$479
Contingency agencies	11.7%	$11,827
Internet	9.5%	$331
Job fairs	4.8%	$429
College recruiting	3.3%	$370
Other	18.5%	NA

Of course, there is often a tradeoff between effectiveness and cost: Contingency search firms rank third after advertising and employee referrals in terms of effectiveness, but they're the most expensive sourcing method on the list. Internal referrals and Internet ads are among the lowest in terms of cost and the highest in terms of effectiveness. (In addition, the two years since this survey was taken have witnessed a dramatic increase in successful Internet recruitment sourcing.)

That being said, the simple answer to this question is this: Beef up your internal referral programs and Internet classified advertising outreach. In most cases, there's no better place to invest your recruitment dollars. On the other hand, although the cost-per-hire for agency hires has been steadily increasing over the past ten years (to approximately $12,000), this methodology may be the most effective choice when candidates are scarce and time is of the essence.

To order a copy of the EMA's *Cost-per-Hire and Staffing Metrics Survey*, contact the Society for Human Resource Management (SHRM) in Alexandria, Virginia, at (703) 548-3440, or reach SHRM at www.shrm.org/ema. The survey is free to SHRM members and costs $45 for nonmembers.

3. What are my company's responsibilities regarding negligent hiring and retention?

Before the recent upswing in negligent hiring and negligent retention lawsuits, companies were generally held liable only for the negligent and intentional acts of their employees committed during the course and scope of employment. However, during the 1990s, the negligent hiring/negligent retention doctrine dictated that injured third parties could sue employers if an employee committed a crime even if the employee was not engaged in the furtherance of the employer's business. In other words, employers may now be generally held liable for the criminal or violent acts of their employees that occur outside the workplace, after working hours, or outside the course and scope of employment. Therefore, it is critical to conduct pre-employment background investigations before extending employment offers to job applicants. In addition, an employer's failure to take appropriate disciplinary measures against existing employees in the form of retraining, reassignment, rescheduling, or termination may likewise subject a company to legal exposure.

Hiring candidates without performing reference or background checks is like having a loose cannon on the deck of your ship. Not only do you have a legal duty to select fit and competent employees, but you should also be aware that punitive damages may be awarded if it is determined that you hired or retained an employee with a "conscious disregard of the rights or safety of others" or because you "knew or should have known of the employee's unfitness for the job." Therefore, conduct thorough reference and background checks. Likewise, the best way to combat negligent retention claims is to conduct timely and thorough investigations of complaints and to reach a reasonable conclusion.

Tell Me More

The most effective way to combat exposure to a negligent hiring claim is to conduct reference and background checks on all finalist job applicants. Whereas reference checks are business communications between companies regarding applicants' job performance track records, background checks rely on outside agencies to research court records for information related to criminal convictions, DUIs, and the like.

It's critical that you document your reference check feedback and place that information in the job requisition folder—not the new hire's personnel file. (After all, employees have access to their personnel files, and information shared by past employers about their strengths or weaknesses is confidential.) This way, should you ever be charged with negligent hiring, you can demonstrate that you acted responsibly in checking with past employers, confirming dates and titles of employment, accounting for gaps in employment, and investigating the applicant's performance history.

Background investigation reports may likewise be placed in job requisition folders. However, it is advisable to ask your background investigation company to retain all records related to individual searches. This way, there is less likelihood that the information will be misplaced or inappropriately discovered. Simply stated, there may be highly sensitive information in a background check that you simply don't want any coworkers to have access to.

Legal liability also exists when companies fail to investigate or to appropriately discipline or terminate an employee once they learn (actual knowledge) or should have learned (constructive knowledge) of an employee's criminal actions, history of drug or alcohol abuse, or other problems involving an unreasonable risk of harm to others. An employer's failure to take appropriate disciplinary action may be viewed as an authorization or ratification of the employee's conduct after the fact.

Negligent hiring and retention claims represent a serious threat to your business operations, especially if you hire individuals whose work activities may affect the health and safety of coworkers and the public (such as employees who deal regularly with customers in their homes or who operate motor vehicles). Such claims may surface any time you hire a new job applicant or learn of harm that results from an employee's negligent or reckless conduct. Treat such instances seriously by exercising reasonable care and taking appropriate remedial action before others are placed at risk.

4. What records must I keep and for how long?

Records retention is a critical part of the hiring (and for that matter, termination) process. The paper record that you create and save as an employer will help you avoid legal liability or at least reduce its risk. Federal as well as state law governs retention of information gathered or evaluated in the employee selection or termination process. Sometimes these laws stipulate conflicting requirements. As a result, you should use caution when discarding any routine or nonroutine records that will help you substantiate any employment-related decision that could later be challenged.

Tell Me More

The following laws stipulate different, and sometimes conflicting, record retention requirements:

- Title VII of the 1964 Civil Rights Act
- Fair Labor Standards Act (FLSA)
- Age Discrimination in Employment Act of 1967 (ADEA)
- Americans with Disabilities Act (ADA)
- Immigration Reform and Control Act of 1986 (IRCA)
- Unemployment insurance codes
- Employee Retirement Income Security Act of 1974 (ERISA)
- Consolidated Omnibus Budget Reconciliation Act of 1985 (COBRA)

For the sake of simplicity, we'll choose the longest time retention requirement period that these sometimes conflicting laws stipulate. For example, Title VII requires that employers retain payroll records for one year; FLSA requires three years; the Unemployment Insurance Code requires four years. Therefore, the table presented here stipulates that four years is the appropriate minimum time period to retain these records. Be aware, however, that certain records, such as pension plan documents, should be retained permanently. Speak with qualified counsel regarding your specific questions and about your state's particular requirements.

Employment Data	Retention Requirement
Job applications, resumes, and employment referral records	Two years
Help wanted advertisements, job posting notices sent to employment agencies or labor unions	Two years
Employment eligibility verification (Form I-9)	Three years
Individual employee contracts	Five years (State law governs the retention period for individual contracts and generally vary from five to fifteen years after the contract expiration.)

Employment Data	Retention Requirement
Employee personnel files, including disciplinary notices, promotions, demotions, discharge, training, tests, transfers, layoffs, or performance evaluations	Two years (although many employment experts recommend retaining such documents for seven years after an employee leaves your company)
Company policy and procedure manuals or employee handbooks	Ten years after they have been superseded or replaced by another manual or by other policies
Payroll records	Four years
Union contracts/collective bargaining agreements	Six years after contract expiration (in case the union challenges the employer on its failure to bargain properly)
Layoff selection criteria and the necessary postlayoff statistical analysis of the remaining workforce	Five years
ERISA (related to severance packages or early retirement incentive plans) notification	Six years (should actions alleging breach of fiduciary duty arise)
COBRA notification	Six years

5. How should I complete Immigration Eligibility Form I-9?

As an employer, you are responsible for completing a Form I-9 for everyone you have hired after November 6, 1986. I-9s appear to be an administrative burden for most employers, but that's because many companies fail to appreciate their responsibility in protecting our heritage of legal immigration. America has always been and will always be a melting pot, but the goal of the Immigration Reform and Control Act of 1986 (IRCA) is to ensure that American companies employ only persons who have the legal right to work in the United States. That way, illegal aliens will not displace competent, qualified American workers or undermine prevailing wage standards.

IRCA also attempts to prohibit discrimination against "protected individuals," including citizens or nationals of the United States, lawful permanent residents, temporary residents, and persons granted refugee status or asylee status. Employers may not discriminate against employees on the basis of national origin or citizenship status. Note, however, that on an individual basis, you have the right to hire a U.S. citizen or national over an equally qualified alien to fill a specific position. However, you may not adopt a blanket policy of *always* preferring a qualified citizen over a qualified alien.

Tell Me More

Specifically, the law requires that you:

1. Ensure that your new hires fill out Section 1 of Form I-9 on the day they start work.
2. Review documents that are presented to you in order to establish each employee's identity and eligibility to work.
3. Properly complete Section 2 of Form I-9 within seventy-two hours of a new hire's start date.
4. Retain Form I-9 for three years after the date of hire or one year after the person's employment is terminated, whichever is later.
5. Make Form I-9 available for inspection to an officer of the Immigration and Naturalization Service (INS), Department of Labor (DOL), or the Office of Special Counsel for Immigration Related Unfair Employment Practices (OSC) upon request.

When new hires fill out Section 1 of the I-9 form, they must be sure to sign and date the document (in the middle of the page above Section 2) on their first day of employment. Furthermore, they must be sure to check one of the three check-boxes indicating whether they are:

- Citizens
- Lawful permanent residents (i.e., those authorized to work via a green card)
- Aliens authorized to work here for a specified period of time (for example, those on H-1B worker visas)

When new hires present you with documents that establish their identity and eligibility to work, you must examine the documents personally. If they appear on their face to be genuine, you must accept them. If you unnecessarily challenge a new hire's documentation or demand more than what Form I-9 asks for, you could be engaging in an unfair immigration-related employment practice. That could be seen as a form of unlawful discrimination. On the other hand, if the documents don't appear to be genuine or to relate to the person presenting them, then you must not accept them.

Okay, easy enough, but what should you do if the person is unable to provide you with the required documents? For example, if the employee lost her Social Security card simply inform her that as a means of demonstrating employment eligibility she must produce a *receipt* showing that she has applied for a replacement document. For example, she can fill out Form SS-5 at the local Social Security Administration in order to receive a receipt of application for the Social Security card. Once hired, that individual must present the actual document to you within ninety days of hire. In addition, the new hire must have checked in Section 1 of Form I-9 that she is already eligible to be employed in the United States.

Furthermore, if the individual doesn't produce the original document or a receipt within three days of hire, you have the right to terminate employment. Similarly, if the employee has presented a *receipt* for a document but isn't able to produce the *original* document by the ninetieth day of employment, you again have the right to terminate employment. However, you're obliged to apply these practices uniformly to all employees.

Fill out Section 2 of Form I-9 once you've inspected the new hire's documents. Section 2 is in the middle of the page, and you'll see that you're asked to examine either (1) one document from List A or (2) one document from List B *and* one document from List C. The reason is simple: List A documents establish both identity and employment eligibility. List B documents only establish identity, and List C documents only establish employment eligibility. Once you've filled out this documentation information, fill out the new hire's date of hire under the Certification section (right above where you're asked to sign your name). Remember, you have seventy-two hours (three *working* days, not including weekends) from the date of hire to complete Section 2. Therefore, INS inspectors will typically look at the date of hire in the Certification section and then look at the date you signed your name as the employer. If more than three days have lapsed between those two key dates, then you will be in violation. Once you've signed the document in Section 2, it is generally ready to be filed away.

Finally, if the INS, DOL, or OSC show up at your door, be ready. The officer will typically give you three days' (seventy-two hours') notice of an inspection. The INS, DOL, or OSC officer does not need to show you a subpoena or warrant at the time of the inspection. You may request an immediate extension of time in which to produce the I-9s, but you should consider calling a qualified attorney who specializes in immigration law immediately. In addition, penalties for prohibited practices include both civil and criminal fines and/or imprisonment.

The fines are stiff: Civil monetary penalties to employers who fail to properly complete, retain, or make available Forms I-9 are not less than $100 and not more than $1,000 for *each* employee. In addition, if an investigation reveals that an individual manager has knowingly committed or participated in acts relating to document fraud, that individual may be ordered to pay a civil monetary penalty. That penalty is not less than $250 and not more than $2,000 for each fraudulent *document* used in a first offense; not less than $2,000 and not more than $5,000 for each fraudulent *document* used in subsequent offenses.

The lesson here? Be careful, folks—this law has sharp teeth! Awareness of the requirements and a few simple precautions should help eliminate the risk of penalties should your company incur an unwanted INS visit. For more information, contact your local INS office for a copy of the free booklet *Handbook for Employers: Instructions for Completing Form I-9.*

6. How should I retain Form I-9?

Form I-9 must be retained for three years after the date of hire or one year after the person's employment is terminated, whichever is later. Two issues face you in this matter, however: Should you keep copies of the documents you've examined, and where should your I-9s be stored?

Though you are not obligated to keep copies of the documents you've examined, they can be vital evidence should your company be audited. These records, however, should be kept in a separate file specifically for I-9 records.

Tell Me More

You're under no obligation to keep copies of drivers' licenses, Social Security cards, passports, or any other documents that you use to comply with Form I-9. Many employers prefer not to retain any documents for fear that the record retention itself may become too burdensome.

On the other hand, there are several valid reasons for keeping copies of the documents used to establish compliance with the law. First, if a supporting document turns out to be fraudulent, the photocopy will establish that you examined the document and that it appeared to be genuine on its face. Since you, as an employer, are not required to be a document expert, a photocopy will help you establish that the document that you examined had no visual cues to doubt the document's authenticity. Second, if you can show that you've complied with Form I-9 requirements, your company will have established a "good faith" defense with respect to a charge of knowingly hiring an unauthorized alien.

As far as storing I-9 documents, most employment experts agree that I-9 documents should not be kept in employees' personnel files; instead, a separate binder or folder should be used where all company I-9s are housed. Why? Employers are frequently caught unprepared for I-9 audits and often must scramble on three days' notice to compile the necessary records. Weeding through employees' personnel files takes too much time when speed is of the essence. Ready-to-use binders, on the other hand, make the task of inventory management that much easier.

In addition, maintaining a separate I-9 file will better serve all employees' privacy interests and lessen your company's liability for failing to protect those interests. After all, most employers wouldn't care to have government auditors combing through their employees' personnel files where other information, such as performance reviews, 401(k) savings information, or other private records, are housed. Not only is such confidential information irrelevant to the I-9 audit, but also, if unrelated information in those personnel files triggers the INS to notify other branches of government regarding potential violations found in personnel records, your company may end up with an additional audit on its hands! Besides, I-9 forms often include information about an employee's national origin, so it makes sense to separate them from the regular personnel files.

7. Am I obligated to have an affirmative action plan?

Possibly. Affirmative action plans aren't required of all employers. However, employers and subcontractors who enter into contracts with the federal government and certain public sector employers such as community colleges and school districts are required to have such plans. In addition, affirmative action obligations may be imposed on companies as part of a court-approved agreement (for example, following the finding of employment discrimination in a class-action lawsuit). Finally, companies may voluntarily elect to have affirmative action plans in an effort to correct imbalances against protected classes in traditionally segregated job categories.

More specifically, government contractors and subcontractors with fifty or more employees and contracts of $50,000 or more are prohibited from discriminating against any employee or applicant for employment on the basis of race, color, religion, sex, or national origin. These employers are required to have a written plan and to take affirmative efforts in employment and promotions so that minorities and women will be employed at all levels in the workforce.

Affirmative action imposes on employers the duty to take positive steps to identify discrimination against protected classes and to improve work opportunities for women and minorities. Affirmative action, as its name implies, requires a company to proactively reach out to qualified members of groups that were formerly excluded from hiring and promotional opportunities. The concept is fairly simple: Unless companies aggressively combat the effects of unintended discrimination, the status quo will remain, and protected groups of employees will continue to be excluded from equal employment opportunities.

The mechanics of affirmative action plans are complicated and go well beyond the scope of this book. However, suffice it to say that one of the key challenges in any company's affirmative action plan is quantifying the results of its outreach efforts. That, in turn, involves determining areas of workforce underrepresentation via a current workforce analysis, geographic labor force analysis by race and sex, a corrective action plan with goals and timetables for correcting any underutilization, and a self-audit system.

Tell Me More

If your company already has or needs to develop an affirmative action plan, chances are that you'll retain the services of a law firm or qualified consulting firm. One of the most common challenges you'll face on a day-to-day basis, however, will lie in your applicant flow log. Under federal equal opportunity and affirmative action laws as well as the laws of many states, companies are obligated to maintain personnel activity data, including data on the race and sex of applicants.

The reason for this is that government audits and discrimination investigations partially focus on gathering information on all applicants who have applied for positions and comparing those flow statistics to current workforce demographics. In addition, employers must also analyze these applicant flow statistics for adverse impact. Adverse impact occurs when the selection rate for any protected group is less than 80 percent of the rate of selection for the group with the highest selection rate (for example, white males). A protected group or class is any group of people who are protected by the law against discrimination (for example, women and minorities).

Defining what is an "applicant," therefore, takes on critical importance in cases of audits and investigations. The EEOC doesn't help much here. Historically, federal enforcement agencies like the Equal Employment Opportunity Commission (EEOC) and Office of Federal Contract Compliance Programs (OFCCP) have looked to the EEOC's *Uniform Guidelines on Employee Selection Procedures* for a definition:

> The concept of an applicant is that of a person who has indicated an interest in being considered for hiring, promotion, or other employment opportunities. This interest might be expressed by completing an application form or might be expressed orally, depending on the employer's practice.

Furthermore, in September 1997, the OFCCP stated that "whether an individual will be considered an applicant turns on the employee selection procedures designed and utilized by the contractor." This definition serves employers well because the newer interpretation has generally said, Look to the employer's definition of an applicant when determining applicant flow statistics. On the other hand, these definitions are susceptible to review and redefinition over time. As a matter of fact, in the absence of an employer's defining just who is an applicant, courts may use their own discretion in formulating a definition. Of course, that's bad for employers because mass mailings, online resume dissemination, Internet job database retrieval, and the like all expand the pool of candidates to a point of distortion. Therefore, your best bet is to define an applicant in writing and to apply that definition on a consistent basis. For example, you might define an applicant as "an individual who applies in person by completing an official company employment application or by delivering a resume and thus whose race and sex may be determined." You can also add wording to specify that "an applicant is also an individual who is interviewed by an authorized company representative."*

By employing such a practical, focused definition, you'll avoid having to include job applicants in your applicant flow log who:

- Have had their resumes downloaded from the Internet but haven't been called in for an interview.
- Have forwarded unsolicited resumes on their own volition but haven't been called in for an interview.
- Have forwarded "solicited" resumes in response to an advertisement but weren't called in for an interview.

These individuals are screened out of the applicant flow log according to the definition given earlier because their race and sex cannot be identified (unless and until they are called in for an interview). Of course, you'll still need to retain those resumes; you can't just discard them. But you'll make your life a whole lot easier at the time of an EEO audit or investigation by restricting the number of "applicants" who must be counted in your flow log.

There are volumes of information relating to affirmative action plans. As in all matters with such serious legal implications, refer your specific questions to qualified legal counsel for further information.

*Robert J. Nobile, Esq., "Who Is an Applicant," HR Advisor: Legal and Practical Guidelines, January/February 1998, Vol. 3 No. 4. The HR Advisor is published by the law firm of Warren Gorham & Lamont in Boston.

8. How do I make diversity a key goal of our hiring process?

Diversity simply means "differences in people." It's not about forced quotas that ensure minority and female workforce participation. It is, instead, a recognized business objective based on the premise that a diverse corporate culture positions every company to more effectively compete in a global economy. By 2005, ethnic minorities will account for 47 percent of the nation's population. Socially responsible employers of choice recognize the strategic advantage of having their workforce mirror their customers' ethnic makeup. This ensures not only that the employer is fair but that it inherently understands the points of view of its clients, customers, and consumers.

What kinds of individual differences can companies hope to incorporate into the fabric of their organizational cultures? Employers with well-defined diversity initiatives look to attract a broad array of candidates with differing backgrounds according to:

- Gender
- Age
- Ethnicity
- Race
- Sexual orientation
- Religion
- Military/veteran status
- Immigrant status
- Language facility

The way such initiatives are pursued and achieved is typically through a:

- Policy of nondiscrimination and equal opportunity employment
- Corporate diversity mission statement
- Corporate diversity policy
- Performance management appraisal system that considers diversity hiring and promotion as part of its evaluation metrics
- Private/local/civic outreach

Sample wording of a nondiscrimination policy and a corporate mission statement are provided in Appendix A.

Tell Me More

As far as minority and female sourcing initiatives, contact your regional chamber of commerce to locate local offices of organizations like these Southern California centers:

<ul><li>Women at Work</li><li>NAACP</li><li>Urban League</li><li>Japanese American Cultural Center</li><li>Pacific Asia Consortium in Employment</li><li>Mexican American Opportunity Foundation</li><li>Chicano Service Action Center</li><li>Hispanic Urban Center</li><li>Southern California Indian Center</li><li>Braille Institute</li></ul>	<ul><li>Gay and Lesbian Center</li><li>Filipino Community Action Services</li><li>Los Angeles City Senior Citizens Affairs</li><li>Forty-Plus of Southern California</li><li>Los Angeles Urban League</li><li>California Counsel for Veteran Affairs</li><li>Los Angeles City Veterans Program</li><li>Federal Veterans Affairs</li><li>Department of Rehabilitation</li></ul>

Regularly forward your hard-copy job postings to these organizations to heighten community awareness of your hiring opportunities.

Remember as well that the Internet offers excellent opportunities to successfully fulfill your strategic recruitment objectives. Log on to some of these sites to strengthen your brand awareness as an employer of choice and advertise your current job openings:

Organization	Web Site	Cost per Job Posting
Asian American Economic Development Enterprises	www.aaede.org	$50 flat fee per ad
The Black World Today	www.tbwt.com	$50 flat fee per ad

Equal Opportunity	www.eop.com	$300 per ad per month
Hispanic	www.hisp.com	$170 per ad per month
Black Collegian	www.blackcollegian.com	$200 flat fee per ad
National Black MBA	www.nbmbaa.org	$200 per ad for thirty days
Hispanic Business	www.hispanstar.com	$4 per word or $100 with print ad
Black Voices	www.blackvoices.com	$550 per ad per week
Latino Link	www.latinolink.com	$270 per ad per month
Minority Career Network	www.minoritycareernet.com	$50 flat fee per ad
Saludos Hispanos	www.saludos.com	$200 per ad per month
Minorities Job Bank	www.minorities-jb.com	$200 per ad for sixty days

In addition, speak with representatives from job posting portals like Career Builder or Monster Board to learn about their simultaneous job posting dissemination to minority and female sites. This way, your ad may reach multiple audiences automatically at no additional cost. For example, your posting on Career Builder (www. careerbuilder.com) may also be automatically listed free of charge on sites like Hispanic Online (www.hisp.com), Microsoft Black Entertainment Television (www.msbet.com), or Women Connect (www.womenCONNECT.com).

Job fairs and open house hiring events can be a very effective way to source a large number of candidates at one time as well. National directories of career fairs are available from recruitment advertising agencies and chambers of commerce in most major metropolitan areas. Following are some opportunities typically found, for example, in the Los Angeles area that might be offered in your area as well:

NAACP Diversity Job Fair
Diversity Career Expo
Black MBA Job Fair
Minority Career Expo

Remember the golden rule about diversity initiatives: It's not only about companies doing the socially responsible thing. More important, it's all about maximizing growth and profitability. After all, the only way you can sell to a diverse customer base is to understand its preferences, attitudes, and inclinations firsthand. When your workforce mirrors your clients, customers, or the consumers you sell to, there's a natural symbiosis that fosters a cooperative and mutually beneficial business relationship. That translates into dollars and cents for your company's top-line revenues.

9. Can I insist that new hires sign mandatory arbitration agreements?

Yes, but there's a caveat: Although recent decisions from federal (including the U.S. Supreme Court) and state courts have encouraged employment arbitration agreements, the issue of whether such agreements are enforceable has not been fully and finally settled in all jurisdictions. For example, at least one federal Court of Appeals has ruled that employers may not force employees to arbitrate discrimination claims under federal law (e.g., claims for unlawful race, sex, disability, or age discrimination).

In contrast, many state courts, including the California Supreme Court, have ruled that agreements to arbitrate employment claims, including discrimination claims under state law, are enforceable provided they guarantee certain fairness and due process standards. To be fair and to meet due process guidelines, arbitration agreements must not be "unconscionable" or be otherwise procedurally biased against the employee in the eyes of the court.

What are the advantages to a company of compelling arbitration rather than allowing for a trial court to hear a case? Saved time and money—lots of it. It's generally true that arbitration is advantageous to employers because it often reduces the costs of litigation, imposes some reasonable limitations on discovery, and grants plaintiffs smaller awards than a court or jury verdict. In addition, arbitration generally reaches resolution much faster than traditional litigation.

There are also advantages for employees: Generally speaking, arbitration is inexpensive, efficient, and allows workers to be "heard" on a timelier basis, that is, closer to the triggering event. This sometimes increases the chances of a successful resolution because the employee doesn't stew over the problem for months or years before getting to trial.

On the other hand, certain companies feel less inclined from a moral standpoint to mandate that employees give up their access to the court system. Other employers feel that all the "at will" and "mandatory arbitration" paperwork in the new hire process alienates new hires from day one. As a result, determining whether mandatory pre-employment arbitration clauses belong in your employment practices and policies is a matter of opinion, corporate culture, geography, and the laws of your jurisdiction. After all, certain states are simply more employer friendly than others.

Tell Me More

Confer with outside counsel regarding both the decision to use arbitration agreements and for the drafting of those agreements. If your company chooses to implement a practice of mandating arbitration of workplace disputes, follow these guidelines:

1. Choose the American Arbitration Association (AAA) or some other respected arbitration firm as your arbitrator.
2. Do not restrict the damages the arbitrator can award. Remedies available in arbitration should be identical to those allowed at law.
3. Your company should pay all arbitration fees. However, you may create a policy that requires employees to pay reasonable filing fees and other administrative costs. As a side note, if you decide to adopt an arbitration policy for your current employees (as opposed to your newly hired ones), remember that you will need to give them some new consideration in exchange for their signature. Cash consideration is the norm; the appropriate amount should be discussed with qualified counsel before implementation.

Finally, mandatory arbitration language is normally found in offer letters, employment applications, and employee handbooks. In order to increase the enforceability of the agreement, it should also be presented as a freestanding written agreement between the company and the employee. See Appendix B for examples of mandatory arbitration language. The samples are intended as blueprints only and just represent an effort to save you time. Please ensure that qualified counsel customizes such language to your company's particular needs.

10. How do I determine whether someone is an employee or an independent contractor?

Independent contractors differ from employees in two primary ways:

1. They control both the outcome of a project and the means of accomplishing it.
2. They offer their services to the public at large—not just to one company.

Problems arise because some workers fall into a gray area, thereby creating the danger of misclassification. The Internal Revenue Service (IRS) provides forms to help classify workers, but sometimes these tests complicate rather than ease the task of classifying workers.

Worker classification and benefits rights have gotten much attention in the press of late in light of a noteworthy case: Long-term Microsoft freelancers sued the company arguing that they were, in essence, *employees* of the company. Their class action award for back benefits and stock options was expected to settle in the $30 to $40 million range; the actual $97 million settlement caught many CEOs, employment lawyers, and human resources managers by surprise and cast a strong light on this issue.

Many employers operate under the misunderstanding that they will be protected from the significant penalties of misclassification if the worker asked to be treated as an independent contractor and signed a written contract acknowledging that relationship. In fact, this doesn't protect your company from a charge of misclassification.

If you misclassify workers as independent contractors, be prepared to be subject to back taxes, interest, and penalties enforced by the IRS. In addition, you could face workers' claims for unpaid benefits, overtime, and minimum wage requirements through the U.S. Department of Labor (DOL), which has the discretion to impose substantial penalties. You could also be required to pay the company's and employee's share of Social Security and Medicare contributions, income tax that should have been withheld from those employees' wages, and federal unemployment tax.

Finally, if the worker is injured on the job, you may have to pay workers' compensation benefits. Note that a disadvantage to independent contractor status is that an individual injured on your premises can sue your company for injuries in a civil lawsuit outside the worker's comp arena. In a civil lawsuit, there are no damage limits similar to those that exist in the worker's comp system.

Tell Me More

Why would a company want to classify someone as an independent contractor rather than an employee? There are several very good reasons:

- With independent contractors, you have no obligation to withhold payroll taxes or to pay any portion of the individual's Social Security or Medicare taxes. In addition, rather than sending the person a W-2 showing earnings and taxes withheld, your only tax responsibility is to complete a Form 1099 MISC at the end of the year if you paid the independent contractor $600 or more.
- You are not required to carry workers' compensation, contribute to an unemployment insurance fund, or offer health, welfare, or pension benefits to independent contractors. Instead, independent contractors are paid only for the time they spend working.
- Terminating independent contractors is fairly easy to do because the individual is hired for a set assignment to be completed by an agreed-upon deadline. There is no need for coaching or progressive discipline in the form of written warnings or suspensions and no fear of wrongful termination. Arrangements are usually set up so that written contracts between your company and the independent contractor allow cancellation on two weeks' notice.
- Finally, whereas employees are subject to various government regulations, including wage and hour laws, family and medical leave, and illegal discrimination, independent contractor status, when properly classified, avoids most legal restrictions.

Sounds too good to be true, doesn't it? As with most things in business, there's a catch. Worker classification is no exception. Now that you know the upsides and downsides of classifying individuals as employees or independent contractors, tread carefully when determining whether you've got a bona fide independent contractor working relationship. Remember, though, that the IRS strongly prefers to have workers classified as employees rather than independent contractors if there's any doubt at all about their employment status.

To determine whether a worker is an employee or an independent contractor, the IRS generally looks at the degree of control you have over the worker. If you, the employer, control, or are otherwise able to control, not only what's done but also how it's done, then the worker is probably an employee. On the other hand, an independent contractor status will more likely be upheld when individuals:

- Decide when, where, and how to work
- Hire, supervise, and pay their own assistants
- Conduct work at their own office or shop
- Realize a profit or loss for their services
- Get paid by the job or receive a straight commission
- Make their services available to the general public
- Perform services for several businesses at a time

For more information, you'll find additional guidance in IRS Publications 1779 and 1976, *Independent Contractor or Employee?* You can get a free copy from the IRS Forms Distribution Center by calling (800) 829-3676 (1-800-TAX-FORM). You can also download and print IRS publications, forms, and other tax information materials on the Internet at www.irs.gov. If you still have difficulty making a determination after employing the IRS's twenty-factor test, the IRS will give you a written report of its determination once you complete Form SS-8, *Determination of Employee Work Status for Purposes of Federal Employment Taxes and Income Tax Withholding*, available from the nearest IRS office.

11. What are reasonable accommodations?

The Americans with Disabilities Act has made the hiring process a legal minefield for employers. Not only must the employer phrase interviewing questions with extreme care, employers are also required to make reasonable physical accommodations for disabled job applicants. Whether job applicants have mobility limitations or sight or hearing impairments or suffer from chronic conditions like degenerative muscular disorders, your company should be able to provide assistance while allowing individuals to maintain their self-respect.

Such accommodations might include providing sign readers or interpreters for the mute or deaf or providing a reading enlarger machine or exams in braille for the blind or nearly blind. In addition, blind candidates may be given exams orally rather than in writing.

Tell Me More

The ADA is a civil rights–oriented antidiscrimination law. It is intended to bring disabled individuals into the workplace by promoting and expanding employment opportunities for approximately 43 million Americans who have one or more physical or mental disabilities. In addition, the ADA doesn't merely prohibit discrimination against people with disabilities. It imposes additional affirmative obligations upon businesses to accommodate the needs of the disabled and to facilitate their economic independence.

As far as job applications and tests are concerned, employers are obligated to accept and consider applications from disabled individuals equally with nondisabled persons. The ADA doesn't prohibit companies from establishing job-related qualification standards, including education, skills, work experience, or physical or mental standards necessary for job performance, health, and safety. However, companies may not use those standards to screen out individuals on the basis of a disability unless those standards are consistent with a particular business necessity.

It follows that the Equal Employment Opportunity Commission (EEOC) will closely scrutinize the job relatedness of any written or physical tests given to disabled job applicants that are not also given to nondisabled candidates. Still, your company retains the right to hire an applicant without a disability over one with a disability if the nondisabled applicant is more qualified for the job. In such cases, the determination of superior qualifications must be based on objective hiring criteria, not on criteria that could discriminate on the basis of disability.

12. How do I determine what accommodations will be necessary for applicants with disabilities?

When it comes to interviewing questions, the ADA requires that employers phrase their questions with extreme care. For example, it is unlawful to ask the following questions to job applicants:

- Are you disabled?
- Do you have any disability that would prevent you from doing this job?
- Will you need any sort of accommodation or special equipment to perform the job duties?
- How many days were you sick last year?
- Have you ever attended a drug or alcohol rehabilitation program?
- Are you capable of lifting two-pound cans?

Okay, now that you know what you *can't* ask; what *can* you ask? The simple litmus test is this: ADA interviewing questions must focus on a candidate's *ability* to get the job done, not on the likelihood that the *disability* will get in the way. Consequently, the question, "Can you perform the essential functions of this job with or without accommodation?" is allowable. Furthermore, you can ask, "Are you capable of lifting two-pound cans and placing them on five-foot shelves in the order of their date of receipt?"

Phrasing the question this way (as opposed to how it's phrased earlier, "Are you capable of lifting two-pound cans?") is allowable because it relates to the actual job duties. Focusing on specific abilities relative to job performance is allowable; focusing on abilities in general could land you in hot water if a rejected applicant files a complaint with the EEOC or pursues a private lawsuit.

Tell Me More

You also can't ask how many *sick days* the employee took that year. However, you have the right to ask, "How many days of unscheduled leave have you incurred this year?" The difference in phraseology is simply this: "Sick days" relate directly to medical conditions that may be covered by the Act. "Unscheduled leave days," on the other hand, may have nothing to do with illness or injury; instead, they may have to do with taking unscheduled vacation days or an unapproved personal leave of absence.

An additional note of interest: Once an applicant is given a conditional job offer, you are permitted to require the individual to undergo a physical or medical exam. Physical fitness tests are not medical exams. These types of tests measure abilities, not disabilities, and may therefore be given in the pre-employment process (i.e., before extending a conditional employment offer). Similarly, a test to determine whether an employee is using drugs is not considered a medical exam under the ADA. You may likewise conduct drug tests designed to accurately identify illegal drugs before a conditional job offer is made. Of course, you must ensure that such exams are given uniformly to all candidates. The results of the exam must be kept in a separate, confidential file and used only for legally permissible purposes of evaluating candidates' suitability for the job.

Finally, if a medical exam screens out an applicant from employment, you must be able to demonstrate that the requirements that excluded the individual from employment are job related and consistent with business necessity. Furthermore, you must also be able to demonstrate that the individual can't perform the job duties even with a reasonable accommodation. Remember, however, that the ADA is still a relatively new and untested law. Because the courts are still evaluating plaintiff attorneys' interpretations of particular ADA provisions and because it is unclear what is required of employers to demonstrate "business necessity," you should discuss the merits of particular cases with qualified legal counsel.

Chapter 2

Recruitment Tools

13. How do I structure an employment application to get the most information?

Too many employment applications are rooted in the past and do not provide "informational windows" necessary to capture candidate achievements. Employment applications are typically incestuously passed down from one generation to the next without upgrades to reflect the changing labor market. So how do you redesign a tired form to complement a candidate's resume and to heighten decision-making skills? The key lies in creating an application that supplements—not duplicates—the candidate's resume and highlights issues that stimulate interviewing conversation.

Employment applications need to ask the questions that might otherwise be overlooked: How has the candidate progressed through the ranks and reinvented her job in light of the company's changing needs? What is the individual's reason for leaving his current company, and, more important, is joining your company the next logical move in the candidate's career progression? How does the candidate's annual compensation break down in terms of base salary versus commission or overtime? And how comfortable are candidates at defining, in writing, the criteria they're using in selecting another company?

Tell Me More

More stimulating conversation makes for better informational exchanges, more enjoyable interviews, and infinitely better hiring decisions. Add the following five informational windows to your current application to help place a candidate's duties and achievements into a clearer perspective:

Starting Position	Current Position

Progression through the ranks is an admirable trait and will allow you to discuss issues regarding vertical promotions, lateral assumptions of increased responsibilities, or overseas assignments to gain certain kinds of line experience.

Company size in terms of number of employees or annual revenues

Expect senior management candidates to answer this question in terms of divisional or corporate revenues; junior-level administrative support workers will typically respond in terms of the number of employees. Whatever the case, this information puts the candidate's achievements into some kind of contextual framework so that you can evaluate business environments in addition to individual duties and achievements.

Number of Hours Worked per Week

Most of us work forty hours by mandate. However, some work sixty hours in a typical workweek to maximize productivity. Others, in comparison, pride themselves on completing their work within the forty-hour time frame and feel that if you can't get the job done in that period, the job's probably too big for you. Stimulating conversation, isn't it?

By the way, recall that one of the most common reasons that new hires don't work out lies in the time commitment to the job. If everyone in Finance works sixty hours a week and the "newbie" is leaving at 5:00 sharp, camaraderie will suffer. After all, everyone will question the new hire's motives and dedication if he doesn't appear to work as hard as everyone else. On the flip side, hiring a sixty-hour wonder could place extra strain on the staff if everyone pretty much leaves at 5:00. Feelings of resentment or envy could follow, and camaraderie will again suffer. Don't leave this important issue to chance: Add the question to your application!

Reason for Leaving

The reason for leaving (RFL) is the link in a candidate's career progression. More than anything else, it provides insights into the individual's career management skills and business values.

> What are your long-term career goals, and how do you see a career with our company helping you meet those goals?

This is a written question on the back of the application, with space for candidates to hand-write their responses. You'll sometimes get interesting insights into candidates' plans and views about work. More important, you'll gain some quick insights into applicants' levels of literacy. In an era of computer spelling and grammar checks as well as "fudgable" resumes, it's always nice to know that the grammar fundamentals are alive and well. Illiteracy is protected from discrimination; you can't terminate someone on the basis of illiteracy.

If the employment application does the talking, managers can concentrate on becoming better evaluators of human resources. You'll find that informational windows will actually serve as windows of opportunity for hiring managers to add critical mass to their candidate meetings and come away with a better understanding of the candidate selection process.

14. Do candidates need to fill out an employment application, or will a resume suffice?

With your revised employment application on hand, you may still be asking whether all candidates need to fill one out. The simple answer is Yes. Employment applications naturally complement resumes but do a whole lot more. In addition to stimulating more interesting conversation, they:

- Help establish the employment-at-will relationship (see Question 63).
- Are the first work product that you actually ask the candidate to produce and in turn reveal important information about the individual's attention to detail or inclination to take short cuts.
- Confirm the accuracy of the information presented by the applicant via a signature line.

Tell Me More

You should instruct any candidates coming in to interview with your company to fill out the employment application as completely as possible. With those instructions, there is less of a chance that individuals will write "See Resume" in the employment history section of the application. Still, you'll find people who take that all-too-common shortcut, and that's not an optimal way of beginning any employment relationship. Therefore, simply return incomplete applications to candidates, and ask them to fill in all the information areas before you begin your meeting.

Some employers have applicants fill out the application online, but if your applicants fill out a paper form, you can analyze their handwriting. The neatness and accuracy of a candidate's print or script may be a telling sign regarding the individual's method of working. Generally speaking, those who write "like typewriters" tend to be very analytical and precise compared to those who write in a sloppy or haphazard fashion. Candidates who take their time filling out a questionnaire neatly will obviously make a better impression than those who view the process as a mundane or useless exercise.

Finally, bear in mind that employment experts estimate that approximately 30 percent of information shared by candidates in interview situations is false: Falsified educational degrees, wrong employment dates, and overstated salary histories are among the most common falsifications.

Historically, courts have differentiated between false statements made on resumes and falsified information on employment applications. Their interpretations placed much greater import on falsified employment applications than on resumes. Why? Because it is simply too easy for candidates to blame incorrect resume information on the resume preparation service. However, because candidates complete applications themselves and sign that the information is true to the best of their knowledge, courts have held candidates to a higher standard of truthfulness. Consequently, your decision to terminate an employee for education falsification, for example, will withstand legal scrutiny better when this decision is based on a falsified application, rather than on a resume.

The legal concept associated with resume fraud or falsified employment applications is called "after-acquired evidence." In essence, if candidates falsify their resumes or provide false answers on employment applications in order to get a job, they may be barred from receiving damages from your company if they claim later that they have been terminated wrongfully. Federal courts have held that such behavior may preclude a terminated employee from being entitled to recover damages from the employer, even if the company was guilty of wrongful termination.

One final thought. Many companies do not ask senior management candidates to fill out employment applications. Applications, instead, are reserved for rank-and-file employees only. This is not recommended, but it may be acceptable only if reserved for the most senior levels of management (i.e., vice presidents and above). First, candidates at this level are often hired via employment contracts, so they're not at-will workers. (The at-will language on the employment application does not apply to their employment.) Second, there tends to be less "fudging" when it comes to JD, MBA, and CPA licenses that are often found among the ranks of senior managers. Still, let the buyer beware!

15. Should I test applicants?

Pre-employment testing is an entire industry unto itself. The in-depth knowledge that comprehensive aptitude testing provides regarding individuals' strengths and weaknesses helps managers make better hiring decisions and provides optimal support to bring out the best in new staff members.

However, most companies limit their pre-employment testing to administrative support candidates in the form of Word, Excel, typing, and grammar tests. Similarly, drivers get road tests, and chefs undergo cooking demonstrations. Fearing discrimination and invasion of privacy charges, many companies avoid psychological testing to determine levels of skill-based competence, honesty, or candidates' work philosophies. After all, employment tests have been a frequent target of discrimination lawsuits. In addition, although psychological testing has been proven to be an accurate indicator in certain situations and has lessened turnover, it can also be expensive and time consuming to administer.

Tell Me More

Keeping these guidelines in mind, let's look at some of the more common aptitude tests available. The typing and computer tests referred to earlier are typically known as "skill" tests. The Wonderlic Basic Skills Test, for example, is a well-known published test that measures verbal skills. In addition, the Wonderlic Personnel Test measures cognitive or problem-solving ability (intelligence).

Another form of paper and pencil examination includes "honesty/personality testing." As the name implies, honesty and personality testing looks to measure personality traits such as truthfulness and integrity. As you'd guess, a sticking point with personality tests is accuracy. Applicants who respond the way they believe the testing instrument "wants them to answer" may distort the test's results and inadvertently disqualify themselves.

You should limit honesty testing to situations where you have a legitimate business reason to be concerned about honesty—for example, when hiring cash handlers. Before actually using a test, be sure to ask the vendor for backup information demonstrating the test's accuracy. Two of the most common tests used in honesty screening today are the Stanton Survey and the Reid Psychological Survey. Most of these tests can be taken in five to thirty minutes and claim to reveal whether applicants are likely to steal or act dishonestly on the job.

"Dependability tests" attempt to measure a variety of values. Sometimes known as trait tests, they evaluate applicants' attitudes, practices, and values that are job related. Dependability tests are developed specifically for individual companies. Companies that use such tests must consequently create their own scoring systems for interpreting results. These tests are usually used by large companies that experience a high rate of turnover among nonmanagement personnel. The tests typically cost $20,000 to $30,000 to develop; however, since the company owns the test, its cost of administration declines with use.

Another form of testing is handwriting analysis. Size and slant of letters, pressure applied to the paper, and a smooth or erratic flow of ink may provide certain clues about candidates' suitability for a particular job. Proponents of handwriting analysis say that it is fairly inexpensive and less time consuming to administer than other selection tests. On the other hand, critics argue that there is no scientific basis or validation procedure from which to draw conclusions. Your decision to use such tests, which cost from $25 to $400 to administer, will probably depend on your own personal experience with them.

When working with aptitude-related tests, keep the following guidelines in mind:

- Testing should never be used as a sole basis for a hiring decision, simply because testing is more effective at identifying the nature of a problem than in calibrating its severity. Determining the severity of the problem should be left to the reference checking process.
- Psychological measures are relative data. It's crucial to the testing process that an individual's strengths and weaknesses be measured in relation to the occupational group to which they belong and weighed against the job description specifications provided. Otherwise, the appraisal technique occurs in a vacuum, and its findings are diminished.
- Retesting should be the exception rather than the rule. Aptitude tests measure personality indicators that remain relatively stable over time; mental abilities, interests, temperament, and motivation should not change with repeated exams. However, there may be cases where re-evaluation (i.e., appraising the same test data for a different job) or additional testing is warranted.
- When you choose to hire despite an aptitude test's recommendations, be sure that references have confirmed that test-identified weaknesses have been accounted for. In other words, move forward with the hiring process only once prior supervisors have confirmed that the weaknesses identified by the testing instrument won't really pose a problem to the individual's performance.
- Review aptitude tests on a continuing basis. Don't make the mistake of filing such reports away once the candidate begins work. Aptitude tests serve as a useful aid in guidance and development throughout an individual's career.

16. How do I validate tests?

Tests that fail a disproportionate percentage of members in a protected class may have an adverse impact and therefore may be considered discriminatory unless validated. Although the Equal Employment Opportunity Commission (EEOC) doesn't require that tests be "validated," your company could be held accountable for validating the tests used if it can be shown that they produce an adverse impact.

As a result, all tests should be validated according to the *Guidelines for Employee Selection Procedures* (1978) published by the EEOC. The *Guidelines* make it clear that any selection process that adversely affects employment opportunities for any protected group must be validated if possible. All testing instruments, whether published or employer created, should be checked for relatedness to job duties. This needs to be done for each type of position.

Tell Me More

An employer policy or practice (like testing) may cause a disproportionate adverse impact on the employment opportunities of any race, sex, disability, or ethnic group if the selection rate for that protected group (say, women) is less than four-fifths, or 80 percent, of the selection rate for the group with the highest selection rate (for example, white males).

If adverse impact has been established, you should consider test validation for job requirements and performance. Three validation methods have been approved by the EEOC:

- *Content* validity studies establish that the content of the test is consistent with the job's duties and responsibilities. A typing test for secretarial candidates, for example, has content validity.
- *Criterion* validity studies, in comparison, measure the relationship between the test scores and some measure of job performance. A test is considered valid if there is a significant statistical correlation between the test results and the individual's job performance.
- Finally, *construct* validity studies are complex and not used very often. This testing methodology attempts to correlate a match between the test taker's individual characteristics and a job's requirements (for example, leadership).

Keep in mind that pre-employment tests must adhere to the employment provisions of the Americans with Disabilities Act (ADA). If these tests tend to screen out those with disabilities, then the company will have the burden of proving that the exams are job related and consistent with business necessity. Even if the test is job related and consistent with business necessity, you'll still have to provide a reasonable accommodation for the test takers if their disability prevents them from taking the test or negatively influences test results. Possible accommodations include modifying the test or testing conditions or even eliminating the testing requirement altogether.

Therefore, you should always check with federal and state laws and regulations before implementing pre-employment testing programs. Employment lawyers and testing professionals will help you through this somewhat complicated field of the law. Remember as well that testing should supplement, not supplant, your decision to hire or reject candidates. After all, the purpose of aptitude testing is not to tell you whom to hire; it is to tell you whom you are hiring.

17. What are the benefits of working with recruitment advertising agencies?

Recruitment advertising agencies are a wonderful resource to help you attract quality candidates, lower your company's cost-per-hire, and provide value-added services that save you significant time. Recruitment ad agencies come in all shapes and sizes, from sole proprietors to large corporations with thousands of employees and offices in all corners of the globe. Traditionally known only for helping companies place ad copy in newspapers, these consulting firms have broadened their services to include:

- Branding and employment image development
- Sourcing and recruitment strategies in print, broadcast, and the Internet
- Market, media, and competitor research
- Internet data mining
- Web site development, hosting, and maintenance
- Resume database and applicant tracking systems (including response handling and activity reports)
- Salary surveys and relocation comparisons
- Executive and contingency search, as well as recruitment contracting services
- Focus group research

In short, the benefits of working with such marketing partners could be incredibly valuable to your company.

Tell Me More

Because traditional help-wanted classified ads are seeing a significant decline in their effectiveness, alternative marketing and branding strategies are becoming necessary to attract talented candidates. Recruitment ad agencies will help your company develop "Run of Paper" (also known as "Run of Press") ads that are printed outside the classified ad section (for example, in the business, sports, or main event sections of a newspaper) in order to reach a more targeted demographic. National advertising agencies will have insights into particular markets that could prove very valuable to your expanding business.

In addition, larger ad agencies have the research capability and available human resources to learn all about your company from the outset. They will thoroughly study what staffing strategies you have been using and to what degree you have been successful. Turnover analysis will reveal where you're losing the most people. Cost-per-hire studies will show where you're getting the most bang for your buck in terms of your recruitment spending. And, for an additional fee, group exit interviews can be conducted by the agency to learn where the real management or compensation problems are— issues you might not be hearing about directly from your departing employees.

Free services typically include media recommendations, customized activity reports, and secondary (i.e., prepublished) market research. Charges for agency services may include the following:

- If a media rate is "noncommissionable" (in other words, the newspaper won't pay the agency its 15 percent commission), that 15 percent markup will probably be passed along to you, the client.
- Certain invoices may include a line service charge to help the agency offset the costs of copywriting, creative, research, and ad placement that are part of the basic fee structure.
- Production costs for display ads typically cost anywhere from $10 to $25 per inch depending on column length size. (Of course, you will have to pay separately for media space, which can run $50 a line or $300 a column inch in a major metropolitan newspaper.)
- Internet postings may be marked up to $50 plus the cost of the ad.

- Creative services such as creative direction, design print, copywriting, or HTML may cost from $100 to $150 per hour.
- Separately stated charges may include fax, telephone, production, typesetting, photostat, finished art, Federal Express charges, or other administrative fees.

One other thing: As you're asking questions to prospective vendors about these costs, be sure to find out whether their account people are salaried or commissioned. Remember, commissioned salespeople make more money if you run bigger ads because they get a piece of the sale; salaried account executives, on the other hand, have nothing to gain by making a client's ads larger than necessary. That could benefit you over the long term.

18. How do I maximize my working relationship with contingency and retained search firms?

Contingency search firms come in two basic flavors: (1) professional/technical search and (2) administrative support recruitment. You're probably well aware of clerical support agencies that place secretaries, staff accountants, customer service reps, and the like. Such organizations typically place candidates earning $40,000 a year and under. Professional/technical agencies, in comparison, usually specialize in individual disciplines like accounting and finance, data processing, retail, software engineering, and pharmaceutical sales. Such candidates typically earn somewhere between $40,000 and $100,000 a year.

Tell Me More

What these firms have in common is that they operate on contingency, meaning they get paid only if you, the client, hire one of their candidates. The contingency recruitment field is a high-volume brokerage business that achieves economies of scale by placing candidates with similar skills, knowledge, and abilities into organizations with like needs. That's why they specialize in particular technical disciplines: In searching for candidates with a predetermined profile, agencies develop candidates who simultaneously meet multiple client companies' needs. The bottom line: You pay only if your needs are met, and that's about as efficient a system as you can get. To locate a contingency search firm with professional industry certification, purchase *The National Directory of Personnel Services* ($20.95) published by the National Association of Personnel Services, (703) 684-0180.

The retained search business, in comparison, is a much more exclusive game. Retained recruiters (a.k.a. "headhunters") typically target candidates earning more than $100,000 a year for their clients. Headhunters typically spend a great deal of time researching your competitors, developing names and profiles of candidates, approaching those candidates with your opportunity, and then qualifying them in terms of their willingness and ability to do the job, fit your company's corporate culture, and potentially relocate.

Unlike contingency recruiters who must place a candidate to earn a fee, the retained recruiter gets a fee that is guaranteed up front. Because of this financial arrangement, there is little financial bias to preclude a pure consulting relationship. Consequently, headhunters act like management consultants who attempt to shift the competitive balance of management power in their client company's favor. Therefore, employ a retained search firm for six-figure positions with exacting criteria when your sense of urgency is great and your need for dedicated attention is critical.

If you find it difficult to pay a retainer when contingency recruiters will apparently do the same work for free, remember that it wouldn't make sense for contingency recruiters to work a search assignment that's too difficult to fill when they have other, more "fillable" openings to tend to. Retained recruiters, in comparison, will be beholden to you until the assignment is completed because they will have already been paid their fee. To contact qualified retained search firms, order the *Directory of Executive Recruiters* ($47.95) from Kennedy Publications at (800) 531-0007 or *The Euro Directory: Executive Search and Selection Firms in Europe* ($125) from The Recruiting and Search Report, (800) 634-4548.

19. How do I negotiate fees and guarantee periods with search firms?

How much will contingency firms negotiate? That depends on the marketplace, namely the unemployment rate, the scarcity of candidates in the particular discipline in question, and geographic differentials. In general, you'll pay more for IT (information technology) and Web development candidates than you will for generic secretaries. As a rule of thumb, though, you should ask for a 20 percent fee. That amount typically justifies the recruiter's time and efforts. Fee agreements typically range anywhere from 10 to 33 percent. Avoid trying to negotiate deals down to 10 percent or 15 percent—the recruiter may agree to it, but you won't see first-tier candidates. In fact, you may not see any candidates at all.

Remember as well that recruiters will trade off fees and time guarantees. Contingency recruiters typically offer both (a) free trial periods and (b) prorated refund periods. Those time guarantees may be negotiable as well. Here is how they work: A thirty-day free trial period will guarantee you that if the candidate "falls off" for any reason—termination, resignation, or layoff—you'll receive your money back, plain and simple. If the candidate "falls off" between days 31 and 90, you'll receive a prorated refund. How the search firm determines the prorated refund period is important.

Tell Me More

Contingency search firms charge a fee based on the candidate's annual earnings (base salary usually, but sometimes the bonus may be factored in if it's a significant portion of the estimated first year's income). The formula most often employed is a "1 percent per $1,000" figure with a 33 percent maximum.

At full-fee contingency, for example, the cost for a $30,000-a-year secretary would be 30 percent x $30,000, or $9,000. The cost for a $90,000 senior UNIX systems administrator would be 33 percent x $90,000, or $29,700. Bear in mind that many search firms will negotiate fees lower than the "1 percent per $1,000" full-fee formula.

In terms of refunds, some firms employ a "1/90 per day" prorated formula so that each day (from days 1–90) guarantees them one-ninetieth of the total fee. If the $30,000 secretary in the example above leaves on day 60, then the recruiter will have earned 60/90 of the $9,000 fee, or $6,000.

Other contingency firms charge the client "50 percent of the candidate's gross earnings" up to the time of the fall-off. In the example just given, the secretary who earns $30,000 per year will have earned $5,000 by the end of her second month ($2,500/month x 2 months). Therefore, the fee earned by the agency would be $2,500. That's a lot cheaper than the 1/90 formula that rewarded the agency with $6,000! Therefore, it's to your advantage to insist on the "50 percent of gross earnings," rather than the "1/90 per day" prorated refund formula.

Contingency recruiters are optimists by nature. They'll always negotiate a greater time guarantee in exchange for a higher fee. So if you ask for 20 percent and the recruiter won't budge below 25 percent, then ask for a higher refund guarantee. For example, you might ask for a sixty-day free trial period and a 120-day prorated refund (instead of the more common thirty-day free trial period and ninety-day guarantee). You might also ask for a "50 percent of gross earnings" formula, rather than the more common "1/90 per day" practice. Savvy negotiations will not only save your company money; they'll demonstrate to the recruiter your thorough understanding of their business.

What about negotiations with retained search firms? Unfortunately, there's far less to talk about there. Retained search firms, or headhunters, charge their clients a flat 33 percent fee based on the candidate's annual earnings. A $150,000 chief technology officer costs $49,500. That fee is a "retainer" that is typically paid in three increments: 1/3 upon acceptance of the search, 1/3 approximately thirty days into the search, and 1/3 approximately sixty days into the search.

The largest search firms rarely discount or negotiate these terms. Smaller boutique firms, however, will often make that final third of the fee contingent upon their filling the search. In other words, if they don't find the candidate that you ultimately hire, you'll be charged only two-thirds of the $49,500 fee, or $32,670. Always be sure to ask that the final third of the fee be made payable upon completion of the assignment. In most cases, you won't face stiff resistance from the recruiter, and you'll likewise end up saving your company significant recruitment dollars.

20. How could research firms and outplacement organizations help me recruit new hires?

As another alternative to traditional contingency or retained recruitment, research firms package their services into hourly paid increments. For example, you might enlist a research firm only to research and identify prospective candidates from competitor firms. The fee would then be based on the number of hours necessary to generate the candidate list. You, the client, could also pay extra for the research firm to approach, qualify, interview, and reference-check those candidates.

In essence, the firm "unbundles" the search process into its component parts, thereby providing you with significant cost control measures by allowing you to bring in-house parts of an activity that formerly had to be totally outsourced. As such, research organizations are a very logical and necessary component in today's environment of cost reductions and expense controls.

Companies that are downsizing sometimes pay outplacement firms to assist displaced workers in finding jobs. As far as the displacing company is concerned, the cost of outplacement for a former employee is far outweighed by the altruistic and practical benefits that allow it to continue its business operations without undue interruption.

It's in the outplacement firm's best interests to get its candidates placed as quickly as possible. It costs outplacement firms big bucks to provide services to displaced executives. As a rule of thumb, if the outplacement firm can get the candidate out of its office (and into yours!) within six months, it will make money on the deal. Therefore, these firms employ job developers to help their candidates find work. Remember that because the candidate's former company pays the outplacement firm, not you (the potential new employer), this free supply of talent could significantly reduce your cost per hire. In short, outplacement firms are an incredible source of free, highly skilled candidates, and it would be an absolute mistake not to list your openings with them.

Tell Me More

To locate a listing of research firms that handle "unbundled" search, purchase *The Executive Search Research Directory* ($125) from The Recruiting and Search Report, (800) 634-4548.

In addition, following are the corporate headquarters of the four largest outplacement firms in the nation with national job banks. Call them for their local office, and then forward your current job openings to:

Lee Hecht Harrison
Corporate Headquarters
200 Park Avenue, 26th Floor
New York, NY 10166
(212) 557-0009
www.careerlhh.com

Drake Beam Morin
Corporate Headquarters
101 Huntington Avenue, Ste. 2100
Boston, MA 02199
(617) 450-9860
www.dbm.com

Right Associates
Corporate Headquarters
1818 Market Street, 33ʳᵈ Floor
Philadelphia, PA 19103-3614
(800) 237-4448
www.right.com

Spherion Corporation
2050 Spectrum Boulevard
Fort Lauderdale, FL 33309-3008
(954) 351-8300
www.spherion.com

21. Will an employee referral program work for my company?

Most employers realize that employee referral programs are the most cost-effective way of attracting new talent. Still, there are some stubborn CEOs and CFOs who begrudgingly argue, "I'm not paying for referrals now; why would I want to start paying for something that I already get for free?"

At first glance, their arguments have merit. After all, it does appear like they'll be giving away money with no apparent return. What they don't realize, however, is that they're not really getting "referred" new hires for free. Your company's cost-per-hire will identify how much you're paying to hire exempt and nonexempt workers in your organization (see Question 2).

Your goal should be to lower the *average* cost-per-hire. To lower that aggregate cost, you've got to look at your overall recruitment expenses per hire—not just to your intermittent "freebie" employee referrals. Employee referral programs are the least expensive methodology for identifying and hiring new talent and reducing your company's cost-per-hire. Further, new hires tend to be more reliable and less likely to leave when they have friends or associates with a vested interest in making them successful. Such "sheltered transitions" ensure a smoother landing and an automatic social network within the company.

Tell Me More

How do you set up an employee referral program? The specifics of your program will depend on the types of hires you're trying to make, your company's current cost-per-hire, and the number of hires you project. Here's how some companies lay out their programs:

- Cash bonuses are given to current employees who refer new hires. Nonexempt cash bonuses range from $250 to $500. Exempt cash bonuses range from $500 to $2,500. In some cases, higher cash bonuses are awarded for information technology or finance candidates (say, $3,000 to $5,000 per hire) than for other exempt new hires.
- Most companies pay cash bonuses in one or two increments. Those that pay in one increment pay at the conclusion of the new hire's first six months with the company. Companies that pay in two installments pay 50 percent when the new hire starts and 50 percent when the new hire reaches the six-month period. (Note: Employees who refer new hires must be employed at the time the referral fee becomes due; if the referring employee leaves the company in the meantime, no fee will be due because the program is only for existing employees.)
- Some organizations augment the cash bonus program by having lotto drawings for "super" prizes like trips or gift certificates at the end of the year. Other organizations pledge a monetary bonus (of perhaps $5,000 or $10,000) to the employee in the company who has referred the most new hires in the previous year.
- Program participation should be limited to regular, full-time employees who refer other regular, full-time employees. Although referring temporary employees or independent contractors may be beneficial to your company, it shouldn't necessarily warrant a referral fee. After all, your company won't receive the same return-on-investment for a casual or short-term worker.

Are there any downsides to an employee referral program? Yes. If you believe that your current employees would not feel comfortable referring their friends or business associates to work for your company because your organization has an "unfriendly" reputation, then don't implement such a program. After all, you don't want to have to implement "PR damage control" to overcome the negative feedback that could arise from suggesting that workers refer their friends. Timing is therefore a critical element of any employee referral program's implementation.

Second, if your organization suffers from a lack of diversity among its staff, encouraging internal referrals may be problematic, since people tend to refer people like themselves. If you want to broaden the spectrum of diverse individuals who contribute to your organization's success, then you may want to rely on external recruitment (through search firms and classified ads in minority publications) more than on internal referrals. After all, although the dollars and cents of internal referral programs can't be disputed, these programs won't necessarily fix perception problems related to your organization's diversity recruitment programs. Instead, documented minority outreach efforts will probably be a better route to recruitment success.

22. Should I consider sponsoring foreign workers and offering them green cards?

If you work in an academic or high-tech environment, it may be necessary or desirable to recruit from abroad. Postdoctorate research fellows are high in demand and low in supply for specific high-skill jobs. In order to obtain a visa or green card for a foreign worker, you must first prove you were unable to find a qualified American worker. Visas are also limited, so be sure you can't fill a position by other means.

Tell Me More

The visa system in the United States comes in two basic types: (1) nonimmigrants and (2) immigrants. To keep these concepts in perspective, simply think of it this way: Immigrants are foreign nationals who obtain the legal right to live and work in the United States without restriction. Nonimmigrants, in comparison, are only here temporarily and will eventually have to return to their original countries.

"Lawful permanent residents" (LPRs) are people who have obtained a "green card" and are allowed to work here without restriction. After LPRs have lived in the United States for five years (three years if they are married to a U.S. citizen), they may choose to apply to become naturalized U.S. citizens. (Once they become citizens, they will have earned the right to vote and serve on jury duty.) Of course, not all LPRs are citizens; citizenship is an option for LPRs, and it's an extra step in the immigration process.

A "green card" is a slang term for an alien registration card issued to permanent resident aliens. The card includes the alien's photograph and fingerprint. At one time, the identity card was green (today it's rose colored). And you've seen this document referred to in your I-9 form: "List A: Employment Eligibility and Identity" requires, among other things, a U.S. passport or Alien Registration Receipt Card (Form I-551) to establish both (1) employment eligibility and (2) identity.

How do employers sponsor aliens who want green cards, and how much does the process cost? First, remember that immigrant visas are limited in number and subject to quota limitations established by Congress. Also, there are two ways to obtain immigrant visas: through (1) family relationships or (2) employment. Although the family relations subtopic goes well beyond the scope of this book, most immigrants come to America to join family members; a much smaller percentage come here to fill jobs where employers have demonstrated an inability to find American workers. Still, employment-based immigration has become a hot topic for U.S. companies in aggressive growth modes, and companies now have to add this concept to their sourcing vocabulary.

There are five categories of immigrant visas, known as "preferences." Whereas research scientists and academicians often qualify under preferences (1)(a), "Extraordinary Ability," or (1)(b), "Outstanding Professors and Researchers," information technology professionals normally qualify under the second or third preference (i.e., "Advanced Degrees," "Exceptional Ability," "Professionals," or "Skilled Workers"). To qualify for these preference categories, aliens must have a combination of a master's degree *or* a bachelor's degree plus a certain number of years of progressive experience in their fields. The positions being recruited for must likewise require at least a bachelor's degree. The specifics of the preference categories should be discussed with qualified immigration counsel.

In addition, the second and third preferences typically require that the employer obtain a "Labor Certification" from the Department of Labor (DOL) confirming that hiring the alien will not adversely affect similarly situated U.S. workers. Therefore, employers must demonstrate sufficient recruitment to show that the U.S. labor market was adequately tested before they can obtain permanent residency for an immigrant. This is typically accomplished by running recruitment advertisements in prominent newspapers and, in some cases, on the Internet to document your attempts to hire American workers first.

The second and third preferences also require that you, the sponsoring employer, file a "Petition for Prospective Immigrant Employee" form (INS #140). And, whereas aliens who claim extraordinary ability (first preference) may file for a green card on their own behalf, aliens under preferences two and three (again, IT professionals) must be sponsored by employers.

Attorneys' fees for obtaining green cards can range anywhere from $3,500 to $8,000, and the green card approval process ranges anywhere from two to five years. Because there are quotas for workers from certain countries, such as India and China, those candidates take the longest to process.

23. How do I temporarily sponsor foreign workers using an H-1B nonimmigrant visa?

Skilled workers such as IT professionals can usually be sponsored using the H-1B form for "Specialty Occupations." The H-1B filing process has four steps that the petitioning employer must follow:

Step 1	Education Evaluation (foreign degree)
Step 2	Confirmation of Prevailing Wage
Step 3	Labor Condition Attestation (LCA) with the Department of Labor
Step 4	Preparation of H-1B petition, I-129 petition for immigrant worker + supplement, and supporting letter to the INS

Similar to the Labor Certification filed with the DOL for green card processing, the Labor Condition Attestation (form ETA-9035) required for H-1B processing documents that hiring the alien employee will not adversely affect the wages of similarly situated U.S. workers. The employer will also have to agree to pay the nonimmigrant's return travel costs if the individual is fired. However, unlike with green card sponsorship, employers aren't required to run recruitment ads in recognized newspapers to prove that the employment market was adequately tested.

Tell Me More

The position must require a bachelor's degree, but, unlike the "Professional" preference for immigrant visas, H-1B nonimmigrant candidates need not have a degree themselves: they may, instead, substitute at least twelve years of progressive experience for the degree. The H-1B visa is awarded for three years and may be extended for an additional three years (for a total of six years).

Furthermore, H-1Bs are "employer-specific." That means that if employees leave another company to join yours while in H-1B status, they will need to apply for a new H-1B with your organization. Similarly, the Labor Condition Application is valid only in the region where it is certified and for the job location where it's certified. Therefore, transferring the employee to a new location of your company may require you to file a new Labor Condition Application for H-1B. Also, if the employee changes from full-time to part-time status or his position substantially changes in terms of salary or job title, a new H-1B may be needed.

The legal costs of sponsoring an H-1B visa petition range from $1,500, to $2,500. (Extensions for years four through six will typically double that fee.) Additional fees include a $110 filing fee, a $1,000 retraining/scholarship fee for American workers, and miscellaneous fees, such as an educational evaluation fee ($150), diploma translation costs ($50), and H-1B family filing fees for spouses and children ($120 per person). You'll probably be looking at a total package of $4,000 to $6,000 for the typical six-year H-1B petition.

Most important, when keeping an open mind to the vast resources of human talent available beyond the U.S. border, remember that it's critical to obtain the services of a competent legal professional. Immigration law can be particularly complicated and fraught with exceptions, so proceed with the utmost caution. For information on immigration lawyers in your area, check with the American

Immigration Lawyers Association in Washington, D.C., by calling (202) 371-9377. Its Web site can be found at www.aila.org.

Specifically refer to the Lawyer Referral Service section of the Web site, and you'll be able to find participating immigration attorneys in your state or territory who are members in good standing of their respective state bar associations. You'll be asked to either call (800) 954-0254 or to e-mail your request to ilrs@aila.org regarding your specific immigration needs. In addition, the charge for an initial, in-person, thirty-minute consultation with an attorney will be no more than $50 if you use this Web site referral service.

24. Should I directly recruit candidates from competitors?

That's always an interesting prospect, isn't it? After all, if you could go directly to your competitors and attract candidates to your company with a phone call, you'd be a real hero. In essence, you'd be acting as a headhunter for your own company without having to pay a fee.

Still, many companies opt not to directly "source" candidates from competitor firms for reasons of propriety. After all, if you're perceived as "stealing" from the competition, they may respond in kind and target individuals in your company when they have job openings to fill. In addition, industry relationships will be at stake if old friends at competitor companies find out that your company is raiding theirs.

In general, it's best to leave headhunting to headhunters. After six years in the search business myself, I can confidently state that there are simply too many risks that employers run in terms of damaging industry relationships and being perceived as overly aggressive by directly sourcing candidates themselves. As a matter of fact, it's not uncommon for companies to strictly forbid any form of direct sourcing from the competition. Still, many employers ask about this option, so let's evaluate how it could be handled if it were to be done.

Tell Me More

Let's say you were looking for a director of finance. You would typically post the job internally, run print and online ads, and possibly engage the services of a headhunter. Before engaging that headhunter, though, you might want to try a limited telephone outreach to other organizations in your industry or geographical area.

Your first step would be to line up companies that compete directly with yours. You have to decide whether you want to directly recruit the candidate (director) or network with the individual one tier higher than the candidate (vice president). You'd then contact the competing companies and ask the person answering the phone for the name of either the director or the vice president of finance.

At that point, you could ask to be connected to that individual. The secretary will act as a "screener" or "gatekeeper" and ask about the purpose of your call. Simply state that you work for XYZ Company, a competitor organization, and you've got a networking question for the director or vice president of finance.

Let's look at how two calls would differ. First, let's call the vice president to network. When the vice president picks up the phone, introduce yourself and your company, and state the purpose of your call:

> Laura, I'm the vice president of finance at XYZ Company, and we're not far from you in Tarrytown, New York. I'm calling you, Laura, because we haven't had a chance to meet before, and I could really use your help. Is this a good time to talk?
>
> Great! We've got about 200 employees and $50 million in revenues, and we specialize in manufacturing plastics primarily for automotive parts. Our director of finance is leaving the company after three years because his wife has just gotten a great job offer in Phoenix, and we're looking to fill that position. We need someone with a strong background in finance, especially budgeting and forecasting, and ideally an MBA or CPA. The pay range is around $70,000 to $85,000, and the candidate would be bonus-eligible after the first year. The bonus would probably fall in the 8 to 12 percent range.
>
> Is there anyone in your network you could recommend, Laura, either because they're in career transition right now or otherwise feeling "boxed in" in their careers? I'd be happy to return the favor in the future.

That's a fairly respectful call, and it's certainly to the point. Rarely will others be offended by such an open and communicative approach. The added benefit is that the call will help you build goodwill relations with others in your industry. Remember, by call-ing the vice president—one tier above the director-level candidate that you're trying to recruit—there's nothing intrusive about the phone call. It really is a goodwill outreach at this point.

Although such calls are fairly simple to make, they're usually not as effective as a "direct sourcing" call. In the latter case, you'd be calling the director-level candidate directly and asking about that person's interest in exploring other opportunities. This call would begin the same way, explaining who you are and why you're call-ing. Then you might say something like:

> I don't know if my timing is right or if you're currently looking to explore other career opportunities right now. I guess my question to you is, Are you the kind of person who would sit down with a competitor organization for an hour or so to see if we could build a career path or develop a compensation plan for you that might be a little more progressive than your current situation?

And there you have it. A direct recruitment call to a targeted candidate that, on its face at least, is nonthreatening and almost casual in tone. After all, it is somewhat enticing to spend an hour with a competitor to see if a stronger career path or compensation plan could be at hand, isn't it? Even the most satisfied employees might have their curiosity piqued enough to meet with you or at least want to hear more about it.

One final note: Don't mention salary or bonus specifics during a direct sourcing call until you know the candidate's current com-pensation package. If the candidate asks about pay, simply state, "Louis, I'll tell you all the specifics, but it really depends on the compensation package you currently have. I don't like shooting in the dark or answering these types of questions in a vacuum, and I may have some flexibility in the salary or bonus depending on the person's background." Once you have the individual's salary infor-mation, feel free to give the compensation specifics of your package or, if you need to go back to the drawing board, call the candidate back at a later time.

25. What role should temp-to-hire staffing play in my organization?

Temp-to-hire is an excellent way of attracting new talent to your company. The key advantage lies in the "try before you buy" opportunity that only temp-to-hire allows. The most common area where temp-to-hire will play a role in any organization is in the administrative support ranks. However, this employment option is gaining popularity in the executive management ranks as well.

The advantages for your company are obvious: interviews, background and reference checks, pre-employment drug screens, and the like will only tell you so much; there's no substitute for working side by side with people to really learn what they're all about. The advantages to candidates are equally appealing: Individuals who wouldn't otherwise qualify "on paper" for consideration gain an opportunity to "strut their stuff" in front of prospective employers. Their chances of landing full-time work skyrocket because they wouldn't otherwise have any way of qualifying for a position.

On the other hand, there are limitations to temp-to-hire staffing arrangements. The biggest disadvantage lies in the fact that candidates enjoy and get used to the flexibility associated with freelance work arrangements. It's not uncommon that people used to that kind of flexibility face difficulties when attempting to conform to a 9-to-5 routine. Therefore, you should be extra careful when interviewing candidates in temp-to-hire situations in this regard.

Tell Me More

It's fairly easy to initiate a temp-to-hire staffing arrangement. In the case of clerical support agencies, simply explain to the agency that you're looking to find a secretary, staff accountant, or customer service representative on a temporary basis who is looking for full-time work. Interview that candidate as you would any other; temp-to-hire clerical staffing is more effective if you interview candidates face-to-face before investing in the training period to follow.

Assignment length is typically anywhere from two weeks to six months, depending on your comfort zone with the candidate and your department's needs (for example, filling in for a maternity leave). Employ the temp-to-hire staffing strategy simultaneously with your ongoing search to fill a position. In other words, temp-to-hire shouldn't *supplant* a traditional search for a full-time candidate; instead, it should *supplement* your search by allowing you an alternative means of identifying the right fit. This way, if you find a more qualified candidate through your traditional search methods, then great—your temp will have helped ensure a smooth workflow transition. Otherwise, the temp himself may be your next full-time hire, and there's your win-win for candidate and company.

Don't backdate an employee's start date to include the time that he was temping for you. During the temp arrangement, the agency was the employer of record; you were only part of a coemployment relationship. Therefore, you shouldn't bridge service credit for periods when you weren't the employer of record. The date the person switches payrolls and becomes your employee exclusively is day one of employment as far as you're concerned.

Clerical agencies distinguish between the pay rate and the bill rate. The "pay rate" is what they pay the applicant on an hourly basis; the "bill rate" is what they charge you. The difference is called a "mark-up." In many cases, clerical agencies charge mark-ups of 55 to 60 percent, depending on geography and the scarcity of a candidate's skills.

Executive temporary agencies may charge hourly mark-ups of 70 to 80 percent for degreed professionals, such as MBAs, CPAs, and JDs. When the candidate converts to your payroll, executive temporary agencies often charge liquidation, or conversion, fees equivalent to a contingency search assignment, often 25 or 30 percent of the candidate's base salary in the first year. (In contrast, clerical agencies rarely charge liquidation fees as long as their temps work for a minimum number of hours, usually around 480 hours, or sixty business days.)

With the U.S. economy in flux, "dot-coms" and other industries in transition have freed up in-demand professionals for interim assignments. Candidates in industries like wireless technology and software engineering will continue to command pay rates in the $60-to-$100-an-hour zone, and companies like yours will need to pay mark-ups on those rates to attract qualified candidates.

Remember that most executive temporary professionals want career stability and full-time work. Short-term assignments with interesting work and good pay have a temporary allure, but many of those candidates will end such relationships in order to find a "real job." Therefore, keep this "fluctuation limitation" in mind when dealing with executive temps—unless you have full-time opportunities to offer, you may lose them before they've solved your interim staffing problem.

For more information on executive temporary placement firms, see *The Directory of Temporary Placement Firms for Executives, Managers, and Professionals* (9th edition, 1999, $39.95. 504 pages) by Kennedy

Information. The book profiles more than 1,900 firms that focus on placing high-level talent, indexed by industries, job functions, and key principals. As such, it's a central source of information and contacts for both corporate recruiters and job-seeking executives. For more information, call Kennedy at (800) 531-0007 or contact the firm on the Web at www.kennedyinfo.com.

26. How do I initiate a campus recruitment program?

College campus recruitment can be an excellent resource for locating highly educated and motivated new entrants into the workforce. Companies in the public accounting, investment banking, and management consulting fields have historically relied upon college campus recruitment for entry-level professionals. Of course, those same organizations will also recruit from MBA programs or law schools to attract newly minted candidates.

However, campus recruiting is no longer reserved for those prestigious Fortune 500 corporations looking only for the top 5 percent of graduating classes to join their ranks. Today companies of all sizes and shapes look to recent college grads to staff positions. In fact, any organization that has the flexibility to train and to allow new hires a generous learning curve could benefit from college campus recruiting.

You have to be prepared for higher-than-average turnover when dealing with young adults who are trying to find their niche in the world. Still, with tight employment markets expected for some time to come, this resource could provide you with a substantial source of recruitment bench strength. After all, few segments of our society are as motivated as new grads to set the world on fire and prove their mettle.

Tell Me More

There's typically no fee for recruiting on college campuses. Among the criteria that many universities and colleges use in deciding whether to allow companies to recruit on campus are these:

- Recruiters should be honest and respectful of the institution, its employees, and the student applicants.

- Job positions and proposals for remuneration and benefits must be factual and fairly current.
- Corporate recruiters should be prepared to invite local finalists to their companies for in-person visits with hiring managers and also be prepared to discuss the training programs and performance expectations before extending an offer of employment.

Copies of annual reports, benefits information, job descriptions, employment applications, and information regarding your company's Web site will be necessary in advance. After all, you'll want to provide the school with that information up front so that candidates will have enough information to choose your organization as a target employer and to ask informed interview questions during your meeting.

Your goal in college campus interviewing is to meet a fairly large number of candidates in a rather short period of time. The college coordinator will forward you resumes of interested candidates in advance. You can then notify the coordinator of the candidates that you'd like to meet. Most employers set up meetings on the half-hour and eventually invite finalists into the office for more in-depth interviews.

On the day of the interview, be prepared to ask the following questions to all candidates:

- Why did you choose this college? How did you pick your major?
- What kinds of career alternatives are you considering right now?
- What qualifications do you have beyond academics that will help you make a successful transition into business?
- Is your grade point average a good indicator of your ability to excel in business?
- After having researched our company, why do you believe you'd want to work with us?

Graduating seniors are looking to use their majors in the world of business. They want to be proud to tell their parents that they're doing exciting and meaningful work. And they want the chance to be creative and to reinvent the business world around them. Your job probably won't offer them any of those things! And that's okay.

Part of the maturation process for recent grads involves learning that work is hard and that it's not always creative and fulfilling and that they won't be the next Bill Gates.

Still, they've got to start somewhere. If their expectations are realistic and they show signs of promise, then your bet that you'll recoup your investment in training them will probably pay off. And who knows—you just might find a superstar who makes a long-term contribution to your company even though it's her first job out of school.

For more information, contact the directors of local or nation-wide university career centers. The College Placement Council is the umbrella organization for all campus recruitment. Learn more at the National Association of Colleges and Employers Web site at www. naceweb.org.

27. How could a recruitment brochure help me market my company to prospective new hires?

With the time restrictions that hiring managers face in high-volume recruiting environments, it's too easy to forget to mention all the "little details" that could influence a candidate's decision to accept a position with your company. If candidates, for example, don't realize that your organization offers a 50 percent tuition reimbursement program, a $.25 match on the 401(k) dollar, or public transportation reimbursement, they may consider only the base salary as the ultimate swing factor in deciding whether to join your company.

Unfortunately, it's all too often the case that job candidates accept or reject jobs solely on their perception of the position and the base pay. The total compensation package can't be considered because most new hires don't find out the details until after they come aboard.

A recruitment brochure may be your answer. Such brochures function as sales and informational tools that can be attached to blank employment applications for candidates to read while they are sitting in your lobby applying for a job. They can communicate your organization's hiring practices and help sell the company's value. Brochures are easily and inexpensively produced as mini-newsletters that can be modified to address your changing practices as an employer. In addition, they enhance your interviews because job candidates will formulate better questions and come to more informed career decisions about joining your firm.

Informed candidates make for better hires with fewer surprises. And think about the deterrent factor: If a candidate realized he couldn't pass a criminal background check or drug test, he could leave right away without proceeding any further in the selection process.

Tell Me More

Appendix C contains a suggested format and sample language to build a recruitment brochure for your company.

Other information found in a recruitment brochure might include:

- Annual holiday schedule and floating holidays
- Vacation grant (x weeks per year)
- Mandatory versus voluntary union membership, one-time union membership fees, and monthly dues
- Parking costs and parking lot locations
- Operating hours and shifts
- Employee services (gymnasium, childcare facility, entertainment discounts, and "ride share" public transportation subsidies)
- Casual dress on Fridays

Some organizations even list the monthly medical and dental premiums associated with their various healthcare plans so that candidates can conduct a comparison of benefits costs against their current employers' programs.

By sharing that you're a caring employer willing to help job candidates come to the most informed career decision possible, your good faith efforts demonstrate your corporate culture and values. By outlining the hiring process, you pace individuals through the hiring process so that each step (reference checks, background checks, employee physicals, and the like) doesn't appear to be a new hurdle aimed at screening out candidates. Most important, you'll get the opportunity to "wow 'em" by selling the full value of your company and by marketing its uniqueness—truly the best way to make a good first impression.

Chapter 3

Online Recruitment

28. What are the advantages and disadvantages of recruiting on the Internet?

Companies are changing their recruiting paradigms to "sell" to an incredibly tightened job market (rather than expecting candidates to come to them). One way to sell themselves to the market is through Internet ads. Internet recruiting is one of the cheapest and most effective forms of recruitment.

Recent polls show that up to 95 percent of U.S. employers are going online to recruit job candidates. So we've all pretty much wet our feet already. Half a billion dollars will be spent in the next few years as companies invest in building and upgrading their own Web sites and posting positions with job search services. Online recruiting is far less expensive and easier to manage than its print ad counterparts, and the turnaround time could be almost immediate if you or your staff are available to monitor incoming resumes. Indeed, with 30,000 job boards worldwide and 2.5 million resumes online, it's hard to dispute the fact that virtual recruitment will lead the way in this century as the job-searching method of choice.

However, there could be serious limitations for companies that rely only on this means of recruitment:

- Women and minorities may not have equal access to Internet resources; as a result, your diversity recruitment efforts may be curtailed.
- New companies offering software solutions pop up all the time; however, many of their products may still be in beta version, and those companies may not be around in the future to support their products.
- A lack of systems integration between your company's HRIS

system and your recruitment software may increase the difficulty in coordinating recruitment activities and tracking results.

- Breaches of privacy may occur due to resume sharing by companies and headhunters once resumes are posted on the Internet.
- Increased quantity may not translate into better quality; shotgun, easy-access resume posting opportunities for candidates may increase the amount of time your company will need to spend in the screening and selection process.

Tell Me More

Raising these issues certainly is not meant to downplay the importance of the Internet's increasing role in your organization's recruitment efforts. However, the Web, the various Usenet sites, and your company's Web site shouldn't be the only outreach efforts that you make. Instead, the Web needs to be integrated into your company's overall recruitment strategy.

For example, according to the National Institute of Business Management's *Success in Recruiting and Retaining* newsletter, some job search Web databases admit that 75 percent of the hits they receive are from males.* Furthermore, until just a few years ago, the demographic of the average Web surfer was a young, white, college-educated male. As a result, relying on the Internet as an exclusive hiring source could limit your diversity recruitment outreach efforts.

Could recruiting on the Internet help you with your diversity outreach efforts? Sure, but only if you target those Web sites dedicated to reaching minority and female populations. In addition, you can post on a general job board established by the Department of Labor to remain compliant with the EEOC. That board is called America's Job Bank and is located at www.ajb.dni.us.com.

Most EEO auditors will expect that you post jobs internally and that you advertise in traditional print classifieds so that the widest population of potential applicants is reached. Your search shouldn't preclude those without home computers or other access to the Internet.

*Reprinted with permission from *Success in Recruiting and Retaining*. Copyright © 2000 The National Institute of Business Management, McLean, Va., (800) 543-2049.

System compatibility problems will remain as software platforms and Internet solutions continuously reinvent themselves to add greater features and functionality. Software companies tend to overpromise full integration with little effort. System conversions are often not completed by preset deadlines, and bugs and systems quirks make it difficult for software products to integrate with your internal HRIS system. Expect, therefore, to run either a separate system for recruitment or an integrated system that may have difficulty capturing all submitted resumes.

There are some fairly new Internet recruiting resources that tout themselves as personality-based placement services by offering personality assessment tools online. Such added screening mechanisms could certainly help if the questions in their assessment tools are well thought out.

Internet recruitment is limited not only by legal issues (in terms of restricting your affirmative action outreach efforts or discriminating against certain protected classes via invalidated online personality tests) and practical problems (vis-à-vis integrating incoming resumes into your company's HRIS system); there can also be ethical issues. Specifically, job candidates complain about loss of privacy, fear of technology invading their lives, and a feeling of being overwhelmed by technological changes. As a result, maintaining traditional recruitment programs such as internal referrals and classified ads in print media will make sense even if you pride yourself as being on the "leading edge" of electronic recruiting.

29. How can I begin recruiting online without generating expenses for my company?

As a general rule, you get what you pay for. The Internet is no exception. However, there are no-cost alternatives available to you if you have no recruiting budget or if you're just starting out in this new medium. Of course, one free and highly recommended option is to add a "job opportunities" site to your corporate Web page. This way anyone who visits your organization's Web site will view your company as a prospective employer. In addition, you'll be able to list your job openings on free online services and on Usenet groups.

Tell Me More

Listing your company's job openings with free online services and on Usenet sites is fairly simple. America's Job Bank, located at www.ajb.dni.us.com, is sponsored by the Department of Labor and allows companies to post their jobs for free. The posting period is for sixty days, and your postings can be linked to your company Web site. In addition, specialty channels exist by geography and occupational field.

Posting your job openings on Usenet groups is also easy. Usenet groups are listings, by date, of hundreds or even thousands of comments on a particular topic. Usenet is a diverse, worldwide electronic discussion forum divided into several thousand news groups. Participants can add their comments on the subject by e-mailing their written opinions (or, in the case of employment Usenet sites, their resumes). The good news about Usenet sites is that they're free, they're easy to use, and many commercial online ad services include Usenet postings in their packages.

The downside includes the fact that they scroll by date, so it's easy to lose your job posting in a mass of other information as others post their own resumes or job postings after yours. In essence, applicants will be forced to scroll down a list of jobs put in chronological order to find the position you've posted because there are no key word search capabilities. Furthermore, the length of time that positions are posted depends on the newsgroup's activity. Older positions will be automatically shed as newer ones arrive. Therefore, your posting could be up for as little as a day. (You'd have to repost it at that point to garner further attention.)

In addition, because they're free, headhunters and other organizations looking to build their own resume databases scour them as well. As a result, these really won't be "fresh" resumes for you—they'll probably have been contacted before by a host of other sources.

One of the most popular Usenet sites for job and resume postings is "misc.jobs." To access a Usenet group, type the group's name after "news:" in the URL space of your Web browser. For example, to bring up a misc.jobs Usenet group, type "news:misc.jobs." Following are some typical Usenet sites that you might want to explore:

URL Address	Comments
us.jobs.resumes	U.S. focus
misc.jobs.resumes	General focus
bionet.jobs.wanted	Biotech industry focus

URL Address	Comments
nyc.jobs.wanted	New York City geographical focus
alt.medical.sales.jobs.resumes	Medical sales focus
sci.research.postdoc	Job posting for postdoctorate research fellows in the sciences
ba.jobs.contract	Contract jobs in the San Francisco Bay area
la.jobs	Los Angeles geographical focus
de.markt.jobs	Positions in Germany

For a more complete listing of free online resume sources, please see the Riley Guide, *Weddle's Recruiter's Guide to Employment Web Sites*, or Job Hunt at the following addresses:

www.dbm.com/jobguide
www.job-hunt.org

30. What are the most effective fee-paid Web sites?

Assuming you have a moderate recruitment budget, placing ads with commercial Web sites is just a phone call or e-mail away. The differences that separate job-posting sites such as Monster.com, Headhunter.net, and Careerbuilder.com from Usenet postings lie not only in the quality of the text and links to your home Web page but also in traffic. Traffic is sometimes measured in "hits," or visits to a particular site. Alternative and more meaningful ways of measuring traffic can be found in terms of the:

- Unique visitors or pages viewed
- Number of job search queries
- Average page views per visitor

The user friendliness, advanced technology, and premium traffic provided by such services may make them more cost-effective than the "free" sites because your time will be used more efficiently. In addition, if you're afraid that your job posting will get lost on large job boards, note that large boards group some occupations into specialized "channels" or "communities." For example, channels such as health care, technology, HR, finance, or sales will focus traffic and viewers' attention on those particular disciplines.

Tell Me More

Commercial job posting sites make use of keyword searching and agent technology, as well as a whole range of Internet tools including Java, sound, and video capability. Most of these organizations offer incentive packages, such as ten postings per month plus access to the resume database, for a discounted fee. Many offer free trial subscriptions that last thirty to ninety days. Others will reduce the fees per posting if you list a minimum number of openings in a given time period.

The question becomes whether you want to employ the services of a general or a boutique site. As their names suggest, general sites are huge career hubs with the most traffic; boutique sites target industries or geographic regions and consequently have greater focus but less volume. Check the resources section in the back of the book for the most popular general employment Web sites according to total reach, with specific information regarding the cost of postings, posting periods, and the ability to mine resumes. A listing of sample boutique sites can also be found in the resources section.

Note that consolidations in the online recruitment industry are ongoing. For example, in late 2000 and early 2001, Headhunter.net acquired Career Mosaic, CareerPath acquired CareerBuilder (but kept the CareerBuilder name), and Monster Board purchased Job-Trak. Expect the industry to continue to fragment because no provider has been able to carry more than 4 percent of the overall market and because the top of the market can have as many as a dozen recognized brands. Organizations that do not charge to post jobs or to mine their resume databases are highlighted in bold for you in the resources section.

Boutique Web sites allow you to target specific employee populations. The trade-off, of course, is that you're tapping much smaller groups (in terms of unique visitors per month or the number of resumes in the database) than with the general employment sites like the Monster Board or CareerBuilder. The best advice is to try both general and boutique sites to maximize the quantity and quality of resume responses and to see what works best for your organization. For more information regarding general and boutique Web sites, see *Weddle's Recruiter's Guide to Employment Web Sites* (AMA-COM, 2001).

31. How should I write an online job ad?

The column-inch paradigm of Sunday newspaper classifieds is dead. Their terse, deliberate language should be saved for obituaries, not for invitations to join your company. Instead, online job ads require that you turn into a marketing guru—someone who sees every job ad as a corporate promotional piece. Why? Because online ads don't charge for space, and, without those limitations, you can let your creative writing juices run wild.

Remember, most job candidates don't change *jobs*—they change *companies*. When you ask candidates about the criteria they're using in selecting another employment opportunity, they'll describe:

- Opportunities for career growth and advancement
- Appreciation and recognition for a job well done
- An open and communicative relationship with the boss
- A working environment where they can make a positive contribution

Now ask yourself, Are these descriptions of jobs or companies? You guessed it: The right answer is that people make career changes to find *companies* that give them the "warm fuzzies" and make them feel as though they're developing their skills and making a difference. Therefore, your primary focus in composing online job ads is to sell your company as a positive place to work.

Tell Me More

Informed candidacy is a concept that dictates that the more job applicants know about a company and a position in advance, the greater the chances of long-term success. That's because there are far fewer surprises when communication is clear and questions are welcomed. Of course, the more information candidates have up front, the better their questions will be throughout the pre-employment process. Your job ad and a hyperlink to your corporate Web site can consequently go a long way in providing lots of information for prospective employees before you ask them to say "I do."

Okay, so how do you structure an online ad? If you have a recruitment brochure that you share with prospective new hires in the interviewing process, it could easily be adapted into an online job ad. You should provide information such as:

- Company history and recent news
- The hiring process
- Benefits information (including premiums, 401(k) matches, and the like)
- Employee services and other perks

Turning this information into a template for online advertising would not only save time but also pique candidates' interest in answering the question, Why would I want to work for this company?

After the company information, you'll want to list information related to the position at hand. Structure the information in this order:

- Title
- Reporting relationship
- Department
- Job responsibilities, both primary and secondary
- Areas of expertise
- Qualifications of the candidate

See Appendix D for a sample Internet ad demonstrating "position" information.

Provide as much information from the job description as possible. If you don't have a current job description, simply remember to distinguish between the primary and secondary responsibilities of the position and to quantify as much information as possible.

If this seems like a lot of information, it may be because you're used to the abbreviated format of newspaper classified ads. Interestingly enough, a print ad could cost considerably more for its one-day run in the Sunday paper than the sample online ad in Appendix D that's due to run for thirty or sixty days! Obviously the ad with more descriptive information about the job will make for a more informed candidate.

Of course, you'll want to include information regarding candidate qualifications (years of experience, professional licenses or certifications, and educational levels). A link to your company's Web site should become a standard addition to every job ad as well. Simply write *"Click here* to visit our Web site for more information."

There's yet another important section to online advertising that doesn't exist in hard copy newspapers: a section called "Community." Ray Schreyer and John McCarter recommend, in their book *The Employer's Guide to Recruiting on the Internet* (Impact Publications, 1998), that you devote a section of your job ad to your company's community. Specifically, they recommend providing information that relates to:

- Real estate values in your area
- Public and private school information
- Professional or school sports teams
- Cost of living comparisons
- Night life and other social amenities

Better yet, they argue, add hyperlinks from your company's home page to other local Web sites that might attract prospective candidates. After all, the Internet gives you the ability to link to any other site with a simple click of the mouse. Some links cost money, so you'll have to investigate this. Still, you might be surprised what added value you bring to job candidates by providing so much thoughtful and insightful information in your job ads (especially when relocation may be an issue).

32. How do I make the most of my corporate Web site?

When designing or updating your Web site, there are some general guidelines that you should follow and some caveats to look out for. Specifically, you should ensure that you:

- Place a link to companywide job openings on the home page so that they are immediately visible to viewers.
- Balance content with design and maintain a visual appeal by providing quick and easy navigation and avoiding slow-loading graphics.
- Organize your Web page's recruitment site by job function, geographic location, or business unit.
- Make searching for job openings easy: if you have more than twenty-five job postings listed on your Web site, break them

down into functional categories; if you have more than 100 jobs, make them searchable.

- Update job openings weekly and avoid internal "jargon" that outside candidates won't understand.

- Include in a navigation button on your home page called the "Life at Work" section as much information as you can about your corporate culture, benefits, work environment, and what makes your company unique; other buttons might focus on company achievements, interactive self-assessment tools, or "refer a friend" promotions.

- Consider offering an online resume builder service that allows candidates to customize their resumes and helps your department route data directly into your proprietary database.

- Consider outsourcing aspects of the design or upgrading of your Web site to consultants.

Following these bulleted highlights, you'll see that speed and easy access are crucial. Too much text is a turnoff; too many graphics may slow the loading process down to the point where viewers are turned off. (After all, most people won't wait thirty to sixty seconds for a page to load.) Therefore, your best advice is to follow the "two-click rule." That is, if it takes more than two clicks of a mouse for a job candidate to access the job opportunities page and locate a related job opening, then your design may be overly complicated.

Tell Me More

Of course, Web pages do much more than recruit. They serve the purpose of communicating public relations information, internal announcements, product and service promotions, annual reports, and news-breaking bulletins. In short, they are the focal point for public information about your company. Adding a button to your main page for job announcements makes sense, since people who come to your Web site as customers or interested third parties might very well "recruit themselves" and express interest in joining your team.

On the other hand, some Internet experts recommend limiting Web page expenditures to less than 10 percent of your annual recruitment budget. They reason that Web pages, in and of themselves, are only part of a company's online recruitment strategy. As such, Web page development should follow the implementation of other strategies, such as online job ads and resume database searches (a.k.a. "data mining"). Unfortunately, too many consultants have touted Web pages as *the* ultimate online recruitment tool, only to disappoint clients who became frustrated that job candidates had no way of knowing how to find the site.

In addition, most small to mid-size companies may not have enough job openings at any given time to justify the costs associated with turning a corporate Web site into a recruiting portal. Simply stated, most candidates will learn of job openings at your company from one of the large commercial databases or print classified ads that you run. Your company Web page should therefore serve, in most cases, as the backbone to educating an already interested candidate, as opposed to a mechanism that draws candidates to itself by its very existence.

If any successes exist in corporate Web page recruiting where the Web page itself is the lure or hook that attracts candidates, then those successes belong to Fortune 500 companies with household names that draw traffic because of their brand-name recognition. The best way to give you a feel for what's really working out there is to observe what your competitors are doing. Better yet, let's take a look at the top ten Web sites in popularity, as ranked by *Success in Recruiting and Retaining* in its May 2000 newsletter.

Study respondents were asked to list the three companies with the best recruiting sections they had seen and used. Of 1,407 responses, these ten were the most frequently cited.*

Company	Web site address
1. Goldman Sachs	www.goldmansachs.com
2. The Boston Consulting Group	www.bcg.com
3. McKinsey and Company	www.mckinsey.com
4. Bain and Company	www.bain.com
5. PriceWaterhouseCoopers	www.pricewaterhousecoopers.com
6. Microsoft	www.microsoft.com

*Reprinted with permission from *Success in Recruiting and Retaining*. Copyright © 2000. The National Institute of Business Management, McLean, Va., (800) 543-2049.

Company	Web site address
7. Morgan Stanley Dean Witter	www.msdw.com
8. J.P. Morgan and Company	www.jpmorgan.com
9. Merrill Lynch and Company	www.ml.com
10. IBM	www.ibm.com

Although your company will most likely not have the same monetary resources to dedicate to Web site development as these prominent organizations do, studying the masters is a logical first step. Remember that the new paradigm of online recruitment focuses on *employment branding*—that is, a company's ability to distinguish itself from its peers. Establishing a recognizable and attractive recruitment image or brand begins with your Web site.

33. How do I increase traffic to my corporate Web site?

According to Advanced Internet Recruitment Strategies (AIRS), in Hanover, New Hampshire, more than 90 percent of online job seekers will check out the Web site of a prospective employer at some point in the interviewing process to learn more about the company. It's estimated that 75 percent of Fortune 500 companies already have their own sites to connect with active and passive job seekers, and this number is rapidly approaching 100 percent. Furthermore, there are more than a million corporate Web sites that actively post jobs.

There are several things you can do to increase traffic to your site:

- Register your corporate Web site address with Internet search engines such as Alta Vista, Excite, or Yahoo so that they can guide users to your site on the basis of users' queries about employment opportunities (typically a free service).
- Purchase hypertext links or "hot links" that lead directly to your server from other Internet services, thereby allowing viewers to jump from one site to another with the click of a button.
- Run banner ads on other Web sites, including chat rooms,

news groups, or job boards, in order to attract candidates to the Careers section of your company's Web site.

- Establish portals that feed into your corporate Web site to increase traffic (for example, with local colleges and universities); this way, when viewers connect to an educational institution's career section, they will be able to hit a "click here" button that links them to your company's Web page.

Make your efforts at driving traffic to your Web site's employment section a rewarding experience for candidates, and you'll find that you're competing for talent on a whole new and exciting level.

Tell Me More

Remember that your company Web site is only as valuable as the eyeballs that view it. The secret of making your company's Web page successful is linking. Traffic to your site will result from the number and quality of Internet connections to your site. Therefore, include in annual reports, company brochures, and your hard copy and online job ads statements such as "Discover more about our company and other career opportunities by visiting our Web page at www.xyz.com." Furthermore, consider purchasing hot links to business partners and prospective recruiting resources, including:

- Suppliers
- Customers
- Trade organizations
- Stockholders
- Colleges or universities that "feed" new graduates to the local employment community
- Commercial or Usenet online job search and recruiting Web sites

The large job boards have expanded their business practices to help small and mid-size companies develop a Web page presence. For example, HotJobs will provide you with a logo and a URL for your company profile page. Hyperlinks are provided free. (A simple e-mail is all it takes to establish a hyperlink.) HotJobs also offers customized "plug-n-play" job boards and can cobrand a job board with your company to enhance the functionality and content of your site.

Specifically, HotJobs' Softshoe product enables corporate clients to integrate job boards within their corporate Web sites to turn visitors into applicants. Every Softshoe installation includes a public job board customized to your site's look and feel. Softshoe offers a configurable network of company job boards, all feeding a central resume database. These job boards can include:

- Public job posting boards for job seekers visiting your company's Web site
- Internal corporate job posting boards
- International job posting boards
- College/university job posting boards

Of course, HotJobs and the other larger online employment hubs will generate traffic to your corporate Web site through banner advertising, channel buttons, splash pages, diversity programs, and other targeted online media programs. Not a bad resource considering the cost-effectiveness and timely turnaround offered!

34. How do I harvest resumes from online databases?

Much like all the topics we've covered in this chapter—free online recruiting sources, fee-paid Web sites, online job ad creation, and Web page development—mining resumes from online databases should be a staple in your virtual recruitment campaign. Employers have a lot to gain by harvesting resumes stored on *all* Web servers on the Internet—not just the resumes in their proprietary databases. You can develop a very active Internet recruiting presence via harvesting, even if you don't post ads or have your own corporate Web site, by mining other sites.

Many employers are comfortable with the idea of posting job ads on the Internet and providing links to their corporate Web pages. However, without dedicated staff to pour through stored resumes on the Web, corporate recruiters tend to steer clear of this lucrative "mining" option. Different databases require different ways of accessing resumes, so in the interest of time, data mining activities have been put off. Truth be told, if you know how to refine your search criteria and you've got a speedy Internet connection, harvesting should become a simple and regular part of your recruiting regimen.

Tell Me More

Probably one of the most powerful yet least understood aspects of keyword searches on the Web is the challenge of writing a Boolean Search String (BSS). Don't panic; it sounds more complicated than it is! BSSs depend on "logical operators and modifiers" to describe what kinds of pages you want to see. When writing a BSS, remember that:

1. Boolean operators are ALWAYS capitalized, and
2. Search terms should generally be in lowercase.

For example, a search string that reads "resume AND programmer AND (Florida OR FL)" will return resumes of programmers who live in Florida or FL. When using an OR operator, it's important that you always close parentheses or else, in this example, you could get a listing of all resumes in Florida! AND, OR, and NOT are the key operators that you'll encounter in Boolean syntax. Some search strings will alter these somewhat—it's not uncommon, for example, that you write NOT as AND NOT in certain arenas. However, Boolean operators are logical and fairly easy to manipulate once you get the hang of them.

In addition to operators, there are also modifiers. Parentheses as seen in the example just given are a kind of Boolean modifier. Similarly, quotation marks act as Boolean modifiers. When used in pairs, they define an exact phrase and hold that phrase together, meaning that all the words must appear in the document in the exact order described. You've seen search strings with quotation marks like "software engineer" that are fairly straightforward. However, if you want to find a programmer with C + + experience, you'll need to write it as "C + +" in your search string. Otherwise, the search engine might interpret the + sign as another symbol for the word "and."

With your Boolean syntax rules in hand, you'll be ready to begin harvesting resumes at some of the sites listed earlier in this chapter. Once you arrive at a given employment Web site, go to the "Employers" tab. Follow the rules listed on the site regarding how you should document your search string criteria, and then click "enter." If too many resumes appear, modify your search string criteria by making them more restrictive. If no resumes appear, then remove some of the modifiers so that you can launch a more general search. You'll find that fee-based Web sites will often allow you to save frequently used queries and create search agents to automate your sourcing process. Wow—just be careful not to get too hooked on all these neat functional sourcing capabilities. You have other work to do!

35. How can I reach passive job seekers online?

The idea of capturing *passive* job seekers through online research is the "next generation" of virtual recruitment and probably the most cutting-edge feature of any company's online sourcing strategy. Passive "job seekers" aren't posting their resumes to job boards or otherwise engaging themselves in a career search. They're busy developing their careers with their current companies and become interested "job seekers" only when solid opportunities present themselves.

Let's look at the math. There are approximately 140 million working Americans. Most companies experience 20 percent turnover per year on average, so that means that 28 million workers will find themselves in active career transition in any given year. However, that means that 112 million workers *won't* be in any kind of career transition mode at any given time. That is the passive job market, and, as you can see, it's four times larger than the active job market.

Strong performers will often listen to opportunities where they can assume greater responsibilities, build their resumes, or significantly enhance their earnings. These very same people can often be convinced that meeting with a competitor firm is wise. The Internet can help you reach these people if you're looking in the right places. Just remember that you won't be looking for resumes or keywords like "employment," "job opening," or "career opportunity" on the Internet. Instead, you'll be looking into virtual communities where people with similar interests gather to talk shop or improve their skills.

Yes, this process takes longer because it's *indirect* in nature; however, your chances of success increase because you'll be treading on fresh snow and presenting unique opportunities at a time when people have the luxury of exploring stronger jobs—while they're currently employed and excelling in their current roles.

Tell Me More

Advanced Internet Recruitment Strategies (AIRS) offers the following information in its virtual recruitment seminars:*

*Reprinted with permission from Advanced Internet Recruitment Strategies (AIRS).

Premise 1: Many of the documents on the Web represent people. They are either created by individuals (e.g., resumes or home pages) or by others to describe individuals (e.g., press releases or alumni lists). From a recruiter's perspective, then, documents equal people, and the Internet is actually a database of people waiting to be identified and found. (A common misconception, therefore, is that a resume is the only document that relates to a candidate.)

Premise 2: Candidates can be found in communities. People on the Web behave just like people anywhere: They join groups related to their skills, interests, professions, and experience. The Internet is simply another forum for people to get together. Instead of church leagues, book clubs, cooking classes, and the Girl Scouts, however, the Web's virtual neighborhoods are in such areas as Visual Basic discussion groups, alumni of particular universities, speakers at the SHRM conference, and senior executive forums. Among the common "gathering grounds" on the Web are companies, schools, teams, organizations, events, projects, and discussion forums.

Premise 3: Communities exist in servers. The Internet is not a centralized, monolithic system. It is, instead, a large, loosely configured network or Web of individual servers linked by a common protocol (TCP/IP), standards, and an infrastructure. A software tool—the browser—lets you view documents across the Web and around the world. Each document or candidate, however, has a specific home on the Web, and this location is in an individual server.

The key issue about these "communities in servers" is that they use a hierarchical directory structure that shows the relationship between the server and its component directories, folders, and individual documents. It follows that if all candidates are related and linked, then your mission will be to "crack the code" of the community that you're trying to identify.

There are two ways that candidates are linked on the Web. The first way that candidates are clustered together on the Web is *across* servers on the Internet. These people can be found using search engines like Alta Vista. Candidates that are uncovered by using search engines to search across the Web come from clues like URLs, links, or keywords that specify which destinations you should examine further. For example, if you include resume.htm or resume.html in a search string, you will locate candidates' resumes that are posted to their home pages, rather than to public job databases.

The second way to locate candidates who are linked on the Web is as a group *within* a particular server. This link is evident from examining the directory structure in the URL. It is common practice, within a particular server, to have lists of people in a folder that is then composed of individual resumes, bios, descriptions, and home pages. So, once you find one candidate who has the skills and experience level you require, you can find others.

To maximize your online research expedition, always search the entire Web first, using multiple search engines, and then investigate specific destinations on the basis of the clues you find. Many companies hire "source strategists" who work with your corporate recruiters to locate potential candidates. Such strategists often engage in "flipping" techniques where they locate and trace links to other Web sites where target populations reside.

If your organization isn't ready to hire a sourcing strategist, you can turn to training and consulting firms such as Advanced Internet Recruitment Strategies (AIRS), in Hanover, New Hampshire, Creative Recruitment Solutions (CRS), in Alpharetta, Georgia, or Netrecruiter.net, in Bethesda, Maryland. AIRS trains recruiters to use online sourcing strategies, while CRS and Netrecruiter perform searches and compile lists of potential candidates for their clients.

In addition, AIRS offers a certification program that leads to a "Certified Internet Recruiter" designation. For more information about this professional designation, call AIRS at (800) 466-4010 or reach the company on the Internet at www.airsdirectory.com.

36. How do I develop an integrated online recruitment program?

Okay, this is the fun part. What's an integrated online recruitment program supposed to look like when you add all these elements together? Very few companies will have *all* these elements. There are two phases to an ideal integrated online recruitment program. The first phase includes harvesting resumes, placing ads, cross-listing ads, and using your corporate Web site. In this phase, use job boards like Monster.com to get more space, longer running time, and instant exposure to a national market at a fraction of the cost of a local classified ad.

In the second phase, employers and recruiters will learn to

drive traffic and build communities themselves that lower costs even further by intercepting target candidates well ahead of commercial job boards.

Tell Me More

Our picture of a well-integrated online recruitment strategy includes the elements already presented in this chapter in the following order:

Phase 1: Ad hoc online recruitment strategy

- Free resume development via Usenet and America's Job Bank job postings and resume harvesting
- Fee-paid ads and resume harvesting in commercial online services with high-traffic databases that contain links to your Web site
- Well-designed, interactive corporate Web site for recruiting (using Java, Shockwave, video, and sound)
- Integration of your print and online advertising by including your Web address in all newspaper ads and marketing materials

Phase 2: Fully integrated, comprehensive online recruitment strategy

- *Resume builders:* Use online prescreening forms and applications to help candidates who don't have resumes available or who want to "self-select" in the employment process.
- *Brand management:* Place banner ads on key Web sites to drive traffic to your home page, and participate in online career fairs to develop a greater online presence and company awareness profile.
- *Publicity:* Use corporate bulletin boards, newsletters, and diversity Web sites as free resources to publicize your job openings.
- *Passive candidate identification:* Employ the services of source strategists or outsource to consulting firms the process of mining the Web for passive job candidates. Their role will be to find resumes across the Web or in destinations like resume banks, virtual communities, or ISPs, and thereby lo-

cate potential candidates in source companies, colleges, organizations, forums, and events.

- *Community outreach:* Use the concept of community to contact candidates and form and grow relationships on the Net. The World Wide Web is an enriched environment with great tools for building pools of prospects and candidate networks. Once you find candidates, you must be able to communicate with them. You must get their attention, convey compelling opportunities, answer their questions, and develop relationships. Cisco Systems does this, for example, through its "Make Friends" program, which connects potential candidates with a Cisco employee from the department where they wish to work.
- *Information management:* Manage the digital flow of resumes straight into your client server or Web-based applicant management system, where they can be analyzed, binned, sorted into work flow queues, shared by recruiters and hiring managers, and then stored to fill future openings. From automatic e-mail notification when resumes are submitted to full tracking of an applicant's progression through the process, technology is available to make the entire process more manageable for you. For example, notes, time/date stamp features, letter templates, distribution functionality, and real-time statistics are available to help you manage active candidates.
- *Reporting:* Develop customized online reports that monitor recruiting activities and get automatically refreshed on the basis of current data. Standard reports typically track source effectiveness, cost-per-hire, time-to-fill, recruiter productivity, and affirmative action outreach efforts.

Whether you choose to use online recruitment selectively or to build your entire employment program around it will depend on your industry, the geographic scarcity of candidates, and the resources you have to dedicate. What's clear, however, is that your goal must be to make recruitment an engine of corporate growth and a competitive corporate tool. There is a fundamental shift of power in the job-finding process, and the Internet is leading the way. Climb aboard and experiment!

Chapter 4

Interviewing

37. What are the three criteria used in selecting high-potential hires?

No matter how refined your interviewing skills, no matter how accurate your testing or how thorough your reference check and background investigation information, the best you can hope for when hiring strangers is that you make high-potential hires. After all, any new hire represents little more than a gamble you're willing to wage that your initial costs and training will pay off for you down the road.

Depending on the kind and nature of work that employees perform, that pay-back period may be three months or one year down the road. If you lose individuals to premature turnover before you've had a chance to recoup the time and money necessary to bring them up to speed, then your return on investment of human capital will be diminished.

There are three criteria to focus on when identifying high-potential hires:

- Longevity
- Progression through the ranks
- Technical skills

The key issue that you'll need to focus on is, How do I question candidates in order to measure their potential in each of these three areas?

Tell Me More

Longevity is the ultimate return on investment when measuring human capital. Because people tend to repeat patterns of change in their careers over time, it's simplest to focus on candidates' reasons for leaving (RFL) past positions. The RFL is the link in a candidate's career progression. It shows you better than anything else does what the person's motivations, goals, and limitations are.

Challenge answers like "No room for growth," which are trite and hackneyed attempts at getting around the real issue. Probe deeper by asking, "What does growth mean to you?" (Vertical progression through the ranks, horizontal progression, broadened responsibilities in other areas, or more money?) and "What would have to change at your present company for you stay there?"

In addition, don't accept "Layoff" as an umbrella excuse. True, many companies shed employees like layers of skin when revenues are down. On the other hand, companies sometimes disguise terminations for cause as layoffs because a no-fault layoff is quick and nonconfrontational in nature. Therefore, challenge the "layoff" answer by asking:

- How many people were laid off at the same time?
- How many people survived the cut?
- How many rounds of layoffs did you survive before you were let go?

Measure a candidate's progression through the ranks by replacing the traditional interview opener "Tell me about your job and what you do" with the following queries:

- Describe how you've progressed through the ranks and landed in your current position at your company.
- How have you had to reinvent or redefine your job to meet your company's changing needs?
- Distinguish between your vertical progression through the ranks at your current (or prior) company and your lateral assumption of broader responsibilities.

Measure technical abilities by asking candidates to self-assess their strengths and weaknesses in their respective disciplines:

- Do you consider your technical abilities basic, intermediate, or advanced?
- On a scale of one to ten, ten being you're a perfect technical match for this position, where would you rank yourself?

(Most people will rank themselves as an eight.) Ask, Why are you an eight? Then ask, What would make you a ten?
- What would you add to or subtract from your technical background to make you more qualified for this position?

With these revised questions on hand and a greater knowledge of the ingredients that make up high-potential hires, you'll find that your confidence will build in the candidate selection process.

38. Can I prescreen candidates with a telephone interview?

Telephone screening calls and online interviews can be a practical defense to the sheer numbers of people applying for positions. These introductions attempt to determine candidate suitability in ten- or fifteen-minute increments rather than one-hour, in-person intervals (and without the validated parking, coffee service, and small talk). Telephone screening calls are essential when setting up interviews across the country. When you have only a little time in faraway hotels to meet with potential staff for a remote office location that you're trying to staff, your initial candidate choices become critical. Therefore, telephone profiling techniques help you determine the optimal candidate pool for off-site interviews *before* you fly out of town.

Your strategy for handling telephone and online interviews, similar to in-person meetings, is twofold: First, employ a questioning matrix to cover all the basics of a candidate's suitability. Second, prepare to sell your company to the candidate and provide the individual with additional resources and information to prepare for the meeting. (Refer candidates to your company's Web page, forward annual reports, or fax them recruitment brochures with details related to the hiring process.)

Tell Me More

There are three major segments of the candidate telephone or online screen: (1) your company and the job specifics, (2) the candidate's success profile, and (3) assessment of candidate's needs. All three are critical because any one area could knock a candidate out of contention. Therefore, simply make copies of the candidate pre-screening interview matrix in Appendix E and attach them to candidates' resumes (if available).

After your initial information gathering session, ask candidates what questions they have about the position or about the company. Close the phone call by stating, "We've got a few more candidates to speak with before we set up in-person meetings. Allow me to get back to you by tomorrow afternoon if we're in a position to invite you in for a meeting." This will gently allow you to end the conversation and possibly heighten the candidate's interest level in the opportunity.

39. How do I interview a candidate when I don't have a resume in front of me?

Interviewing candidates without a resume is a critical skill. First, it's a necessary skill: If you're telephone screening a candidate referred to you or "direct sourcing" candidates from the competition, you won't have the luxury of a resume from which to generate your questions. Second, interviewing "from scratch" allows you to gain a more thorough understanding of a candidate's background because your information gathering is more like filling in the pieces of the puzzle. As such, you'll naturally heighten your candidate evaluation skills.

Tell Me More

The key to interviewing a candidate "cold" lies in your ability to build structure around a naturally amorphous process. If you've never done it before, try interviewing candidates without looking at their resumes for about a week. After eight or ten tries, you'll get the hang of this unique skill and increase your self-confidence in the entire selection process.

To get you started in building the structure of an interview from scratch, use the interviewing matrix found in Appendix F. The advantage of this matrix structure lies in its ease of use: Gaps in employment, changes in industry, and salary and title progression (or regression) reveal themselves easily. In addition, you can easily focus on the reasons for leaving past positions. Remember, the reason for leaving one job should be fulfilled by the next position; the reason for leaving the current position should be "fulfillable" by joining your company. With these key "pressure points" accounted for, you should feel confident that you'll have captured the essence of the candidate's career progression.

40. How do I balance the company's needs with the candidate's requirements?

If it sometimes feels as though you're playing more of a career-counseling role than a recruitment role during the interview process, then welcome to one of the tightest labor markets in thirty-odd years. Historically, employers focused on candidates' credentials and their abilities to make an immediate impact on the company. However, it's a two-way street: It's not enough to gauge whether a candidate will make a positive impact on your company; the candidate must also have an opportunity to build his resume, learn new skills, and assume greater responsibilities by joining your company.

Historically, that part of the equation was the candidate's responsibility. Employers didn't "baby-sit" and ask interviewing questions about why joining the new company would make sense for the candidate from a career progression standpoint. No more. The only real way to determine if candidates will provide you with a satisfactory return-on-investment for hiring them is to question their career development and career management goals. Once you understand whether your job makes sense to them from a career-building standpoint, you can estimate how long that person will remain with your company once the honeymoon phase is over.

Tell Me More

After finding out the person's reason for leaving, ask, "What would be your next logical move in career progression if you stayed with your present company?" If, for example, a vice president of information technology were to respond that her next move would be to chief information officer, that would make sense. Follow up your query with, "How long would it take you to become the CIO?" If she responds, "Oh, probably six months," then stop the interview right there. After all, why would she be interviewing elsewhere if she's heir apparent to the throne within six months?

Point out the discrepancy, and then ask, "What's the *real* reason you're here today and pursuing a job search?" At that point, the true answer may come out—"Paul, although I'm heir apparent to the throne, my boss, the current CIO, may be gone soon, and if she goes, I'll probably be asked to go with her." Bravo—you'll have gotten to the heart of the matter. There's nothing wrong with a "political" response like that. It's just better for you to know the real motivation behind the move than just the superficial answers that candidates initially proffer.

On the other hand, if this candidate says, "Oh, my boss has been there ten years and will probably retire with the company," then it may make sense for her to pursue a job change now. Ditto with responses like, "I want to manage a larger team," "I want to get more involved in Web-related development," or "I want more exposure to multitiered architecture."

In short, as long as candidates are on the fast track with their current employers, they won't leave. When, on the other hand, they're blocked by their bosses because of interpersonal relationship problems, they feel that their job may be in jeopardy, or they feel that they're not capable of making a difference at work, they'll look to move on. Be sure you know the *real* reason for the change before inviting the individual on board.

Third, ask, "Why would moving to our company make sense to you from a career-progression standpoint?" Job changing should be well thought out. Candidates at all levels should be able to articulate the criteria they're using in selecting their next company, what they've learned about your organization via advanced research, and why joining your company will advance their career. Look for answers that demonstrate that candidates are geared for progression in their careers and can make the same contribution to your company that they're making to their current employers.

The manager who's looking for a director title, for example, makes sense. The accounts receivable supervisor who's looking to add accounts payable and financial statement analysis experience to his resume—even at a lateral title and salary—makes sense. Even a finance manager in a small company who'd consider a financial analyst position for less money in a Fortune 500 company may make sense if that person's goal is to join the Fortune 500. Avoid candidates who appear to change jobs for change's sake. Steer clear of job changers who don't have compelling reasons for leaving their current companies, or you may find yourself filling the same position again before you've had a chance to recoup the costs associated with hiring and training.

Finally, remember that people tend to repeat patterns of change in their careers over time. If you see that a candidate lasted twelve months per position over the past three jobs, then don't kid yourself: You'll most likely have this individual around for only the next twelve months as well. That might be okay for you, depending on your immediate needs (for example, for Web-savvy techies with specific Web design skills). Overall, though, beware spotty job histories with predictable job changing patterns: Those folks tend to leave positions for change's sake, and that makes for low-probability hires.

41. What kind of notes should I take during the interview?

Careful here—the notes that you write on employment applications, resumes, or evaluation forms become part of a candidate's written record and are "discoverable" documents if subpoenaed. Making personal notes to yourself on yellow stick-ems count just as much—if not more—than other comments jotted down about an individual's candidacy. (So don't use yellow notes in the hopes of removing them at a later date!)

That's why many companies forbid hiring managers from making any notes whatsoever about candidates. Their logic is that if nothing is written down, the documentation can't later be used against the company to substantiate a claim of discrimination. Unfortunately for the rest of us, being forbidden to write notes on particular candidates makes the selection process that much harder. After all, how can you keep people apart in your mind when you don't have notes to remind yourself of their strengths, weaknesses, and personality?

Companies that forbid managers to take any notes about candidates are probably overreacting. After all, discrimination lawsuits based on a company's right *not* to hire someone after an interview are fairly rare. Still, they occur often enough that an ounce of training prevention indeed is worth a pound of antilawsuit cure.

Tell Me More

You may write the following comments about a candidate without landing yourself in hot water should the documentation ever be subpoenaed and used against you:

> Well-spoken, warm, excellent progression through the ranks at her current company, but had difficulty expressing why she wants to leave her current job. Also didn't know her company's annual revenues. Definitely someone we should explore further.

> Stiff, inflexible style, appeared to be preoccupied with getting out of my office for another appointment. Cold and aloof, almost rude. I'd pass.

> Nice person, but credentials are not impressive: all small companies with little name-brand recognition, poor reasons for leaving prior positions, and she can't remember old dates of employment or names of prior supervisors. I'd pass.

> Inappropriately dressed for interview. Used the term "orientated" rather than "oriented" several times and kept saying "ya know" as a nervous pause. Wrote "see resume" on her application. I wouldn't recommend her for our department.

> Very difficult to understand because he mumbled—poor eye contact and posture. Seemed to have very little self-confidence or self-esteem. Not a good fit for our front-desk position. He'd have difficulties dealing with the overly demanding personalities.

What kinds of written comments should you avoid? Here are a few that would probably expose your company to unnecessary legal headaches:

> Looks like he'd have difficulty lifting thirty pounds over his head.

> Wrong image—we need a much leaner, hipper look for dealing with visiting clients and vendors and projecting the company's image effectively.

> Doesn't think young enough—lacks zest and appeal. Pass.

> Accent too heavy. It would be difficult to understand her on a daily basis.

> Acne and weight problems. Don't refer.

The obvious problems with these comments lie in their subjective nature. They imply that individuals should be precluded from employment because of the perceptions of the beholder, rather than because of the individual's lack of talent, abilities, or related experience. Avoid documenting subjective perceptions of people that are not tied to their skills, knowledge, or abilities or to your company's specific business needs.

42. How formal should an interview be?

Interviews can be as formal or as informal as you'd like them to be. Interviews are extensions of the interviewer's personality. People who are very formal and systematic in their approaches to dealing with others should reflect that very same style during the interview meeting. On the other hand, people with bubbly personalities who are, by nature, informal and casual should have no problem allowing their personalities to shine.

Although this question is fairly common among hiring managers, there really isn't a definitive answer that should dictate your interviewing style. Instead, just remember that you will tend to hire in your own image. So finding people who are most like you will result from your genuine concern and desire to identify candidates geared for progression in their careers who can make the same contribution to your company that they're making to their current employers.

Tell Me More

That being said, it's time for some self-awareness and sensitivity training. My interviewing style is very casual. I'm not very formal in anything that I do, including business meetings or conference presentations to hundreds of people. What does that look like to candidates? Well, in my office, candidates will find cookies, licorice, or a number of other doodads to break the ice of the initial meeting.

I typically offer candidates something to drink. Most politely decline, while some ask for water. I'll usually follow up my initial invitation with, "You mean I can't get you anything at all (or anything else)? How about some beer, wine, or a highball of some sort?" That always gets them laughing, and before long we'll be into a deep conversation about their backgrounds and personalities. I know that may sound a little too informal for most of you, but I like to have fun during an interview. Most candidates appreciate the corny humor, and it puts people's defenses to rest.

And, yes, there's a logic to all this. Besides the fun, I really want people to confide in me during an interview. If candidates respond, "Well, Paul, I normally wouldn't say this during an interview, but . . . ," I know I've gotten to the real person behind all the "interview hype."

In addition, informal interviewers often conduct their meetings from the couch or coffee table where employer and candidate are on the same level playing field. There is typically an effort to establish a friendly relationship both in informal "warmup" talk, situational seating, and a nonthreatening questioning style.

What about more formal interviewers? How do their interviews sound? Well, they're typically more structured, and they often follow a predetermined format to ensure fairness. Formal interviewers possess a more point-counterpoint questioning style. Humor isn't typically part of the interview meeting. Instead, candidates respond more formally and, yes, mechanically, to the questions asked of them. Formal interviewers typically sit at their desks, they take notes of candidates' responses, and the roles of interviewer and interviewee are clearly defined and rarely transgressed. Again, these aren't negatives. It's simply a matter of being aware of how your style may come across to strangers.

In addition, interviewing formats often differ between formal and informal interviewers. Formal interviewers tend to ask candidates questions first and then go on to describe the position and the company. There is often a palpable break in the interview meeting where the conversation switches from employer questions to company and position information. Candidate questions then follow.

Informal interviewers, on the other hand, usually weave information together throughout the meeting. The meeting may begin with candidate questions, proceed directly to information about the company and the job, go off on some kind of personal tangent, and then return to candidate questions.

There are some advantages and disadvantages to these styles. Informal interviewers run the risk of "giving away the farm" if they share too much information with the candidate up front. After all, candidates will adapt their answers to fit your company's needs if they're given the opportunity to hear your game plan up front. So informal interviewers, beware: As much as you enjoy the spontaneous communication with candidates, don't share too much about the position until you've figured out what candidates have accomplished and are looking for in their careers.

Formal interviewers, you've got to be aware of an inherent flaw in your more structured style: It sometimes becomes necessary to cut an interview short because a candidate isn't qualified for the job. How do you stop short an otherwise unproductive interview meeting to save yourself time? Well, it's by short-circuiting the format that you hold to so dearly! For example, if you've determined after five minutes that a candidate won't work, skip from wherever you are in your structured interview paradigm to this one magic question: "What are the three or four criteria you're looking for in selecting your next company?" After the candidate responds, thank him for taking the time to meet with you, and give him your business card. That should save you lots of time by cutting short an otherwise unproductive interview. A rejection letter can then be sent to close the communication loop regarding the individual's candidacy.

43. Are there any specific questions that should become a staple of every interview?

Yes, but that's only a recommendation, not a requirement. In other words, it's up to you to employ a core of key questions for all applicant interviews. Of course, you're not legally obligated to ask all the same questions to all job applicants to make sure that you're being fair in the evaluation process. The more consistent your questions are, however, the more accurate your objective evaluations will be. In addition, a core of questions will build your confidence and ensure that you're covering all the key issues related to an applicant's suitability.

Tell Me More

Okay, so what are the questions? That's actually up to you. You've probably been asked questions as a job candidate yourself that impressed you. Maybe you've read interviewing books like my *96 Great Interview Questions to Ask Before You Hire* to generate ideas. (Okay, so that was a free plug!) Overall, though, you might want to ensure that you've got five or six questions that you can pull out of your pocket during every interview to objectively qualify individuals who want to join your company.

The questions that follow are only suggestions. They are particularly popular among employers, and that might encourage you to add them to your portfolio of interviewing questions:

> Tell me about your greatest accomplishment at your current company/in your career. And if you wouldn't mind, please link that achievement to increased revenues, decreased expenses, or saved time.

That's pretty straightforward. Employees are hired to do one of those three things for their companies: Those with P&L responsibility—line managers—are paid to increase revenues. Staff managers in finance, information technology, or human resources come up with ideas to decrease costs. And anyone and everyone, from receptionists to limo drivers to chefs, is responsible for saving time. Remember that people tend to be hesitant about sharing their achievements for fear of appearing to brag. This question is a good indicator of one's ability to see oneself as a provider of workplace solutions; it's also an accurate indicator of one's self-esteem.

> What would your most respected critic say of your job performance? How would that relate to the grade you received on your last performance evaluation?

This is a challenging question because it forces an on-the-spot self-assessment. In addition, it can be easily verified should you ask the candidate for copies of a recent performance review. Beware of rehearsed answers like, "I tend to have difficulty delegating work to others" or "I tend to be too critical of myself." Those rejoinders come straight out of job-finding books or Internet advice columns. When you're faced with a superficial response, say, "Nice try, Sam, but that's not *real* enough. Be more critical and more specific: What's a real weakness that we'll need to be aware of so that we can give you added support from day one?"

Once you've identified the real answer, be sure to run that same question by a former supervisor during a reference check: "Sam said his real weakness lies in his listening skills. He sometimes apparently misses important points because he's two steps ahead of himself during meetings, and he's not actively listening to what's being said. Have you as his supervisor ever found that to be the case?" That's the best way to customize a reference check.

What would you add to your background to make you more qualified for this position?

No candidate is perfectly qualified for a position. As a matter of fact, it's usually a mistake to hire "perfect" candidates because you'll get the most productivity out of people who are enjoying a learning curve. People who rank themselves technically as an eight out of ten will often produce more effectively than those who rank themselves as tens, because tens have been there and done that. The new job that you're offering represents a continuation of skills already learned and repeated. As a result, you might want to ask, "How would you rank yourself on a scale of one to ten in terms of your qualifications for this job?" That query may provide some insights that you otherwise may have missed.

Where do you see yourself in five years?

I know, that's one of the oldest questions in the book. And it's not really a fair question because candidates lose if they answer it: If, for example, a candidate interviewing for a financial analyst position says that five years from now, he wants to be the CFO, that may appear to be unrealistic and quixotic. On the other hand, if he says, "Five years from now I'd be happy being a financial analyst," then he's a meatball. After all, doesn't he have any career aspirations at all?

The best response is no response at all. A candidate who punts that question might respond, "It's hard to say where I'll be five years from now. What's important to me is that I'm given an opportunity to assume as much responsibility as you'd be willing to give me. After five years, you can decide where I'll be able to make the greatest impact." Bravo—good answer!

What three or four criteria would you use in selecting your next job/ company?

It's important to understand what drives people to leave their current positions. Focus them on what they want in the future, not what their problems were in the past. This will help you decide whether your company's opportunity will meet their career needs and be their next logical move in progression.

The top answers you'll find when asking this question are:

- An opportunity for growth and advancement
- An open and communicative working relationship with the boss
- Recognition and reward that are commensurate with achievements
- Creative, rewarding work and the freedom to work independently
- Job stability
- Salary and bonus opportunities

What's important is not only the content of their answer but also the *order* of their answers. The values they place on their next job will be directly proportionate to their frustrations at their current company. It's an insightful exercise from an employer's perspective, but candidates like it as well. After all, it really shows that you're focused on their needs as well as on your company's needs.

> At what point salary-wise would you accept a position, and at what point would you reject it?

This question is often saved for the final rounds of interview at the pre-offer stage, but it needn't be. Although some employers choose to avoid salary discussions until the eleventh hour and then magically draw back the curtain to reveal the salary offer, others prefer to discuss salary expectations up front in the initial interview. Either way is fine, although you may find that you'll save yourself a lot of time by discussing salary right up front. At whatever point you choose to address this topic, remember that it's the sine qua non of employment offers. Make it a staple of your interview so that you have a handle on this critical topic when it's time to select finalists and ultimately make an offer.

44. What is behavior-based interviewing?

The most successful technique for adding dimension to superficial interview responses lies in employing a behavioral questioning format. Behavioral interviewing techniques attempt to relate a candidate's answers to specific, past experiences and focus on projecting potential performance from past actions. By relating a candidate's answers to specific past experiences, you'll develop much more reliable indicators of how the individual will most likely act in the future. Behavioral questions do not deny that people can learn from their mistakes and alter their behaviors. They do, however, assume that a person's future behavior will closely reflect past actions.

Tell Me More

Behavioral interview questions call for on-the-spot self-analysis. There are two main types of behavioral formats: self-appraisal and situational questions. Self-appraisal queries ask the candidate, "What is it about you that makes you feel a certain way or want to do something?" For example, "What is it about you that makes you get totally involved in your work to a point where you lose track of the time?" Similarly, the self-appraisal format may ask for a third-party validation of your actions: "What would your supervisor say about that?"

Other examples of self-appraisal queries include:

- On a scale of one to ten (one meaning that you're lenient and understanding, ten meaning that you're demanding and critical), how do you see yourself as a supervisor? Why?
- If you had the choice of working in a marketing or a finance environment, which would you choose and why?
- In the future, how do you think you would handle an employee termination under those same circumstances?

Situational queries, like self-appraisal queries, look for concrete experience as an indicator of future behavior. The standard behavioral interviewing query begins with the paradigm, *"Tell me about a time when. . . . "* Examples include:

- Describe the last time you assumed responsibility for a task that was clearly outside of your job description. Were you commended for your actions, or could you have possibly stepped on others' toes?
- Give me an example of a time when you had to make a critical decision in your boss's absence. What were some of

the risks of making that call, and what would have happened had you chosen not to make any decision at all?

Notice the specific linkage to concrete past experiences and situations.

The beauty of this questioning methodology is that it can be applied to anything: a candidate's greatest strengths and weaknesses, his supervisory or sales styles, his communication skills, or his self-proclaimed work ethic. As a result, behavioral questions ensure spontaneity, since candidates can't prepare for them in advance. Rehearsed answers to traditional queries go by the wayside in this ad hoc interviewing environment where candidates tell stories about their real-life performance. And, because it ties responses to concrete past actions, this technique minimizes the candidate's inclination to exaggerate answers. Hence, you're assured of more accurate answers in the selection process, and you're provided with specific ammunition to use later down the line in the reference-checking process.

Of course, you can't prepare behavioral questions before an interview. It's not about specific questions; it's about a questioning *format* that gets candidates to discuss details related to their initial answers. Use their answers to your initial questions to formulate behavior-based questions. The further you remove a candidate from a "first-tier" response, the more you get to actually know the person.

Anytime you feel that the candidate's thought is incomplete, or you're otherwise left hanging, simply ask for an example. Used one or two times during an interview, this technique can help your meeting become much more conversational and informative.

45. What are the three biggest mistakes that interviewers typically make?

Interviewers do a lot of things right, but there are a few errors that trip up even the most successful hiring managers, such as when they fail to:

- Spend enough time with the candidate to really gain an understanding of the individual's personality and approach to dealing with problems.
- Make sure that the candidate's level of business maturity

will ensure a smooth interpersonal transition into your company.

- Confirm that accepting your position would be the next logical move in progression from a career development standpoint.

Tell Me More

Let's look at each of these issues separately. Spending "enough time" with a candidate is a relative concept because it's situation- and job-specific. In other words, you might not need to spend as much time with a candidate for a part-time receptionist position as you would with someone applying for a vice president job. Still, too many managers spend relatively little time with applicants, ask superficial questions, accept innocuous responses, and then make a determination that hiring the person would be a good decision for the company.

What's the solution to such a problem? Add critical mass to your interview! First, be sure to line up enough solid questions in advance so that you'll have meaty issues to talk about. Second, be sure to explore candidates' initial responses by employing behavior-based interviewing techniques. Again, the beauty of behavioral interviewing queries is that they allow you to place superficial responses into some kind of contextual framework by asking for examples of actions and situations that occurred in the individual's past.

Third, remember that your goal in the interview is to truly "get inside the candidate's head":

- Can you understand what motivated her to change jobs in the past?
- Does she jump around from job to job too much, and, if so, how long will she most likely remain with your company if you hire her?
- On a scale of one to ten, how technically qualified is she for the job? What would she have to add to or subtract from her background to become more qualified? How much downtime will she require in terms of a learning curve?
- Do you believe that the criteria she's using in selecting her next company or job are realistic and can be fulfilled by your company?

- Will she be willing to put in the hours necessary to get the job done, will she accept direction easily, and does she have the organizational forecasting ability necessary to ensure that the work flows smoothly?

Similarly, looking at a candidate's level of business maturity is also essential. Business maturity isn't age related; rather, it has to do with candidates' willingness to assume responsibility for their actions, rather than pass off blame on someone else. This issue is best handled during a reference check with a candidate's prior supervisor, since most individuals won't admit shortcomings in this area. However, an interesting way to probe this issue during an interview might be this way: "Judy, I'm not asking you to be critical of your boss or of your department's management team. But I'd like your objective feedback: Did your supervisor assume responsibility for things gone wrong, or did the 'blame game' ensue anytime something hit the fan?"

Now watch the candidate's response: People who readily blame their supervisors during an interview may tend to blame others in general. Why? Because that's become the corporate norm or expectation under which they've learned to operate. If a candidate believed that her boss readily blamed others anytime something went wrong, that candidate could still "protect her boss" when answering your question by assuming responsibility for that problem. This would demonstrate her business maturity.

A candidate may have learned lessons about conduct in corporate America that will be difficult to unlearn. A red flag during an interview should definitely be explored during the reference checking process.

Finally, interviewers tend to see the hiring process as a one-way street. They fail to place themselves in the role of headhunter or career counselor to ensure that candidates are making the best moves for themselves when considering employment offers.

What if you expect that accepting a position with your company could be a step backward for the individual? Then pull away during the interview! For example, if you sense that joining your company would:

- Force the candidate to take a significant cut in pay
- Force the candidate to take a significant cut in responsibility
- Not provide the creative outlet the individual is looking for

then say, "Don't mind my saying so, but this doesn't look right for you. You've been working with Price Waterhouse Coopers for the past three years, and I realize that you want to go inside with a client because you're tired of the consulting route. But our company is very small, and you'll have little room to grow, since our CFO has no plans of retiring. As much as I like your background, I don't see how we can keep you motivated by providing you with any type of career ladder. Besides, you can join the Fortune 500 at this point in your career. Why would a small, start-up dot-com make sense for you now?"

That challenge is a pull-away, and it will force the candidate to come to terms with your offer relative to other offers she could probably entertain from larger or more prominent companies. Asking it shows your genuine concern for the individual and simultaneously protects your organization from premature turnover. It's a consideration that will help you get inside the candidate's head, assess his business maturity, and ensure that your organization gets the optimal return on investment for its hire.

46. How do I interview technical candidates when I'm not a "techie" myself?

Interviewing technical candidates poses problems for human resources and general managers alike. Supervisors feel particularly challenged when they're responsible for interviewing and hiring technicians who possess a level of technical competence far greater than theirs. Still, no one can know *all* facets of all the people they hire—the world has simply become too niche oriented as far as particular professions are concerned.

For example, human resource recruiters in a hospital environment might be responsible for hiring IT, finance, and quality assurance candidates, in addition to nurses and postdoctoral research fellows. Few of us would be able to understand the intricacies of those professional positions, and there should be no guilt or shame in that. Still, interviewers have to evaluate those candidates and make hire/no-hire recommendations, despite their lack of technical understanding. The question is, How do you evaluate someone when you really don't understand the nature of the detailed and complex work they do?

The way around this dilemma is to state your knowledge limitations up front and then allow candidates to evaluate themselves according to their own criteria. That will spare you the embarrassment of appearing to know the technical nature of those business functions when you really don't. (After all, it will only be a matter of time until technical candidates realize that you don't really speak their language.) It will also provide you with enough information to make evaluative recommendations based on candidates' self-analysis of their qualifications, career progression potential, and history of achievements and shortcomings.

Tell Me More

Let's assume you're hiring a lab technician who is responsible for gene sequencing because that is an important role on your team. However, as a business manager, you don't consider yourself a bench scientist. Here's what your interview might sound like:

Step 1: State your knowledge limitations up front.

> Laura, as a business manager in this unit, I focus more of my time on the behind-the-scenes administration of the lab. I've got my degree in microbiology, but, truth be known, I'm not that familiar with gene sequencing techniques. Therefore, don't mind if I sit respectfully and listen to your technical answers without appearing to be "leading edge" myself. I'd prefer if you answer my questions in layman's terms and teach me what you're doing by explaining it as if I've never had a day of biochemistry in my life. Would that be all right with you? [Yes]

Step 2: Allow candidates to evaluate themselves according to their own criteria.

Candidates need first to address what they do in their current roles. Your questioning might begin this way:

> Let's look first at gene sequencing, an important part of the position you're applying for in our lab. Tell me about the gene sequencing you're doing at your current organization. What exactly do you do now?

Candidates then need to address the challenges they perceive in transitioning from their current companies to your organization on the basis of differences in product lines, computer systems, research methodologies, and the like. You might follow up with a question like this:

> Your current lab focuses on the human genome project; our lab, as you know, does cancer genetics. What do you think you'd be doing differently from a gene sequencing standpoint in our lab as opposed to what you do now in your current lab?

Next, ask candidates to assess their technical competency on a scale of one to five.

> On a scale of one to five, how do you rank yourself from a technical standpoint? In other words, if a one meant you're far off from what we were looking for, and a five meant you were exactly what we were looking for from a technical point of view, how would you rank yourself?

Note that most candidates will rank themselves as a three or a four, depending on their experience and level of comfort with the position they're interviewing for. Few will rank themselves a five for fear of being perceived as cocky or arrogant. When they rank themselves as a three or a four, ask:

> Why would you rank yourself a four?

After noting their response, ask the logical follow-up query:

> What would you add to or subtract from your background to make you a 5?

At that point, you'll have enough information to measure the gap between the ideal credentials and this candidate's particular background. Still, to help you focus further on the issue of "technical match," ask another follow-up question:

> Where would we need to give you the most support, direction, and structure in your initial employment period to make sure that you excelled in this position from a technical point of view? What else should I know relative to how you see your qualifications for this position from a technical standpoint?

The information you gather will typically be very on target for a few reasons. First, candidates appreciate your willingness to "learn" from them. Most take that responsibility seriously and will help you come to an informed decision about them. Second, these questions get right to the heart of the matter. Even if you don't fully understand the technical information shared, you'll be able to write accurate notes and make formal recommendations.

Save the true technical competency questions for the pros, in this case the Ph.D. biochemists who are waiting to interview the candidate. Focus your interview, instead, on career progression potential and achievement profiles, and set the stage for counteroffer possibilities, reference checking, and salary negotiations. Be sure, however, to be able to touch upon the technical aspects of the interview enough to discuss your concerns or recommendations, ask relevant questions, and come to an informed hiring decision.

47. How do I interview Generation X job hoppers?

If you're recruiting for skilled professionals in today's job market, you'll be forced to engage job-hopper candidates with spotty employment histories and little apparent staying power or commitment to their prior companies. And, because of market competition, you may not have the discretion to simply pass on individuals who have held four jobs in the past three years. Indeed, these individuals sometimes appear to be holding all the cards and negotiating for signing bonuses and other perks once reserved for senior levels of management.

There are three issues you've got to consider when interviewing job candidates with spotty work histories. First, what's their reason for leaving their current company? Second, what would be their next logical move in career progression if they remained with their current employer? And, third, would moving over to your company be a good move in progression for them from a career development standpoint?

Tell Me More

It's not enough to gauge whether a candidate will make a positive impact on your company; the candidate must also have an opportunity to build his resume, learn new skills, and assume greater responsibilities by joining your company. You can determine whether the company's needs and the employee's needs are balanced by using the process described in Question 40.

Candidates who appear to change jobs for change's sake should be avoided. Steer clear of job changers who lack compelling reasons for leaving their current companies, or you may find yourself filling the same position again before you've had a chance to recoup the costs associated with hiring and training.

Remember that people tend to repeat patterns of change in their careers over time. If you see that a candidate lasted twelve months per position over the past three jobs, then don't kid yourself: You'll most likely have this individual around for only the next twelve months as well. That might be okay for you depending on your immediate needs (for example, for Web-savvy techies with specific Web design skills). Overall, though, beware spotty job histories with predictable job changing patterns: those folks tend to leave positions for change's sake, and that makes for low-probability hires.

48. What are the ten most common interviewing questions that could cause legal problems?

No discussion of interviewing would be complete without at least a partial listing of the most problematic interviewing queries that could land companies in legal hot water. Usually these are questions that are, or can be perceived as, breaking laws against discrimination. No one sets out to ask discriminatory questions; sometimes it's just out of oversight that managers ask inappropriate questions.

For example, a hospital administrator in a pathology laboratory interviewed a female candidate who was obviously pregnant. The administrator was concerned that the chemicals in the lab, which were known to cause cancer, could adversely affect the fetus. Out of concern, the supervisor asked the candidate, "Are you sure you'd want a job that exposed you to cancer-causing chemicals, especially now that you're pregnant?"

When the candidate was not ultimately selected for the position, she brought her complaint of discrimination to the hospital's human resources department. The department promptly invited the candidate back to interview for other openings and apologized for the hospital administrator's indiscretion. Although no further legal action was taken, a more aggressive individual might have pursued the matter further. The administrator, in his defense, stated that he was asking out of practical concern and meant no harm or offense. He was written up nonetheless: Companies have an obligation to demonstrate that they take such concerns seriously and provide remedial training and, when necessary, discipline to prevent further incidents of inappropriate questioning.

Tell Me More

So which questions do you have to watch out for? After all, you realize that your intentions, harmless and innocuous though they may be, are not at issue. It's a plaintiff attorney's interpretation of your questions that's the real issue. And it's not uncommon for plaintiff lawyers to attribute unlawful motives to your actions by making a case that you've used the information that you learned by asking a particular question to unlawfully deny the candidate employment.

To avoid legal skirmishes of this sort, review this partial "watch list" that follows, and ensure that these questions never make their way into your interviewing vocabulary:

Inappropriate Question #1: "What's your maiden name so that I can check your references?"

Asking for a woman's maiden name can discriminate against her on the basis of marital status and possibly national origin. Instead, ask whether the candidate has used any other names in the past (not necessarily due to marriage) that will allow your company to verify the person's past work experience and education.

Inappropriate Question #2: "How old are you?" A variation of this question is, "In what year did you graduate from high school?"

State and federal law protects workers more than forty years of age. There's no problem asking about the year in which a candidate graduated from college: People can graduate from college at any point in their lives. In contrast, nearly all high schoolers graduate at about eighteen. An individual's year of birth could readily be determined by subtracting eighteen from the year of graduation.

Inappropriate Question #3: "Where were you born? Are you a U.S. citizen? Where did you learn to speak Spanish?"

These questions transgress guidelines regarding national origin, birthplace, and citizenship. Instead, you should ask, "Could you, after employment, submit verification of your legal right to work in the United States?" Questions regarding a candidate's native language or acquisition of foreign languages should generally be avoided unless such language proficiency is an essential function of the particular position being applied for.

Inappropriate Question #4: "Are you married? Can you make adequate provisions for child care?"

Ooops—a big no-no! It's a legitimate concern to wonder whether a potential employee can meet overtime demands, fly out of town on last-minute notice, or consistently report to work on time. However, you are limited by law to stating such things as standard working hours, any overtime demands, and company travel expectations, and then simply questioning whether candidates would have any reason why they couldn't meet those requirements.

Inappropriate Question #5: "Would your religion prevent you from working weekends?"

Asking such a question discriminates on the basis of religious affiliation. It's just as easy and effective to state: "Weekend and holiday work is required. Is that acceptable to you as a condition of employment?"

Inappropriate Question #6: "Are you disabled? Have you ever filed a workers' comp claim? How many days were you sick last year? Do you have AIDS?"

The Americans with Disabilities Act of 1992 requires businesses with fifteen or more employees to make their facilities accessible to the physically and mentally disabled and prohibits job discrimination on the basis of disability. The ADA says that a company can't exclude a qualified candidate from a job if that individual can perform the "essential functions" of the job either unaided or with a "reasonable accommodation." (The terms in quotation marks are subject to legal interpretation, of course.) The alternative? Hand a candidate a job description that differentiates essential and nonessential job functions, and ask, "Are you capable of performing the position's essential job functions with or without a reasonable accommodation?"

Inappropriate Question #7: "Have you ever been arrested?"

It is allowable to ask a candidate whether he has ever been convicted of a felony, but this felony question (typically found on your company's employment application) must be accompanied by a statement that a conviction will not necessarily disqualify the candidate from consideration for the job. See Question 51 to find out whether you can deny employment to people with criminal records.

What's the difference between being arrested and being convicted of a felony? Simply put, people who are arrested are often not convicted, either because they are innocent or because there wasn't enough information to justify a conviction. Whether the conviction is for a felony or misdemeanor is not the key issue. Various states define unlawful acts differently as felonies, misdemeanors, or "wobblers" (meaning the unlawful acts can be either felonies or misdemeanors depending on the circumstances). In California, for example, embezzlement is a misdemeanor. This misdemeanor would clearly be considered job related for any job applicant who would have a fiduciary responsibility to your company. Employment could consequently be denied on the basis of this misdemeanor. The language in your employment application, therefore, must be scrutinized and adapted to meet the laws of your state.

Even if the candidate has been convicted of a felony, categorically rejecting him would be a problem for two major reasons: First, the felony may have no relation to the essential functions of the job. Second, such a blanket policy has been held to have an adverse discriminatory impact upon certain ethnic and racial minorities in inner cities. Speak with your employment attorney before accepting or rejecting candidates who have been convicted of a felony. These are rare occurrences, but you could end up in legal hot water for wrongfully hiring the individual (a concept known as "wrongful hiring and retention") or for failing to hire him.

Inappropriate Question #8: "What kind of discharge did you get from the military?"

Whoops—another no-no. Military service questions must be limited to relevant skills acquired during service. No questions about the nature of the discharge—honorable or otherwise—may be asked.

Inappropriate Question #9: "Have you ever declared bankruptcy or had your wages garnished?"

There are no acceptable alternative questions that allow you to address these issues before the hire. You are, however, perfectly within your rights to make employment offers contingent upon credit checks provided: (a) applicable state and federal laws are followed and (2) good credit is necessary to perform the essential functions of the job.

Inappropriate Question #10: "Who is the nearest relative we should contact in case of emergency?"

It's fine for you to ask for *someone* to contact in case of emergency. However, asking for the "nearest relative" could border on discrimination by national origin, race, or marital status.

Check out *The Employee Recruitment and Retention Handbook* and *Fair, Square, and Legal* for more information about what questions you can legally ask in an interview.

Chapter 5
Making the Final Selection

49. How can I conduct an effective reference check?

There are still many misperceptions out there regarding what can or can't be discussed during the reference-checking process. Many otherwise well-informed employers mistakenly believe that it's illegal to check references on candidates. Still others believe that checking references isn't a good use of time because only dates and titles of employment are revealed.

Little could be further from the truth! In fact, references are just as important—if not more important—than interviewing. Why? Because a well-placed reference-checking telephone call can provide you with a prism through which you can see the future. Prior supervisors' opinions of candidates' strengths, weaknesses, and areas of development, along with perceptions of how candidates will fare in particular working environments, are exceptionally valuable avenues of exploration in the selection process.

How can you ensure that you won't simply have your call forwarded to a company's human resources department where name, rank, and serial number will be the only feedback you get? More important, how do you get prior supervisors to speak candidly with you regarding weaknesses and areas for improvement?

Following is a methodology for generating critical information during a reference check:

Step 1: Once you've selected a finalist candidate, ask the individual to "bridge the reference" for you. In other words, ask the candidate to locate her prior supervisors and to ask them to accept your phone call regarding her performance.

Step 2: Open the phone call by painting a picture of your corporate culture and its unique pressures so that the former supervisor can do some evaluative decision making regarding the individual's fit with your company.

Step 3: Reassure the supervisor that what he says will not dictate whether you hire the individual. You simply need to know how to best manage the person from day one.

Step 4: Save formal questions like "dates and title" until the end of the reference-checking process.

Tell Me More

Too many employers make the mistake of calling past employers "cold" and expecting feedback. If a former supervisor hasn't heard from a candidate in two or three years, don't expect lots of subjective feedback. It's a "cold" call, and you'll probably get a cold response: "Call human resources. Company policy says I can't give any reference information" is the typical company line you should expect.

Other employers, once given the okay to begin asking reference questions, begin by reading off a sheet of canned questions. Their queries are asked in a vacuum, and former supervisors are forced to respond generically to superficial questions like "What did she do for you? What were her greatest strengths and weaknesses? And was she timely in meeting deadlines?" Not that those aren't important points—they're just mediocre in their presentation and reveal little eye-opening information.

Here's a better way to handle references. First, figure out what concerns you. Then find a way to incorporate that information into the reference. For example, let's assume you're looking to hire a Web developer who is technically qualified for the job but appears to jump from job to job much too much. Assuming the candidate has spoken with his previous supervisor and confirmed that the prior supervisor is expecting your call, here's what your call might sound like:

> Jay, my name is Paul Falcone, and I'm the executive producer of entertrainment.com. We're a training and development organization that focuses on providing small to mid-size companies with management training in the areas of performance management, leadership, train-the-trainer, and workplace conflict resolution. We're privately held and have about twenty-five employees. I'm

calling you, Jay, because Doris Panico is a candidate we're seriously considering for our Web designer job opening. She told us that you were her immediate supervisor at Corporate Training, Inc., and I was hoping that you'd be able to share some insights into her ability to excel in our company. Is now a good time—do you have a few minutes?

Great! First, Jay, before I ask you any questions, let me just tell you that we're a small, start-up dot-com, and our culture is kind of an "anything goes" type of outfit. We're not much on formalities or policies and procedures. I need someone who's easygoing and who'll fit in and get along with everyone else, and that's my main concern when bringing new people aboard. Please keep that in the back of your mind when answering my questions, okay?

We all liked Doris, but we were a bit concerned about her career stability. I know Generation X-ers tend to move around a lot, especially those who are pursuing careers in the somewhat unstable world of dot-com startups. Still, Doris doesn't appear to have sunk her teeth into any work assignment for more than six months at any time. She's only been out of school for two years, but I'm afraid she still needs to kiss a few frogs before she finds her prince. Did you experience the same thing, and were you disappointed when she left your company?

Note here that if the employer is hesitant to provide any reference information for fear of legal repercussions, you should replace the notion of "what you tell me will determine whether we hire this person" with an appeal to the employer's managerial expertise:

Jay, I won't ask you to address anything you'd rather keep confidential. I asked Doris to call you in advance because I know that prior employers will always try to help people that they liked. I also want you to know that I don't need you to unilaterally judge her past and feel pressure relative to our hiring her or not. It's more a case of our wanting to know how to best manage her and provide the right level of structure, direction, and feedback if we were to hire her. We're not looking for someone with a halo who can part water—we just want to make sure that we can manage her weaknesses and make this as good an experience for her as it will hopefully be for us. With that in mind, would you mind answering some questions regarding the best way to manage her from day one so that she has a smooth landing at our company?

If the former supervisor still won't provide any information, then state:

> Jay, I have to assume that no news is bad news. Companies that have nothing to say about prior employees typically don't have anything *good* to say in my experience. Am I going to get burned by hiring this person?

At that point, you have nothing else to lose. Simply listen to the body language on the other end of the phone, and be sensitive to any animosity that may linger. An unwillingness to come to the candidate's aid or otherwise defend the individual's performance record at that organization may suggest that you should pursue other candidates (or at least chalk this one particular reference off to "burned bridges").

50. What questions yield the most useful information in a reference check?

Remember not to begin the call by asking "filler questions" about dates of employment and last title held. Save those for the very end. Instead, open up with either-or types of questions that require the former supervisor to take a stand on a topic. For example, try asking these five opening questions:

1. What kind of structure and supervision would provide Doris with the most support from day one: (a) a structured environment with clear guidelines and immediate feedback or (b) an autonomous, independent, "hands-off" type of culture?
2. Some people constantly look for new ways to reinvent their jobs and assume responsibilities beyond the basic, written job description; others adhere strictly to their job duties and "don't do windows," so to speak. Which style fits Doris more accurately?
3. In hiring _____s, we look for a solid balance between quality and volume (or output) in their work. Still, most people lean more in one direction than another. Where does Doris fall on that spectrum?
4. What about her ability to accept constructive criticism? Do we need to walk on eggshells when delivering bad news to her, or can we "hit her right between the eyes," so to speak?

5. Does she function better in a (a) moderate, controllable, and predictable environment; (b) a faster-paced atmosphere with deadline pressures and time constraints; or (c) a "hyper-space," chaotic, "management-by-crisis" culture like the floor of the stock exchange?

Tell Me More

Furthermore, try some of these questions as the reference-checking phone call picks up steam:

- How would you grade Doris's ability to predict needs before they arise? In other words, how would you grade her timeliness and proactive business style?
- Would you consider her more of a people person or a technically oriented person?
- How would you grade her oral and written communication skills?
- What about technical capabilities: What softwares were used in your department? Would you consider her level of competence basic/intermediate/advanced?
- How many hours a week did she find it necessary to work in order to get her job done?
- What about her organizational, time management, and listening skills?
- Have unscheduled leaves, tardiness, or unreliability ever been a problem?
- What do you consider to be Doris's greatest achievement or accomplishment within your company? (And please try to link this achievement to increased revenues, decreased expenses, or saved time, if possible.)
- What one or two areas of improvement could she work on right now as part of a professional development plan? (In other words, what should we look out for in terms of giving her extra support?)
- Would you consider her "high maintenance" or "low maintenance" in terms of supervision? Is there anything that typically "unwinds" or bothers her?
- Is she rehirable? Yes. No. If not, why not?
- What was her reason for leaving your company? (What

would've been her next logical move in progression at your company had she stayed?)
- What was her ending salary?
- What were her dates of employment?
- Is there any additional information that you feel would help us in determining her ability to excel here?

Using these questions, a typical reference-checking phone call will last between ten and fifteen minutes. The value of the queries, of course, lies in your ability to bounce a candidate's version of reality against a former supervisor's opinion. In addition, nothing works better than a reference check in providing you with a blueprint for managing to a person's strengths.

51. May I deny employment to job applicants who have been convicted of a felony or misdemeanor?

Most employment applications ask the question "Have you ever been convicted of a felony or a misdemeanor? (Conviction will not be an absolute bar to employment)." Remember from Question 48 that it is improper for a prospective employer to ask job applicants to disclose arrest records that did not result in a conviction for fear of violating their privacy rights. It is illegal for an employer to discriminate against a candidate because of an arrest that did not lead to a conviction or to discriminate against a job applicant who participates in a pretrial or posttrial diversion program that is not considered a conviction.

However, employers may ask employees or job applicants about arrests for which they are out on bail or out on their own recognizance pending trial. The question becomes, What do you do with an affirmative answer? Clearly, you may not deny employment because of a positive response to this question; however, it may be wise to postpone a decision until the case has been resolved. If there is no conviction at the time that the case is resolved, if the position is still available at that time, and if the applicant is the best-qualified individual for that job, then you should hire. However, if the applicant was convicted and the crime was "job related," you may deny employment. In most of these cases, the mere postponement of a decision will result in your never hearing from the applicant again.

Certain exceptions to this "arrest versus conviction" questioning rule exist: There are several industries, such as healthcare, aviation, transportation, and law enforcement, where employers are prohibited from hiring when there was an *arrest*. For example, in some states, healthcare employers may question applicants about arrests for sex offenses if the applicants are to interact with patients. They may also ask about drug arrests when considering applicants who will have access to drugs. Similarly, utility employers may ask about arrests if applicants are to have access to private homes.

With the exception of the industries listed here, employers are generally prohibited from seeking from any source whatsoever a record of arrest that did not lead to conviction. Further, due to disparate impact, a categorical denial of a job due to an arrest that is not job related may expose the organization to legal liability that would be difficult to defend.

Tell Me More

This is all somewhat confusing and probably won't come up all that often. So what should you do if a job applicant checks the box stating he's been convicted of a felony?

The EEOC dictates that a conviction for a crime should be analyzed on the basis of (1) the nature and severity of the offense, (2) the time lapse since the conviction or sentencing occurred, and (3) the relevancy of the conviction to the job applied for (i.e., job relatedness). Furthermore, employers are permitted to deny employment opportunities to convicted felons if there is a "sound business reason" for doing so.

Violent convictions are clear; however, the crime of embezzlement is considered clear only if the applicant will have access to funds. What about spousal battery convictions, petty theft, or driving under the influence (DUI) of alcohol or drugs? Using the rules outlined here, an employer must first analyze whether there is a sound business reason for denying employment. Although criminal convictions must clearly be related to job responsibilities, in today's violent society employers remain concerned about negligent hiring and negligent retention exposure.

In addition, companies consider "character" a key ingredient in the hiring process. When such evidence of lack of character appears, a case can be made to deny employment on the basis of crimes where an indication of an abnormality in the person's character was a factor. Of course, we're touching on legal theory here, so before concluding that employment may be denied because of a record of violence or a lack of character, speak with qualified counsel for a fact-specific analysis.

One more point: Driving under the influence is a misdemeanor in certain states, while it is a felony in others. Many employers are surprised to learn that they may ask on their employment application, "Have you ever been convicted of a DUI?" If an applicant checked "no" on the application but a background check reveals that the candidate lied, then the issue of character goes not to the DUI but to the falsification on the employment application.

The lesson? It is easier to deny employment for falsification of an employment application than for any other reason. Even when an employer learns of a crime that on its face would not stand up as a job-related offense in terms of denial of employment, the fact that the applicant did not divulge the information when specifically asked may be grounds for denial of the position.

The wisest advice for you to follow when facing a situation related to a checked box under the felony, misdemeanor, or DUI category on your employment application is to thank the candidate for applying for the position. Explain that you're not sure how the conviction might impact his application for employment. Look into the matter further with the help of qualified legal counsel, and then follow up with the candidate appropriately. If the conviction bars him from employment, forward a standard rejection letter. If the conviction doesn't bar the applicant from consideration for employment, then judge the individual's candidacy relative to those of others who are applying for the job as you would under any other circumstance.

52. Should I hire a background investigation firm?

Many employers who consider using background investigation firms think only of liability protection. Courts have ruled that companies have a general duty to check criminal records for prospective employees who interface with the public or who could have an opportunity to commit a violent crime in the course of their employment. In addition, damages against employers are being awarded where the company has been found to be negligent and failed to perform a reasonable search into an employee's background prior to hiring. Therefore, a background check could minimize the exposure of a wrongful hire or wrongful retention lawsuit.

That's certainly a valid reason to employ background investigation firms. On a more practical basis, however, background investigation firms will help you hire better employees by steering clear of candidates who have falsified their employment applications. Since industry experts approximate that 30 percent of all resumes contain some misrepresentation (most commonly in the education section), a sound background check will help you:

- Enhance security in the workplace
- Reduce turnover
- Minimize occurrences of employee theft
- Provide you with peace of mind in your hiring decisions

And, no matter how good your reference checks are, you won't have the time, resources, or authority to check into candidates' criminal backgrounds.

Tell Me More

Your background investigation firm should provide you with legal disclosure forms (updated pursuant to any Federal Trade Commission staff opinion letters) in both English and Spanish that require candidates' signatures to demonstrate their consent to being investigated. (The Fair Credit Reporting Act makes it legal to procure a consumer report for employment purposes only if the consumer has been notified in a clear and conspicuous written disclosure before the consumer report request, and only provided that the consumer has given written authorization.) In addition, sample rejection letters to applicants should be provided to you should your decision not to hire be based wholly or in part on information contained in the report.

Finally, be sure to include information regarding your company's practice of conducting background checks in your pre-employment literature. There's definitely a preventative value to stating your intentions up front. After all, if candidates learn from your recruitment brochure or from posters in your office that you conduct criminal background checks (or drug screenings, for that matter), they will typically walk out before taking the time to fill out an application if they know they can't meet your requirements.

Dollar for dollar, background checks are an excellent pre-employment tool. Expect 5 percent of all candidates to be knocked out of the running. That could save you significant time and money, depending on the number of hires that you make every year. The added time to the hiring process is minimal because you can begin background checks at the same time you conduct reference checks. Most important, your employees will appreciate your due diligence in ensuring them a safer workplace.

53. How do I select a background investigation firm?

What do you look for in selecting a background investigation firm, and how much will its services cost? First, a basic search will typically investigate a candidate's:

- Criminal history
- Motor vehicle report (MVR)
- Social Security verification

The basic criminal search should be completed by the background investigation firm *in person* (as opposed to via the Internet or via CD-ROM database retrieval) at the local superior and/or municipal court for the most up-to-date records. The number of years of criminal history that can be typically investigated depends on the laws of your state. The MVR is important because warrants for arrest typically appear on them (including driving under the influence, possession of drugs, and failures to appear before a court). The Social Security trace validates the accuracy of the individual's Social Security number and may be used to validate job history dates.

Tell Me More

Additional searches for additional fees may include:

- A credit report
- Education verification
- License verification
- Military records verification
- Workers' compensation filings (post-offer applicants only)
- Sexual offender/child molester identification requests (for

example, for school employees, home health employees, or employees in child care centers, or in any cases where companies have "parties at risk")

Credit reports should generally be conducted only when the applicant would have a fiduciary responsibility to your company or handle cash. Accounting, finance, and senior management candidates typically should have their credit histories checked. (For other positions, the applicant's financial condition is not likely to be relevant.) By acting responsibly in evaluating candidates' credit histories, you'll mitigate risk by protecting yourself not only from in-house loss or theft but also against actions brought by others if the employee acts on your behalf. It is critical that your background investigation firm follow the laws established under the Fair Credit Reporting Act (FCRA) as amended by Congress in 1997 and the Consumer Reporting Employment Clarification Act of 1998, as well as applicable state laws.

The cost of a basic package ranges from $25 to $100 per search. You may be able to create your own "package deals" for a discounted fee by guaranteeing the firm a certain number of searches per year. Ancillary services such as credit checks or education verifications may cost anywhere between $10 and $25 per search. Court fees may apply as well. Turnaround time is typically twenty-four to seventy-two hours; however, education verification for out-of-country searches may take longer.

54. Should I institute drug testing for all new hires?

Every supervisor knows that employees under any influence of alcohol or illegal drugs almost invariably produce inferior work, call in sick a lot, and threaten the safety of coworkers and customers. Fortunately, corporate America has clearly developed a consensus that the workplace is an appropriate site for confronting drug abuse. As a matter of fact, since the passage of the Drug-Free Workplace Act of 1988, there has been a nationwide decline in the use of drugs by employed individuals. That's the good news; the bad news is that workplace substance abuse still costs U.S. employers an estimated $120 billion each year.

American Management Association's survey on workplace drug testing and drug abuse policies indicates that nearly 80 percent of surveyed companies have adopted programs to test employees for illegal drug use. Since 1987, the date of the AMA's initial survey, company drug testing has increased by more than 300 percent. According the to U.S. Bureau of Labor Statistics, approximately 70 percent of large companies (5,000 employees or more) have some kind of drug-testing policy in place.

The Drug-Free Workplace Act requires all federal government contractors and fund recipients to implement workplace drug abuse prevention programs. Such programs typically include a written policy (see Appendix G for a sample policy), supervisory training, employee education, an employee assistance program (EAP) resource, and drug testing. Prevention and deterrence are the key focus of most workplace programs; the Act doesn't include mandatory implementation of a drug-testing program. However, companies governed by the Act may voluntarily employ a two-pronged approach to minimize drug use in the workplace:

1. A new hire testing program where applicants who test positive are denied employment.
2. An in-service program structured to get the substance-abusing employee into treatment and to provide the opportunity to get help, with the goal of getting the individual back to work.

Tell Me More

The Americans with Disabilities Act provides that a medical examination can be required only *after* an offer of employment has been made and before the beginning of the applicant's duties. However, a test to determine whether an applicant is illegally using drugs is *not* considered a medical examination. Therefore, if an employer wishes to conduct a drug test even before making a conditional offer of employment, he can. However, the ADA allows pre-offer tests only for *illegal* substances. Therefore, tests for blood alcohol level are permitted only after an offer has been made. In addition, the ADA protects applicants who have successfully completed a drug rehabilitation program. Therefore, an employer should establish a time frame within which an applicant who previously tested positive may reapply.

Lab rates for pre-employment collection and testing range from $30 to $60 in many industrial clinics and medical facilities. Turnaround time for lab results is usually around forty-eight hours. The drug test screens for the following chemicals when urine specimens are collected:

- Tetrahydrocannabinol ("marijuana/THC")
- Amphetamines ("uppers"); a common side effect includes violent tendencies
- Phencyclidine ("PCP/angel dust"); confusion, agitation, severe mood swings, and erratic and violent behavior are also common side effects
- Cocaine metabolite
- Barbiturates (sedatives)
- Benzodiazepines (tranquilizers)
- Morphine, codeine, methadone (opiates)
- Propoxyphene (painkillers)

Alternatives to body fluid testing include hair analysis, pupillary reaction testing, and video-based eye-hand coordination testing.

Clear drug screen test reports will show "none detected" under each chemical area. By the way, it's a good idea to ask your provider to test for "adulterants." For an additional fee of around $.50 per screening, the clinic will check to see whether candidates have attempted to distort the results of the test by ingesting products meant to dilute drugs already present in the system.

Some companies use on-site drug testing kits, rather than labs, for immediate results. The limitation to on-site kits lies in the fact that candidates have been known to sneak others' urine into testing rooms, thereby getting a clear report. Labs ensure against such deception by measuring the temperature of the specimen, locking toilet lids, and coloring toilet water blue (so that water can't be injected into the urine to dilute it).

Remember that any on-site positive result should be sent on for a gas chromatography/mass spectrometry (GC/MS) confirmation assay in a certified laboratory to rule out a medical treatment or prescribed drug use.

The legal issues surrounding workplace drug testing are numerous and complex. What's clear is that it's much more difficult to terminate a current employee who may be protected by the Americans with Disabilities Act and other rights of privacy than to terminate a job applicant in the pre-employment process.

If you implement a drug-testing program, you should test all applicants for all jobs. Notice of the substance screening policy should be placed on your employment application. Employees should be given an opportunity to retest, as well as to challenge the results. If your employees are governed by a collective bargaining agreement, this may be a "bargainable" issue. Finally, if you aren't already familiar with your state laws on drug testing, contact your state legislature, or get a copy of *A Guide to State Drug Testing Laws and Legislation*, published annually by the Institute for a Drug-Free Workplace.

55. How do I decide between two good candidates?

The ultimate selection decision may be difficult if you're fortunate enough to have multiple candidates to choose from. That may be the equivalent of a "millionaire's choice" in the working world, but it's frustrating nonetheless. Remember that, on top of all the criteria that you're using to select the most qualified candidate for the position, the candidate's desire factor should play a critical role. In other words, don't discount the importance of an individual's desire to join your company. All else being equal, the desire factor might serve as the ultimate swing factor in your decision to select a finalist.

Of course, everything in the first part of this book deals with hiring the most qualified individuals. Interviews, reference checks, background investigations, personality tests, and the like all serve to narrow down your choices in order to help you make high-potential hires. Selecting a finalist, however, means looking beyond these objective selection criteria to more subjective issues because, all else being equal, it's the personality match and a candidate's desire factor that win the day.

Tell Me More

The only way to actually zero in on a finalist among finalists is to use the old Ben Franklin Close. Do you remember that one from grade school: Plusses on the right, negatives on the left? After listing all the pros and cons, you'd tally the totals at the bottom of the sheet and use that factor to make the ultimate decision.

Appendix H contains a twelve-point Ben Franklin Close to help you use that tool in the selection process. Of course, the statisticians among you may feel a need to "weight" the factors by order of importance. Remember, though, that this is only an informal tool to help you sort out your feelings on paper. Feel free to adapt it to your own hiring situations as position-specific factors change. Bear in mind that this documentation will become part of the official hiring record. Therefore, as discussed in Question 41, be careful what you write.

56. Should I hire on the basis of gut feelings or vibes?

There's absolutely nothing wrong with hiring candidates on the basis of a gut feel. As a matter of fact, it happens all the time. We all tend to hire in our own image, and when we meet someone we genuinely like, we tend to project a positive feeling about working with her.

On the other hand, many managers would agree that experience has taught them that hiring on the basis of chemistry or "likability" has historically gotten them into trouble. Why the discrepancy? Because gut feelings should serve as the ultimate swing factor only when other, more objective, criteria have been met. In other words, you need to make sure that likability equates to compatibility once the new hire starts with your company. To do that, you'll need a more objective diagnostic test to see whether you're actually compatible. Once that objective evaluation has been made, you can feel free to rely on your gut feeling as a tiebreaker.

Tell Me More

How do you know whether you really like someone and are compatible with that individual? That topic alone justifies the existence of the entire personality testing industry! (See Questions 15 and 16 for more information on tests.) We all know that no matter how much we try to control variables in people's personalities, there's only so much we can do. Interviews help, as do references, background checks, personality tests, and the like. Still, until you're both working side by side, you just can't know how you'll get along.

Our only chance lies in making high-potential hires. We know there are no guarantees when dealing with people (both in our personal and business lives), but at least, in a business setting, there are resources available to help us make optimal choices.

Once you've gotten consistent feedback from both the candidate and her prior supervisors during the interviewing and reference-checking processes as illustrated in Questions 43 and 50, allow your "gut feeling" to make the ultimate call!

57. How do I take the wrinkles out of the salary negotiation process?

Salary negotiations tend to be the most challenging part of the offer process for most employers, and for good reason: Managers often think that their company pays well below market, and the only way to get good candidates is to buck their company's internal salary guidelines. "If you pay peanuts, you'll get monkeys" goes their all-too-common line of logic. Unfortunately, managers may place themselves at odds with their own organizations when it comes time to land the candidate they want.

Candidates, of course, often see salary negotiation as the ultimate swing factor in accepting or rejecting an offer because they believe that the salary offer represents their perceived value to the organization. That's fine, but most candidates don't understand how salary offers are made: They have no idea that internal equity considerations will force you, the prospective employer, to "slot" their salary offer between other existing employees on the team. They don't know what budget considerations you're under—even if you're over budget for the year. Consequently, they can get hung up on $5,000 and reason that, if your company is so stingy that $5,000 makes a difference, maybe you're not the right company to join in the first place.

With candidates and your own managers sometimes against you, it's no wonder that salary negotiations are the most misunderstood portion of the selection process. It's also little wonder that they're saved for the end of the selection process.

Tell Me More

Salary negotiations actually begin with the first phone call and continue throughout the interview process. You are responsible for "preclosing" candidates on their salary expectations from the first telephone screening or in-person interview.

If your company has a set salary cap for a particular position, share that with candidates up front. Depending on the years of experience you're looking for, your offer may be fairly low for an experienced candidate in your part of the country. Therefore, when you receive resumes and leave messages for candidates who have submitted their resumes, state up front that you like the applicant's background and would be happy to meet with her, but the salary will max out at $30,000. If that's a go, you can set up a meeting.

What about situations where you've got a salary cap of $85,000 for a director of finance position, and a candidate includes in her cover letter that she's currently earning $90,000 plus a bonus? The letter doesn't stipulate her desired salary range, and you don't know whether the candidate would consider $85,000 or is looking for $105,000. Again, the best way to handle it is to be up front about the matter during the screening phone call:

> Sarah, I see that you're currently earning $90,000 plus bonus. I'd like to invite you in to come and speak with us, but our position is budgeted at $85,000 without bonus. I know it's too early to discuss salary negotiations since you don't know much about the job or our company, but whenever a position is paying *less* than what a candidate is currently earning, I want the person to know that before she comes in. This way everything is above board, and no one's time is wasted. What are your thoughts: could you consider an $85,000 salary if the position were a good move in career progression for you?

Now on to a trickier situation: The Law of Inverse Gravity kicks in whenever a candidate realizes that a position could be paying more than the company is willing to offer. For example, it's not wise to tell candidates that a position pays anywhere from $30,000 to $36,000 for one simple reason: The candidate just heard you say $36,000; you ideally want to pay $30,000. And now you're upside down in the deal from the outset. The simple way to avoid this is to avoid quoting salary *ranges* to candidates until you know how much they make and what they're looking for.

Unfortunately, someone in the interviewing loop almost always inadvertently lets the cat slip out of the bag. When you're upside down in a deal, there's only one way out: Explain how internal equity and budgeting works. Here's how your conversation might sound:

> Vic, you're currently making $32,000, and I know that you were told that our position could pay up to $36,000. Naturally, $36,000 is the number you heard. However, I've got to take a minute and explain some basic rules of our compensation program to you. I never want a candidate to think the company is "being cheap" about a salary offer; naturally we want to give as much as we can to motivate people to join our company. Still, when it comes to making offers, it's not just the salary range that's at issue. It's also a matter of what we call "internal equity."
>
> We can't know up front how much experience a particular candidate will bring to the table. However, once we've identified a finalist, we've got to slot that person's years of experience and particular skills and education to those of the existing employees in the department. We obviously wouldn't want to pay a new hire more than what we're paying our existing staff members. As a result, we make a determination as to where to slot the candidate should that person accept our offer. We've looked at your years of experience and determined that the fairest offer to make you would be at $33,000. I realize that's not the top of the range; however, I wanted you to understand that this number wasn't pulled out of a hat or determined in a vacuum. It's actually the fairest offer that our company could make to you for this job, and we hope you'll take it. However, we understand if you'll need to walk away from this offer and pursue opportunities with other companies.

Notice the pull-away at the end of this conversation. There's no need to apologize for your company's salary determination. It's always a better strategy to explain internal equity and then gently "tug the offer away" to see if there's still interest on the candidate's part.

What if you're competing with another offer (or a counteroffer from the candidate's current company)? Those are the most difficult salary negotiations of all, and it's certainly worth exploring on our part.

Let's assume that your candidate currently earns $90,000 at his current job. Your position pays $100,000. However, at the finish line when you're about to extend the offer (which the candidate originally agreed he would accept), you learn that the candidate has another offer on the table for $115,000. The candidate calls you somewhat apologetically and tells you that another company suddenly put a deal together offering him a 30 percent bump as opposed to your 10 percent increase. He's hoping your organization can match that higher salary.

Now it's time to earn your keep as a master negotiator. First, determine how much you want the candidate. After all, even if you had the money in your budget, you might not feel that this particular individual was worth all that money. Second, look at internal equity and see where a $115,000 offer would place this candidate relative to his peers at your company. If other existing employees are MBA/CPAs and this individual has only a bachelor's degree, it may not be worth offering the higher salary for fear of upsetting the compensation balance with your existing employees. Remember, "pay secrecy" is only a theory; sooner or later, salary information leaks out over the water cooler.

Now let's assume that you can afford to raise your offer from $100,000 to $105,000 without breaching internal equity or going over budget. Should you offer $102,500 and then be prepared to go up again to $105,000, or should you offer the $105,000 salary straight out?

The answer depends on your negotiation style. Of course, either approach is acceptable. In general, however, it's best to be open and fair with candidates from the start and minimize any perceptions of back-and-forth negotiations. Here's what you might say:

> Vic, we've gone back to the drawing board and looked at budgets and internal equity to increase our offer. I want to let you know that I don't believe in tug-of-war salary negotiations: I think they start employment relationships off on the wrong foot. Instead, what I'd like to do is make you a good faith offer above what we originally put on the table. Before I do that, though, I'd like you to know that this will conclude the negotiation; if the offer isn't acceptable, I'll understand. I'll have to respect your decision to accept the other organization's offer over ours. Does that sound fair?

> Good. There's another thing I'd like to know before I share the revised offer with you. Let's take salary off the table for a minute. I don't need to know who's making the other offer; however, I would like to know how you compare the two companies and two jobs. If you were strictly looking at the other company and its offer, whose position would be superior, ours or theirs? In other words, which position is the next logical move in progression for you from a career development standpoint?

Assuming the candidate feels that your position is superior, then continue this way:

> We can increase our offer from $100,000 to $105,000. I realize that's not as much as your other offer, Vic, but it's $5,000 more than we were planning on paying, and we're willing to go over budget because we feel you'd make an excellent addition to our team. I assume you've looked at benefits plans and premium costs so that you could make an apple-to-apple comparison. It's really a matter of juxtaposing the initial salary offer with the perceived career value that joining our company might have for you. What are your thoughts about accepting or rejecting our offer?

That's about as open and honest as negotiations will ever get. Depending on timing in the individual's life, his perception of your appeal as a company where he'd be proud to work, and his career development goals, your revised offer will either be accepted or rejected. Respect the individual's right to decide his career fate on its own merits. After all, last-minute offers and changes to the game plan are a part of doing business. If your best efforts fail, you'll live to fight another day.

58. How do I prevent candidates from leveraging counteroffers?

Counteroffers occur when a candidate accepts your company's offer of employment, returns to her current job to give notice, and then decides to remain with her current employer after being countered with a pay increase or promotion. In such cases, your recruitment efforts will be for naught, since the interviewing, reference checking, and salary negotiations will all be undone. In short, you'll have lost the candidate that you hired and will have to start the recruitment process all over again.

Companies often "work on" their employees with counteroffers while those individuals are in their two-week notice periods. Appeals to loyalty, guilt, and even fear have been known to entice workers to stay when combined with increases in salary or promotions.

The bottom line is, you can't know whether a candidate's current employer will aggressively entice him to stay; you have to assume that all candidates will receive counteroffers from their present companies. Therefore, it's an important proactive strategy to stay in contact with new hires who have given notice to their current companies. After all, people are creatures of habit, and, as the saying goes, the devil that you know may be better than the devil that you don't know. Translation: "Maybe it's not as bad here as I originally thought, and leaving for another company might raise a whole new set of problems for me. I think I'll stay put!"

Tell Me More

Addressing counteroffer possibilities occurs early on in the interviewing process. From meeting one, employers should discuss the possibility of a counteroffer:

- Bill, what is your motivation for leaving your current company?
- What are the three criteria you're using in selecting another company?
- What would have to change at your present company for you to stay there?

With such questions on hand from initial interview rounds, you'll have a firmer grasp of the possibility of a candidate's counteroffer acceptance.

In addition, *before* the offer is extended, it becomes time for a "resignation drill." Remember, a counteroffer is nothing more than a variable that you should seek to control before offering someone a position with your company. Therefore, part of your offer negotiation will sound like this: "Bill, we've talked about your readiness to make a move from your current company. But I don't want your emotions at the time of the offer to cloud your better business judgment. Let me ask you this: Tell me about the counteroffer that they'll make you once you give notice. If you gave notice to your boss right now, what would she say to keep you?"

This query mentally prepares the individual to deal with the counteroffer awaiting her. This way, when it comes, the candidate may say to herself, "Oh, this is what my new company already warned me about." If, on the other hand, the current employer doesn't make a counteroffer, then the candidate (who, because of your prompting, is preparing for one) may feel disappointed that she wasn't pursued more aggressively. This will only reinforce her conclusion that accepting your job offer was the right thing to do all along. In either situation, your preclosing drill will have set the stage for a smooth transition out of her present company and into your organization.

59. Can I rescind an offer before the start date if I change my mind?

Nope! Once you've made the offer and the candidate accepts, it would be very unwise to undo your decision and rescind the offer. A legal concept known as "wrongful failure to hire" may result whenever an employer has promised a position, either verbally or in writing, and an applicant has relied on that promise to his detriment. In other words, if that job applicant has placed himself in a worse position by quitting his present job or by relocating and the employer fails to provide the job as promised, then a legal cause of action for wrongful failure to hire may arise.

Wrongful failure to hire is a valid legal claim even if the job in question is at-will (i.e., not for a specified period of time). In essence, the applicant's attorney will argue that the applicant is still entitled to be given the opportunity to show that she could have performed the job satisfactorily. In cases where the applicant is unemployed at the time of the employment offer, a wrongful failure to hire claim may still be sustained if an unlawful discrimination or "detrimental reliance" allegation is proven.

Tell Me More

It's critical that you cross your t's and dot your i's before extending any offers of employment. Follow these two steps before making any offers:

Step 1: Ensure that your original job requisition has the appropriate signatures from the hiring manager, budget coordinator, and senior management member (for example, the CFO).

Step 2: Ensure that your budget will allow you to make the appropriate salary offer not only from a departmental budget standpoint but also from a human resources internal equity standpoint.

In other words, it's not enough that the departmental budget will allow you to pay a senior financial analyst $50,000. You also have to ensure that (a) the $50,000 target salary is in the position's salary range and (b) the new hire will be paid appropriately relative to her peers in the department and across the company.

So what should you do if an offer is made (verbally or in writing), and you absolutely have to rescind it? After all, hiring managers sometimes make mistakes in the form of slips of the tongue, and business conditions could change in a day should a hiring freeze be announced. The simple rule is this: Openness and honesty will be your best ally when having to deliver bad news. Be prepared to hire the candidate if she insists, but try this appeal first:

> *You:* Debbie, we made you an employment offer yesterday, but I need to talk with you about it. I'm the vice president of marketing, and Travis Griffith, the director of marketing who interviewed you last week and made you the offer yesterday, misspoke. He told you that you had the job at $50,000 when in reality, we hadn't gotten budget clearance. It was an internal communication error on our part, and I assume full responsibility for the problem. I'm very sorry this happened, and I thought the best way to handle it would be to speak directly with you and share the details of the situation.
>
> I'm not telling you, Debbie, that we won't hire you. After all, one of our managers extended an offer, and you accepted it. However, I am appealing to you for your help. This position wasn't appropriately budgeted, and the reality is that we'll have to place the job on hold indefinitely until we can figure out if we can go ahead and fill the head count. Would you mind telling me your thoughts at this point? Have you given notice at your present company?
>
> *Applicant:* Yes, actually I gave two weeks' notice yesterday. My boss accepted my resignation, and today I already started working on transitioning my work projects for the next person they hire to fill my job.
>
> *You:* Let me ask this, Debbie. Obviously this is somewhat embarrassing for us, and I'm very sorry to have to make this call to you. Did your boss know you were looking to change jobs, and has your resignation been fairly amicable?
>
> *Applicant:* Yeah, everyone's been very supportive, including my boss.
>
> *You:* Then let me ask you a favor: Would you be in a position to speak with your boss about the faux pas on our side and ask her to

allow you to rescind your resignation? I know that's asking a lot, but I can only appeal to your goodwill at this point and hope that you'll agree to help us in this unfortunate situation.

Applicant: Wow, I can't believe this is happening. Okay, I'll ask, but my boss is going to say, "So as soon as that job opens up, you're going to leave us for them, aren't you?" What should I say?

You: Debbie, I can't answer that question for you. I hope that you're not so soured on our company that you wouldn't consider coming aboard once the budget approval is done. Still, I realize that we may be losing a great candidate because of our mistake, and I also recognize that you might find another position before our job is budgeted. I guess you'll have to answer that question as openly and honestly as you can.

Applicant: Okay, I'll go speak with my boss this afternoon. I can't promise anything. However, if she won't allow me to stay past my two weeks' notice, I expect that you'll keep your promise and allow me to start on January 8. Is that a fair assumption on my part?

You: Yes, Debbie, that's correct. We won't go back on our word, but please understand why I'm making this appeal to you. And again, please accept my apology. I'm very sorry to have to call you with this news.

Applicant: Okay, I'll call you back once I've spoken with my boss.

Phew! That's a tough phone call even when the candidate is as nice as Debbie was. The moral of the story is this: You really don't have the right to rescind an extended offer. Of course you *can* rescind an offer, but it's bad business and it subjects your company to legal challenges that you would be hard pressed to defend.

Therefore, your only solution is to appeal to the candidate with the details of the mistakes made on your part. You can hope that the current company will understand that human error was involved and allow the applicant to continue her employment. (After all, many people, including me, would indeed understand that kind of uncomfortable situation and allow the employee to continue working if no other external candidates have been identified or internal promotions announced.) If not, then keep your word! It's bad business practice and legal irresponsibility to deny employment to candidates who have relied on your offer to give notice at their present companies.

60. How do I compose a job offer letter?

If your company decides to make offer letters a part of your employment practice, you need to consider a few points. First, as a rule of thumb, the more information you include in the offer letter, the better. New hires are much more amenable to "legalese" language stipulating employment at will and mandatory arbitration than tenured employees are. Also, the more you include regarding new-hire orientation, introductory periods, and benefits availability dates, the more informed your new hires will be.

Second, it is wise to provide new hires with two original offer letters. One is for them to keep; the other should be signed and returned to your company. Again, the logic is simple: If you're planning on using the offer letter as a written confirmation of the employment-at-will relationship or of the candidate's agreement to be governed by binding arbitration, a signed letter is preferable from an evidentiary standpoint.

Third, be sure to document the salary offer in either *hourly* (for nonexempt workers) or *weekly* (for exempt employees) terms. At least one court interpreted a salary quoted on an "annual" basis as a promise of guaranteed wages for the entire year. When that company terminated its employee for cause, the company was on the hook for the remainder of those annual wages "promised" in the offer letter. Therefore, you should never stipulate more than one hour or one week of wages in your offer letter.

Tell Me More

There is a sample offer letter with all the bells and whistles in Appendix I. Use this as a model to structure new-hire offer letters at your company. Note that it includes compensation and benefit information, reporting status, an employment-at-will clause, an arbitration agreement, orientation information, and a reminder to bring documents to fill out Form I-9. An offer letter is one of the best places to introduce new hires to legal policies such as employment-at-will and arbitration agreements. Not only are new hires more amenable to such agreements, but placing legal information in employment agreements helps establish them as policies.

Part II
Firing

Chapter 6

Common Questions About the Performance Management and Termination Process

61. What is progressive discipline?

You can't attempt to understand the firing process without studying progressive discipline. Progressive discipline is a series of attempts that employers make to turn around poor-performing employees via verbal and written performance warnings. When these warnings are violated, then companies terminate employees "for cause." Progressive discipline is therefore the precursor to termination for cause.

The logic to these documented warnings is threefold: First, employees should have the right to learn about performance problems before they are terminated so that they can improve and ultimately have a fighting chance at keeping their jobs. Second, should your company be sued by an ex-employee for wrongful discharge (see Question 69), you could defend your company's actions by demonstrating that you acted responsibly as an employer in letting that individual go. Third, if you can turn around a poor performer, you not only get a valuable one but also spare yourself the headache and money of replacing that employee.

Progressive discipline ensures that your company acts reasonably and documents the effect of the worker's unwillingness or inability to do his job. Later, if you're sued, you can prove that, despite your interventions to better the situation, you ultimately were left with no choice but to terminate that substandard performer. In addition, you acted reasonably and responsibly by documenting your affirmative efforts at helping to rehabilitate your worker. You also can prove the employee realized that his job was in danger of being lost. Each attempt to document the ongoing performance problems adds a more serious element to the process: consequences such as suspension, probation, and ultimately termination step up the severity of failure to improve. Therefore, a plaintiff attorney would have difficulty asserting that her client, your ex-employee, was denied "workplace due process."

Tell Me More

Workplace due process comes from a legal theory known as the "job as property doctrine." This theory asserts that the right to work is so intrinsic to American citizens that work should not be denied arbitrarily or capriciously, without just cause as accorded under the Fourteenth Amendment to the Constitution. The way employers accord due process in the workplace is via a series of written performance warnings in the progressive discipline process.

This fundamental expectation of fairness is alive and well today in courtrooms and arbitrators' chambers. Although the concept of "employment-at-will" severely restricted the job as property doctrine when employment-at-will was born in the 1930s, today employment-at-will has been severely restricted in its use. Now, when wrongful termination claims are not dismissed via summary judgment and end up going before a court, companies must show that they had cause to dismiss a worker. Failure to demonstrate cause may result in a court or arbitrator mitigating your decision to terminate to a lesser penalty (e.g., reinstatement plus an unpaid suspension, for example).

62. What does it mean for an employee to be hired "at will"?

Few issues cause such confusion in the workplace as the concept of employment-at-will. That's for good reason: Many managers believe it should say what it does, that is, allow managers to terminate employees with or without cause or prior notice. Defense attorneys who defend your company from wrongful discharge lawsuits initiated by your ex-employees employ the "at-will affirmative defense" to gain a summary judgment of the case. In the courtroom, your attorneys will argue that:

- Sally Brown was hired at will.
- Sally understood that she was hired at will, as attested to by her signature on the employment-at-will agreement in her offer letter, the employment application, and the free-standing employment-at-will agreement in her personnel file.
- Your company did nothing to abrogate the employment-at-will relationship by engaging in oral or written contracts to the contrary.

In essence, if Sally was indeed employed at will, then the merits of her case need not be heard: It was simply the employer's right to terminate her at any time with or without cause. Hence, your defense attorneys will ask for a summary judgment, that is, an immediate dismissal of the lawsuit.

So where's the rub? Well, there are many exceptions to the employment-at-will rule, and a plaintiff attorney will argue that your company engaged in one of the exceptions, thereby abrogating the employment-at-will relationship.

Tell Me More

Without a crystal ball, you can't know what kind of spin a plaintiff attorney will place on a wrongful termination charge two years from now. The plaintiff attorney may argue that your company:

- Discriminated against the employee on the basis of the individual's age, race, sex, or sexual orientation. These are statutory considerations established in Title VII of the Civil Rights Act of 1964 and other legislation.
- Retaliated against the employee for having filed a workers' comp claim, for whistle-blowing, for engaging in group activities that protest unsafe working conditions, or for refusing to commit an unlawful act on the employer's behalf. These are known as public policy exceptions.
- Discharged a long-term employee just before she was due to receive some anticipated financial benefit (e.g., pension plan vesting). This is known as an implied covenant of good faith and fair dealing.

- Failed to follow promises documented in your employee handbook or verbally made during the hiring interview that required just cause to terminate. These are known as implied contract exceptions.

Following are other exceptions to employment-at-will. Remember, it is illegal to terminate or otherwise punish an employee as a result of the individual's either doing or refusing to do the following activities, or for the employee's acknowledgment of any of these conditions:

- Attendance in an alcohol or drug abuse rehabilitation program
- Disclosure of a condition of illiteracy
- Union membership, organizational activities, or other "protected, concerted" activities
- Wage garnishment
- Filing a petition for bankruptcy
- Refusal to submit to a polygraph or lie detector test
- Military service
- Pregnancy, childbirth, or related medical conditions
- Infection with HIV virus or AIDS or the appearance of physical symptoms

So here's the bottom line: Without a crystal ball, you can't know what kind of spin a plaintiff attorney will place on a wrongful termination charge two years from now. Therefore, you can't assume you'll win a summary judgment of the case on the basis of the employment-at-will affirmative defense. As a result, you should "assume the default": In other words, always be prepared to show *cause* despite the existence of an at-will employment relationship.

"For cause" termination is the opposite of employment at will. It dictates that employers must have a good reason to terminate and that employees should be accorded workplace due process before losing their jobs. The way employers typically show due process is in the form of written warnings as part of a progressive discipline system. After all, many judges and arbitrators reason that "if it wasn't written down, it never happened." And that's a fairly reasonable assumption on their part: "If the person's performance was so bad that the company was thinking of terminating this person, then management should have at least taken the time to put it down in writing" goes the court's logic.

And that's why we live with the dichotomy between employment-at-will and progressive discipline. It's not one or the other—it's both. This way, if you win the employment-at-will summary judgment, good for you. However, if the judge throws out the employment-at-will affirmative defense and doesn't grant a summary judgment, you can defend the termination on its own merits by showing just cause.

Yes, this is a somewhat conservative approach. On the other hand, if you made all termination decisions on the basis of employees' at-will status, you'd be sailing with a loose cannon on the deck of your ship. In essence, without a consistent progressive discipline system and written warnings in an ex-employee's file, any cases that didn't get summarily dismissed would need to be settled out of court—you'd simply have no way to defend your actions.

63. How do I communicate the employment-at-will relationship to my workers?

First of all, recognize that most states, but not all, recognize at-will relationships. For example, the state of Montana has enacted a statute that completely abrogates employment-at-will. As a result, Montana employers are prohibited from discharging workers without "good cause."

If you are in an employment-at-will state, you can establish an at-will relationship with your workers by properly communicating their at-will status in employment applications, offer letters, and handbooks and via freestanding documents (typically found in a new-hire package). Sample language can be found in Appendix J; please bear in mind that this is only a blueprint to save you time. Qualified legal counsel should approve the actual language you use. Prospective new hires and employees alike should sign these documents.

Tell Me More

Why do companies spend so much time drafting at-will provisions to protect themselves from litigious ex-employees? The answer is simple: In order to retain the at-will affirmative defense and win a summary judgment, companies are obligated to show that they've communicated clearly the at-will relationship to their workers. It's not enough simply to use the term "at will" in offer letters and the like. Courts want to ensure that workers understand what the term "at will" actually means—hence, the follow-up description "with or without cause or notice at any time."

In addition, some courts have denied companies' requests for summary judgments based on the employment-at-will affirmative defense because it simply had been too long since the organization communicated the at-will relationship to the employee. In other words, courts have ruled that if a twenty-year employee hadn't signed an employment application, offer letter, or handbook acknowledgment in as many years, the company's burden of communicating the at-will relationship hadn't been satisfied. That's why many companies issue annual "at-will updates" for their employees' signatures.

Similarly, certain courts have ruled that at-will language "buried" in employment applications, offer letters, and handbook acknowledgments didn't meet the threshold of communicating the at-will relationship. Companies responded by creating freestanding documents that were to be signed and attached to employees' personnel files. As a matter of fact, courts have denied the employment-at-will summary judgment when that relationship was *solely* communicated via the employment application. The court's logic? Employment applications were only enticements to enter into an employment relationship with a company; the employment applications themselves were not documents that governed the actual employment relationship once it began.

So what's a company to do to protect its right to gain a summary judgment by using the employment-at-will affirmative defense? The answer is simple: Do as much as possible at all times. Communicate employment-at-will language in employment applications, offer letters, and handbooks, and via annual freestanding at-will reminders.

64. What is a "probationary" period?

Like employment-at-will, probation periods cause many employers headaches because probation periods are simply misunderstood. There's good reason for the confusion: Unions have historically allowed for "probation periods" in their collective bargaining agreements that granted management the right to terminate new hires at whim. Of course, that magical window only lasted about sixty or ninety days, but the probationary termination became the employer's contractual right. The union would not argue with the organization's right to terminate new hires who weren't performing up to par.

On the other hand, nonunion (i.e., at-will) employees are not covered by union contracts and do not have magical probationary periods during which they can be dismissed without censure. At-will employees can actually sue your company for wrongful termination even if it occurs at the onset of their employment! Hence the confusion: Whether employers have the right to terminate probationary employees on a whim depends on the union or nonunion status of their workers.

Still, companies try to retain as much flexibility with new hires as possible. As a result, nonunion companies attempt to establish "probationary periods" where there is minimal (if any) obligation to provide workplace due process in the form of written warnings or other progressive disciplinary actions.

Tell Me More

If all or part of your workforce is covered by a collective bargaining agreement, then you've probably bargained for the right to include probation period language in the contract. Good for you: That right to terminate new hires on a whim, without cause or notice, is probably the most significant benefit that a union contract gives you.

If you're an at-will employer, on the other hand, establishing a probation period is somewhat more difficult. In interpreting probation periods, courts typically look for some reason that they exist—specifically, employees must receive some benefit upon completion of the period. As a result, you should ensure that there is some difference in your workers' employment status during the probationary period and after it. Allowing employees to enjoy some benefit (e.g., accrued vacation, sick leave, or 401(k) participation) that they did not have before completing the probationary period typically accomplishes this.

In addition, many companies have done away with the term "probation" because some courts have unfavorably interpreted probation periods. The reason? Historically, applicants and new hires (along with their attorneys) have construed probationary periods as minimum periods of job security during which they couldn't be fired (i.e., "until the end of the probation period"). As a result, companies have replaced that term with "introductory," "evaluation," "training," "initiation," "eligibility," or "orientation" periods.

True, these designations may help avoid the undesired implications and assurances that the term "probation" has historically carried with it. However, a plaintiff attorney representing an ex-employee might still posit that your company did not have the right to discharge without cause or that your company engaged in some discriminatory practice—regardless of the existence of some "introductory" period.

There's an even greater danger: Some labor experts discourage the use of probation periods at all. First, if employees are truly hired at will, then a probation period is superfluous. Second, some courts have ruled that the mere completion of such an initial evaluation period suggests express or implied contractual obligations that make it more difficult for companies to discharge at will. Specifically, the completion of the probation period could be construed to mean that employees have some greater right to job security in the form of workplace due process than they had while in their probation periods.

Proponents of doing away with probation periods argue that employees are subject to the same standards of performance and conduct throughout their employment. Consequently, no probation period is necessary, and no implications of job security will arise for employees once these periods are over. I agree. However, you should discuss this concept with your labor counsel to find what's best for your company.

65. How do I conduct an internal investigation of an employee accused of misconduct?

Internal investigations must always be handled discreetly. That sounds obvious enough, but too often investigations appear to be public shaming sessions where employees who are accused of wrongdoing appear to be punished without having been accorded due process. Accordingly, follow these five rules when conducting internal investigations:

- Give accused employees their "day in court." In other words, provide them with specifics regarding the charge

against them. Follow the "who, what, where, when" paradigm, and list any witnesses who may have observed the
inappropriate acts that are in question.

- Hold all investigator meetings behind closed doors, and include only those individuals who have a strict "need to
  know." Whenever possible, department members and subordinates should not know of the accusations or the results
  of your investigation.

- Involve the accused employee's supervisor so that the supervisor is aware of the problem and can monitor the situation
  on a daily basis.

- Only involve witnesses and expand the circle of your investigation if an employee accused of wrongdoing refutes a
  charge; if that employee admits to the charge, then no further investigation is necessary.

- Share the results of your investigation with the employee
  who originated the complaint. Assure the person that no retaliation will result. In a similar fashion, share the results of
  your investigation with the employee who was accused of
  wrongdoing to "close the loop" and to allow that individual
  to come to terms with the results of your investigation.

Tell Me More

The easiest way to demonstrate how to conduct a proper investigation is to look at an example of how *not* to conduct an investigation.
A telephone utility company learned from a department secretary
that the secretary's manager might have made inappropriate comments of a sexual nature to her.

The utility followed its policy for handling such "hostile work
environment" complaints: The manager's supervisor brought a box
to the manager's office. The manager was instructed to place his
company badge into the box, along with his laptop, cell phone, and
the keys to his company car. That manager was immediately placed
on administrative leave and instructed not to return to the workplace until further notice. This was done in front of the manager's
subordinates.

When the manager asked why this was happening, he was told
that a complaint had been made against him and that he would hear
from the utility's EEO officer the next day. The manager naturally
asked for more specifics but was told to simply go home. Not know-

ing the nature of the complaint, the manager assumed he was about to be fired. His subordinates assumed the same thing.

After a long night without any sleep, the manager spoke with the utility's EEO officer and finally learned of the accusations made against him. Apparently his newly hired secretary had complained that he had made inappropriate remarks to her during the interview. Specifically, she said that he said, "I want you" at the end of their meeting. She stated that he had winked at her in a suggestive manner. She stated that there had been no witnesses but that she had felt uncomfortable.

The manager readily admitted to this. In fact, he told the EEO officer, "Sure, I said that, but she didn't tell you the second half of the sentence. I told her I wanted her because her prior experience in another division of the company made her the most qualified person for the job. I offered her the job later that day after I checked her references with her then-current supervisor. I don't recall winking at her, but I may have. It certainly wasn't done with any underlying message on my part, that I can assure you."

The EEO officer found no wrongdoing and apologetically explained to the manager that being placed on administrative leave and having one's ID card removed was simply a matter of company policy when such claims were made. Unfortunately, the damage was already done: Subordinates questioned what had occurred and wondered whether their boss was really at fault. The manager felt humiliated when he returned to work the following day. And the secretary who lodged the complaint worried that others would accuse her of exaggerating her claim in order to get her supervisor in trouble.

The company's response was obviously not commensurate with the alleged wrongdoing. Furthermore, all the histrionics and public flogging could have been avoided had the organization simply asked the accused manager for his side of the story in private before placing him on administrative leave.

Remember, an investigatory leave is a tool to use once you've learned *both* sides of the story. If you feel that interviewing witnesses is necessary and that the manager's presence could bias your fact-finding mission, then place the manager on administrative leave for a day or so while you meet with witnesses. Don't do what this utility did, however, by using an administrative leave as a perceived punishment in and of itself. That's inherently unfair to the individual in question and creates a corporate culture based on mistrust and authoritarianism.

66. How should I conduct internal investigations regarding sexual harassment or discrimination?

Sexual harassment and discrimination investigations are among the most common investigations that occur in the workplace. The law requires an investigation of a claim of sexual harassment or unlawful discrimination. Failure to conduct a timely investigation can, in and of itself, constitute ratification by the employer of the unlawful conduct. In addition, regulations under Title VII of the Civil Rights Act of 1964 require that your company both (a) investigate and (b) take immediate corrective action to stop the behavior.

Failure to take immediate corrective action after a timely investigation, especially in cases of repeated harassment, could be evidence of the company's "malice" and therefore could be the basis for an award of punitive damages. Note that no other workplace situations (other than harassment or discrimination) legally require that a company conduct an internal investigation.

Tell Me More

Conducting sexual or other unlawful harassment investigations is challenging for employers because your organization can be sued by both the complaining party and the alleged harasser if you create a perception of inequity in handling the case. The regulations under Title VII define sexual harassment as unwelcome sexual advances, requests for sexual favors, and other verbal or physical conduct of a sexual nature when:

1. Submission to such conduct is made either explicitly or implicitly a term or condition of employment,
2. Submission to or rejection of such conduct by an individual is used as the basis for employment decisions affecting the individual, or
3. Such conduct has the purpose or effect of unreasonably interfering with an individual's work performance or creating an intimidating, hostile, or offensive environment.

Failure to recognize and discover behavior that violates these guidelines could expose your company to liability. In California, for example, a sexual harassment claimant can receive awards for back pay, future pay, lost benefits, emotional distress damages, reasonable attorney fees, and, in cases of employer "malice," punitive damages.

On the other hand, the alleged harasser can also file a lawsuit against your company for wrongful termination, wrongful demotion, or defamation. It is not uncommon for former employees to attack your investigation as inadequate, superficial, or irresponsible.

With the gun cocked at your head from both directions in sexual harassment or discrimination claims, remember to proceed with the utmost caution. Equally important, remember to maintain a perception of fairness with both parties. These claims are often "he-said-she said" scenarios, without witnesses, in which both sides are acting on principle. Avoid appearing punitive or unreasonable. Respect both employees' points of view.

Conclude your investigation by keeping both sides abreast of what you've discovered. Finally, explain to the alleged wrongdoer that, regardless of reality, a *perception* problem exists. You have no choice but to act responsibly on the basis of the good-faith investigation that you conducted, and you hold all employees accountable for their own "perception management." By softening the blow this way, you'll remove the defacing mechanism that is so often associated with sexual harassment or discrimination claims. Employees may not agree with your findings, but if they feel that you've handled the matter fairly and objectively, they can usually get on with their lives.

Remember that sexual harassment claims are evaluated on their impact, not their intent. And, since harassment is in the eye of the beholder, you must sensitize your staff to others' feelings and impress upon them a heightened level of responsibility for workplace behavior.

Two conditions have to occur for sexual harassment to take place. First, the harassment has to be (a) sexual or (b) gender-based in nature. Second, the conduct must be "unwelcome." Remember, however, that employees can "consent" to behavior that they don't necessarily "welcome." Since consent, therefore, doesn't preclude an employee from feeling harassed, then ridding your workplace of unnecessary exposure becomes the goal of your sexual harassment policy.

There are two types of sexual harassment: quid pro quo and a hostile work environment. The harassment checklist in Appendix K can be used consistently as a baseline report for gathering information regarding a sexual harassment charge. Whether or not you employ a checklist, bear in mind that such documents may be subpoenaed in the discovery process. They should consequently be reviewed with qualified legal counsel prior to their implementation. For more information, see *What Every Manager Needs to Know About Sexual Harassment*, by Orlov and Roumell (AMACOM, 1999).

67. Should I allow an employee to "resign by mutual consent"?

If you've ever felt inclined to allow an individual to resign voluntarily rather than be discharged for cause, don't be too hard on yourself. You demonstrated humanity and compassion. Remember, though, that ambiguity in the termination process can be held against you. Generally speaking, if you've got just cause to discharge the employee, termination is appropriate.

Lessening the blow by offering the employee two weeks' pay in lieu of notice or continued medical benefits or by placing the individual on inactive status while keeping her on the payroll can be interpreted as signs of weakness on your part. Worse, it can be interpreted as an acknowledgment that the company was partly at fault and may be trying to cover up something.

Tell Me More

Avoid sugarcoating terminations as much as possible. Assuming you've accorded the employee workplace due process in the form of progressive discipline, then follow your company's policies and past practices, and avoid exceptions. Terminations for cause aren't fun, but they should be a straightforward management practice. A former employee looking to avert blame may distort your good intentions. Exceptions all too often provide fodder for plaintiff attorneys, who may attempt to attach ill motives to your benevolent actions.

On the other hand, there's something to be said for allowing employees to resign of their own accord. Note that unilateral resignations, as opposed to mutual resignations, do not allow for severance pay, continued medical benefits, or any other company-sponsored perks. They simply allow the employee to resign, rather than be terminated for cause. As such, it would be much harder for a plaintiff attorney to somehow distort your actions as a sign of weakness. In addition, anytime you can avoid being the "moving party" in a termination, you should, because you'll naturally avoid certain causes of action that a plaintiff attorney could otherwise levy at you.

The question remains, When should this option be mentioned? It wouldn't be appropriate, for example, to hold a termination meeting with final check and COBRA paperwork in hand and then simply allow the employee to resign. By that time, you'll have established a written record of termination for cause. Allowing a resignation during the termination meeting would consequently create an inconsistent paper trail.

On the other hand, if an employee appears to have violated the terms of a final written warning and you're speaking with the employee to learn his side of the story, you might suggest the following:

> Dennis, I understand that you were in a rush to meet a deadline and that you assumed that your coworker would pull the satellite feed. Still, satellite feeds are ultimately your responsibility. You were given a final written warning two weeks ago documenting that your failure to pull a particular feed caused the station to miss airing a TV commercial. Today it appears that you've missed another feed during your shift with the same result. Now that I've heard your side of the story, I'll need to discuss this with station management. However, you need to know that this could result in your termination.

> I know you've had difficulty in your job since you joined us last year. Maybe it's just not a good fit. You know, right person, wrong job. If it's easier for you to resign if we find that you violated your final written warning, I'd certainly understand that. I simply want you to have that choice if you feel it would be better for your career. We'll respect whatever decision you make. What are your thoughts?

Given that choice, the employee may take the path of least resistance and simply resign. That avoids the loss of face associated with a termination for cause. It also saves you from having to conduct a termination meeting. Is there a downside for the company or the employee? There's typically no downside for the company, unless the employee argues that he was "constructively discharged," that is, that he had no choice in the matter. However, treating people with dignity and respect and allowing them to have some control over their future will typically beget appreciation, not anger.

On the other hand, there could be a downside for the employee. If he unilaterally resigns, he will technically be considered the "moving party," or the party that initiated the terminating event. As such, he could be denied unemployment insurance. (Unemployment is typically granted by the state when the company is the moving party and the employee had no control over the separation.) Your company may choose not to contest unemployment (i.e., challenge the employee's claim for unemployment benefits); remember, though, that the state determines eligibility. If the employee says he quit, the state may very well deny a benefits award. That information should be shared up front with an employee who is considering a resignation while a termination decision is pending. It's only fair that you share the long-term results of his decision that could impact him after he's left your company.

68. How do I discipline someone for attitudinal behavior?

One of the most common challenges facing line managers today is dealing with employee attitude problems. It's the entitlement mentality evidenced by rolling eyeballs, sighs, and antagonistic body language that drives managers crazy. Still, trying to stop such "silent" behavior is difficult because it's so easily denied by employees.

There are two key points to keep in mind when attempting to eradicate this all-too-common problem: First, the manager should tell the person how he *perceives* her actions and how she makes him feel. Second, if formal written discipline becomes necessary, the manager should be sure to paint a picture with words so that the documentation clearly portrays the employee's attitudinal actions.

Tell Me More

Managers should avoid the word "attitude" when speaking with an employee or documenting progressive discipline. It's simply too subjective a word and typically escalates disagreement by fostering feelings of resentment and anger. As a matter of fact, courts have interpreted "attitude problems" as mere differences of opinion or personality conflicts. It is therefore critical that you avoid that specific term in any of your disciplinary documentation. Only behaviors and actions that can be observed and documented may be presented as evidence in court.

When attempting to fix a communication problem that exists with a staff member, approach the matter verbally first:

> Richard, I need your help. You know they say that perception is reality until proven otherwise. I feel that you're either angry with me or angry with the rest of the group. I don't know if anything's bothering you or if you feel that I can be more supportive of you in any way, but please let me know if that's the case. Otherwise, though, understand that you make me feel embarrassed in front of other members of the staff when you roll your eyes upward and whine, "Okay, I'll get it done." Do you feel it's inappropriate for me to ask you to complete your work on time? Should I even have to follow up with you, or should that be your responsibility? How would you feel if that were done to you as the supervisor?

If your verbal meeting doesn't work and the problem continues, you may need to document your concerns in a written warning. An example of a written warning for inappropriate workplace conduct is included in Appendix L.

Can employees be terminated for occurrences of inappropriate workplace conduct? Sure they can, and attitudinal problems that appear to be difficult to measure fall under the category of insubordination. Never assume, however, that a jury will relate to you, the supervisor, just because you documented that an employee had an "attitude problem." The key lies in describing the employee's actions accurately so that the documentation remains clear enough to convince a jury that the company had cause to discipline or terminate.

69. What does it mean to fire "for cause"?

The term "cause," sometimes referred to as "good cause" or "just cause," means that you, the employer, have a reason to terminate an employee. What reasons do employers typically have to terminate employees? Broadly speaking, the categories fall into one of four areas:

- Policy and procedure violations
- Substandard job performance
- Inappropriate workplace conduct
- Attendance/tardiness problems

See Question 75 for an explanation of these areas.

Tell Me More

What becomes important in the termination process is the discretion that you exercise as an employer. First and foremost, you should attempt, whenever possible, to document company rules and regulations so that employees are aware of your expectations. That's the role of employee handbooks and policy and procedure manuals.

Second, you must be consistent in the application of your own rules. Workers have the right to consistent and predictable employer responses when a rule is violated. In other words, problems cannot be corrected on an ad hoc basis without your being perceived as arbitrary or unreasonable. In addition, remember that when perceived unfairness occurs to a member of a protected group, a discrimination charge may be sustained.

Third, the discipline must be appropriate for the offense. Occasional poor performance or a minor transgression (known as a *de minimis* infraction) is certainly actionable but probably not cause for termination. An employee's performance track record and prior disciplinary history should certainly be taken into account.

Fourth, remember that you have more discretion when dealing with conduct infractions than you do when dealing with performance or attendance problems. Conduct that is egregious may be grounds for immediate dismissal, otherwise known as a "summary dismissal." The logic is simply this: If an employee engages in gross negligence or is caught using drugs on company premises, you've probably got a clear shot at a quick and defensible termination.

On the other hand, courts and juries expect companies to provide the full span of progressive discipline to an employee who is having difficulty performing the duties of the job or who is excessively absent or tardy. The logic here? You hired him, so if he's not doing the job the right way, you should have been more diligent in the selection process. Now you're obligated to help the individual improve his performance to meet minimum company expectations. Ditto with the employees who suffer from excessive absenteeism or tardiness: They may be going through a difficult period in their lives, and the company is expected to exercise restraint before removing them from the job.

The steps that your company takes in providing progressive discipline that may ultimately result in a termination for cause are up to you: Most companies apply a three-step system that includes a verbal correction meeting, a written warning, and then a final written warning before termination. These steps are part of your written policies and past practices.

As a rule of thumb, follow the paradigm that you've established unless doing so would make you, the employer, appear irresponsible. In other words, don't give employees three chances to steal, embezzle, or punch their bosses in the nose. Those, again, are conduct infractions, and no court or jury would expect a company to provide progressive discipline in such cases.

70. How should I handle poor performance?

Usually the impetus that moves the "progressive discipline" process from one stage to the next is a repeated violation of the same rule or type of rule (e.g., repeated absenteeism or substandard job performance). In essence, there must be a link or nexus between events in order to move to the next stage. Without an interrelationship between events, you may end up with a series of first-level warnings (sometimes called verbal warnings), rather than a progression from a verbal to a written to a final written warning.

Tell Me More

Let's assume that a one-year benefits clerk is having difficulty staying on top of her work, following up with customers, and collecting outstanding receivables. The individual was verbally counseled one month ago and instructed to work more efficiently, to keep her boss informed of her progress, to ask for help when she was falling behind, and to minimize any further occurrences of excessive personal telephone calls and extended breaks.

Since that time, the person continued to fail to meet these expectations and received a written warning (see Appendix L for sample written warnings). About five weeks later, the employee improved her conduct by avoiding any further occurrences of extended breaks or personal phone calls; however, a major error occurred with a large account. This became grounds for a final written warning. (See Appendix L for a sample final written warning.)

Any subsequent performance or conduct violations within a reasonable period of time from this point would probably result in a termination for cause.

71. How can I encourage an underperforming and unhappy employee to leave the company when we haven't begun the progressive disciplinary process yet?

Even in a tight labor market, it becomes necessary from time to time to convince employees to leave your company. Why? Because employees who are experiencing performance and conduct problems will often stay "on principle"—in other words, they'll rationalize that they'll stay till *they're* good and ready to leave. "No one's forcing me out of my job until I'm ready to go—especially not that boss of mine!" goes the logic of the disenfranchised and victimized worker.

Unfortunately, the results can be very problematic. It can mean workers' compensation stress claims or wrongful termination lawsuits for your company. Employees may go through months or years of feeling unappreciated and having their egos and self-esteem dragged through the mud. So your best solution may be to broker a peace where one party can walk out of the working relationship with his dignity and respect intact.

Meetings such as this require a third-party facilitator. First, if immediate supervisors who are part of the problematic interpersonal relationship with the disenfranchised employee attempt to "talk the employee into" leaving the job, their efforts may be perceived as insincere or self-serving at best. Second, whatever is shared with the employee in meetings like this may take on a different meaning two years down the road when the company is being sued for "constructive discharge."

Tell Me More

A constructive discharge claim is similar to wrongful discharge; however, in the constructive discharge case, the employee leaves and is not terminated by the company. Still, a plaintiff attorney will argue that the conditions were so egregious at work that any reasonable person would have left under similar circumstances. Consequently, the plaintiff attorney will argue, "My client was forced into leaving her position, and the company had no right to create such an unfriendly environment. I mean, come on, your Honor, her supervisor told her that she wasn't wanted there anymore and had no future with the company! Telling her that after a year of isolating her from the rest of the team, denying her a raise, withholding training, and holding her to a higher standard than everyone else was just too much. She had to quit, but it's *their* fault."

To avoid creating a record that could be construed as a manager giving an employee no choice but to resign, the immediate supervisor can't be the deliverer of this message. Instead, a neutral third party must be used. Human resources or a member of your company's senior management team is the typical mediator in such cases.

We all know that, when it comes to job performance problems, both sides are often in total disagreement about the situation: Managers argue that the problematic employee is disrespectful and noncommunicative and does not hold herself accountable for her own actions. The disenfranchised employee will argue that her boss holds her to a higher standard than everyone else, that she's never in the communication loop, and that she's never told when she does something right—only when she does something wrong.

Who's right and who's wrong in these situations? Unfortunately, both sides are at fault. In essence, if the working relationship has deteriorated to this point, both the manager and worker have failed. Sometimes, however, trying to fix these problems just becomes an ongoing battle of wills where little good results.

When the problem stems from something more basic than workplace performance issues—when the two people just can't seem to get along because of personal style differences or genuine dislike—transferring the employee may make sense. Even then, other jobs may not be available or the employee may have such a poor reputation that no other manager would hire that individual. It's then time for the facilitator/broker (again, senior management or human resources) to attempt to gently inject respect, dignity, and professionalism back into the relationship by allowing an "easy out" exit strategy. First acknowledge the efforts to make things work out and that it hasn't been a love match. Ask the employee whether she is frustrated and agrees the situation isn't ideal. At this point, try to put the events in perspective:

> There's enough work around here to tire the most energetic of people. When you add the interpersonal friction that you've both been experiencing for the past year or so, it becomes very difficult. I don't want to minimize the importance of your working relationship together, but if you think about it, it's only work. I mean, when you think about families who lose their health or parents who have to see their children through serious illnesses—that's important in life. If we're not suffering from that kind of illness, we're lucky. So let's keep that in perspective as we look at this workplace issue, okay?

> Sometimes it's fair to say that there just isn't a right fit. What's important to me is that both parties feel like they're being treated with dignity and respect. I don't want people feeling like their egos and self-esteem are being trashed. Life is simply too short for that.

> Mary, I need to share with you that Sue isn't going anywhere. She's a vice president, she's under contract for several more years, and senior management believes she's doing an excellent job. That's an important point for you to keep in mind. I also don't believe that you're happy here. You seem to be disappointed in the management team. You appear not to enjoy your work. And I suspect that you feel like you're not appreciated or part of the team, at least at certain times.

You can offer her an exit. Here are a few questions you might ask:

- Would exploring other opportunities outside the company make sense for you at this point in your career?
- Would leaving now of your own accord allow you an honorable exit strategy?
- Would you like us to give you time to begin interviewing at other companies?

Make sure she knows you would be happy to help her as long as she makes sure that work comes first and that you're given at least twenty-four hours notice of an upcoming interview. That way, the employee needn't feign illness or conjure up doctors' and dentists' appointments if she has an interview coming up. It's important to stress that the decision is entirely up to the employee:

> If you'd like our support to either resign on your own terms now or to begin looking for other work, then we'll help you. If not, that's okay, too. We'll do everything we can to help you reinvent your working relationship with Sue, to be given objective performance standards, and to become more effective at your job. I just want you and Sue to feel better about working with each other if you choose to stay. I also want to give you these additional options, Mary, because it's better that we discuss these things openly than leave them unsaid. What are your thoughts?"

This velvet glove approach is typically somewhat challenging to deliver, but it lowers the tension in the relationship immediately. It's always better to tell people where they stand than to make them "divine" from their managers' actions that they're not wanted. When people are treated professionally and respectfully, they'll typically respond in kind.

Are there downsides to this intervention technique? Not really, as long as:

- You're careful to ensure that the employee understands that this is *her* decision (thereby avoiding a constructive discharge claim later down the road)
- You advise her of the objective performance standards she'll be responsible for meeting if she chooses to stay
- You carefully document the meeting, including the employee's response

Just remember that it's *your* meeting—not theirs. Tell them that anything's open for discussion as long as it's said with the other party's best interests in mind and in a spirit of constructive criticism. There's no attacking and no need for defending, and the meeting will be stopped if you sense that either party is breaching that rule. You'll get to the truly human concerns at issue and allow your employees to take back control of their careers. In fact, for some troubled employees, you may be giving them a chance to take back control of their lives.

How often does this approach work? It depends. In my experience, it's an 80–20 game: 20 percent of the time employees choose to resign on the spot or at least tell you that they'll agree to begin looking immediately for other work. That may not seem like a great track record, but if you look longer range, you'll find that many employees leave the company within three or four months after a meeting like this.

After all, no matter how angry employees are at the company, they'll come to realize that fighting an uphill battle makes no sense. When angry people are treated respectfully, their anger dissipates. And when the anger is gone, they feel less inclined to stay with your company "on principle." More important, they'll leave quietly, on their own terms without all the histrionics and threats of lawsuits.

72. How do I maximize exit interviews?

You're not required to conduct exit interviews, but polling your departing employees can reveal very useful information regarding their reasons for leaving your company and pursuing opportunities elsewhere. How do you make exit interviews confidential and effective? Most departing workers won't look to bash their boss on their way out the door. Even if they were dissatisfied, there is always a sense that the information they provide will somehow be placed in their personnel file and come back to haunt them should they ever look to be rehired by your company. There is also a fear that bashing one's boss could lead to negative references with prospective employers.

Tell Me More

First of all, you've got to decide who will conduct the exit interview. A member of your organization's human resources team or a senior member of departmental management is the best choice. Immediate supervisors aren't recommended for this task because their presence may bias employees' feedback.

Second, you've got to determine whether your exit interviews will be done in writing or via a personal conversation. Ideally, you should do both: Exiting employees coming to drop off their company IDs and to pick up their final checks should be required to fill out an exit interview questionnaire first. Then they can verbally share their experiences with the company during the face-to-face meeting after the written questionnaire is completed.

If you develop a written questionnaire, be sure to construct it so that the information can be fed into the computer and tracked for trends and patterns. Some of the questions you might include in the questionnaire fall under the following five categories (which can be mirrored for staff, as well as for management employees): (1) nature of the work and job responsibilities, (2) relationship with the supervisor, (3) employee compensation and benefits, (4) career progression opportunities, and (5) reason for leaving. A sample questionnaire covering all five categories can be found in Appendix M.

A brief look at a resigning employee's responses before the face-to-face meeting should provide some insightful feedback regarding that individual's experiences. The true value in the exit interview data lies, however, in the pooled information developed over time and across departments. For example, you can look to exit interviews to substantiate your suspicion that a particular supervisor lacks the leadership abilities to motivate and retain staff. Such objective evidence may help you sell the benefits of management training to particular supervisors or even substantiate employee complaints against them in the form of progressive discipline.

One caveat here: Exit interviews work well with employees who are laid off or who resign of their own accord. They're less useful when given to employees who are being terminated for cause because such employees often lack the objectivity to assess the working situation fairly.

Chapter 7

Progressive Discipline

73. How do I administer progressive discipline?

Progressive discipline was defined in Question 61 in Chapter 6. There are several basic rules that apply to administering progressive discipline. In essence, your company's progressive discipline system must provide all the elements of workplace due process. Specifically, you should follow these four rules when disciplining your employees:

> *Rule 1*: The employee needs to know what the problem is.
> *Rule 2*: The employee needs to know specifically what he needs to do in order to fix the problem.
> *Rule 3*: The employee needs to have a reasonable period of time in which to fix the problem.
> *Rule 4*: The employee needs to understand the consequences of inaction.

If your company has ever lost a wrongful termination charge, it may not have been because of the merits of your argument; it was probably lost because you failed to follow one of these rules.

Tell Me More

Let's look at these issues individually.

Rule one states that an employee needs to know what the problem is. That sounds fairly self-explanatory, but it's actually a very common miscommunication in the workplace. Employers assume that workers know what's wrong, only to learn later that the employee was confused by management's directives and actions. "I didn't realize that my job was in trouble; everyone does that around here, and no one else has been fired because of it" is a common response. Employers also hear rebuttals like, "You didn't tell me that was a formal warning; I thought you were giving me a coaching session when you told me that I needed to increase my productivity on the shop floor." Therefore, you shouldn't assume that any performance-related issue is self-evident; your concerns should be explained clearly both verbally and in writing.

The second rule states that workers need to know how to fix the problem at hand. The best way to accomplish this is by adding an "Expectations" section to your verbal and written warnings. For example, you might write, "John, I expect that you will arrive at your workstation by 8:00 A.M. and be ready to begin work at that time on a go-forward basis." That kind of directive is clear and incontestable in its intent. After all, a measurable standard must be known in advance for it to be enforceable and capable of withstanding legal scrutiny.

Rule three requests a reasonable time period. How much time is reasonable when it comes to giving your employees a chance to turn their problematic performance around? That depends on the nature of the work that your company is engaged in, the length of time the employee has been with you, and how you've handled similar situations in the past. No one would expect you to allow an employee to run your business into the ground. Still, your warnings can't seem prescribed or mechanical. In other words, you typically wouldn't give someone a written warning for substandard job performance on Monday and then turn around and terminate the person on Tuesday. Under most circumstances, that wouldn't be reasonable. Your remaining employees would know that, and morale would sink. A jury would also find this unreasonable.

Rule four states that the consequences must be clear. Too many employers commit serious errors at this stage. Untrained supervisors allude to open-ended consequences in their verbal counseling sessions and written warnings. Warnings to be avoided sound like these:

- If you engage in such activity again, *serious consequences* will follow.
- I will have no choice but to take *further action* should you repeat such behavior.
- You must immediately increase the *volume* of outbound tele-

marketing calls. Otherwise, disciplinary action up to and including dismissal will occur.

The obvious weakness in these examples lies in their generic nature. What are "serious consequences"? What kind of "further action" is at issue? How many outbound telemarketing calls are acceptable? How many are unacceptable?

To avoid such problems, be sure to ask yourself, Are these consequences clear enough that the employee could explain it back to you? Would a jury understand exactly what I meant? Once you feel comfortable with the specific consequences you've outlined, be sure to discuss this "documented conclusion" with the worker being disciplined. Does it appear to be fair and reasonable to her? Can she understand why you have to take these action steps as a responsible employer? Does she understand that your failing to take these steps could create a poor precedent in terms of your management practices? If so, you've done a thorough job outlining the consequences of inaction.

74. How do I ensure that the progressive discipline is fair?

In addition to the four golden rules of progressive discipline, there are other considerations you need to make on a case-by-case basis. Review this "litmus test" any time you're about to engage in the disciplinary process:

- You've got to be consistent in the application of your own rules. In other words, look not only to your written policies but also to your past practices when handling similar types of offenses.
- The discipline must be appropriate for the offense. Be sure to fit the company's response to the seriousness of the infraction.
- Employees should be given an opportunity to respond. Each employee deserves to tell her side of the story before disciplinary action is taken. Therefore, as a general rule, you should conduct the meeting first, explain the purpose of the meeting, listen to the employee's side of the story, and then write the disciplinary memo. You should also encourage em-

ployees to document their version of the story for the record. Include a sentence in the written warning that states:

> I recognize that you may have your own ideas for improving the situation at hand. Therefore, I encourage you to provide your performance improvement plan input and suggestions on a separate sheet of paper if you wish.

- Discipline can't be administered in a vacuum. Disciplinary memos must be tied logically to prior written records in an employee's file. Therefore, always review prior warnings and performance reviews, and acknowledge consistencies and discrepancies in prior records.

Tell Me More

Remember one additional rule that will always help you administer discipline fairly. Always ask yourself, How would I respond if my best-performing employee committed the same error? If you would respond the same way with your best performer as you would now with an employee who's having difficulty meeting job expectations, then you know that you're responding fairly. On the other hand, if it appears that you may be acting more harshly with your current worker than you would with others, then reconsider your actions before moving forward.

A caveat here, of course, is that similar infractions need not be handled identically. You reserve the discretion to consider an employee's prior service, overall performance, and prior discipline when evaluating new infractions. For example, a newly hired employee who engages in inappropriate workplace conduct by offending someone's ethnicity or sexual orientation may be dismissed immediately. That same behavior from a ten-year employee without similar prior incidents may merit a written or final written warning instead of outright discharge. It's your responsibility as the employer to match the discipline to the offense.

75. What are the most common kinds of disciplinary infractions?

Generally speaking, there are four types of transgressions that occur in the workplace:

- Policy and procedure violations
- Performance transgressions
- Behavior and conduct infractions
- Absenteeism or tardiness problems

Although employee transgressions are rarely identical, most infractions can be categorized in one of these four areas. Some disciplinary infractions violate more than one of these issues simultaneously. For example, an employee who is excessively late to work violates the "tardiness" and "performance" categories. Similarly, someone who engages in inappropriate workplace conduct by getting into a screaming match with a coworker violates the "policy" and "behavior" categories.

The key to allowing progressive discipline lies in establishing a link or connection between events. Using the example just given, an employee who is excessively late to work may at first receive a verbal reprimand and an admonition to be on time. If that doesn't fix the problem, then a written warning and, ultimately, a final written warning may be appropriate. Failure to meet the terms of the final written warning may result in the employee's termination. In essence, the employee will have failed to rehabilitate herself, despite the company's ongoing warnings and stepped-up consequences.

Tell Me More

Substandard job performance is probably the most common problem. When employees have difficulty mastering the basics of a job or when they fail to communicate appropriately so that their supervisors learn of problems before they become serious concerns, termination for substandard job performance is appropriate.

Inappropriate workplace conduct leads to dismissal if an employee commits gross insubordination, engages in unlawful activities on the job, fights with a coworker, commits time card fraud or otherwise steals time or money from the organization, or violates company policies regarding sexual harassment or discrimination.

Attendance and tardiness infractions occur when an employee fails to hold himself sufficiently responsible to report to work on time on a consistent basis. Some companies have very clearly defined policies regarding what constitutes tardiness or an occurrence of unscheduled absence. Others handle these matters on a case-by-case basis. Companies also differ as to how many occurrences justify discipline and, ultimately, termination for cause.

Why is it important to identify the type of infraction and the link between disciplinary events? The answer lies in the perception of fairness. When a repeated violation of the same rule or type of rule occurs, further discipline is warranted. That's fair to your workers and would be perceived as equitable by a jury.

What you don't want to do, however, is create a record in which the manager addresses employees' isolated behavioral events. Sometimes our forms and policies create these problems for us. For example, one fairly common method of administering discipline is via a "performance warning" postcard. These postcards list upward of forty individual infractions in a "check box" format. When an employee violates one of the forty specific performance areas, the manager checks off the corresponding box.

There are two problems with this method. First, giving an employee a postcard is akin to giving him a speeding ticket. It's a quick, down-and-dirty exercise that asks for little input or commitment on his part and offers no help on yours. As such, it has a demeaning element to it. Second and more important is the fact that disciplinary infractions are rarely identical. It is difficult to progress from a verbal to a written to a final written warning when there is little connection between events. You could end up issuing your employees two or three written warnings for different infractions rather than progressing to a final written warning for overall substandard performance.

Instead of using this postcard method with lists of isolated infractions, simply tie specific incidents to one of the four broad categories listed earlier. It will then be much easier to demonstrate the link or nexus between events, and you will have the documented grounds necessary to make your performance management system effective.

76. How do I "bundle" separate performance infractions?

It's sometimes the case that an employee's erratic behavior violates multiple company performance standards simultaneously. For example, the individual may already be on written warning for excessive absenteeism and then engage in inappropriate workplace conduct. Does the new conduct infraction warrant placing him on final written warning overall, or should you issue a separate warning for his conduct?

It depends. Some of the factors you'll need to look at include your company's past practices in handling similar incidents, the severity of the conduct infraction, and the number of incidents of unauthorized absence. Of course, the state in which your company is located will also help you determine how bold you may be in terms of taking adverse action against an employee.

Two schools of thought exist: Conservative employers and defense attorneys usually recommend treating these unrelated infractions separately. In essence, the employee would remain on written warning for absenteeism and then be given a separate written warning for inappropriate workplace conduct. On the other hand, more aggressive employers believe it is appropriate to view employee behavior in terms of responsibility rather than as isolated behavioral acts. As such, they believe that lumping all these issues together allows them the discretion to issue a final written warning for overall substandard job performance.

Tell Me More

"Bundling offenses" is the term often used for this latter school of thought. Bundling allows violations that are fundamentally unrelated to be lumped together for purposes of documenting poor performance. This accumulation factor often plays an important role in justifying terminations because arbitrators generally uphold more aggressive disciplinary measures when numerous performance problems—even if unrelated—have accumulated over short periods of time. There is a sample written warning for this example in Appendix L.

77. How do I determine what level of progressive discipline is appropriate to the offense?

Four criteria can help you determine the most appropriate level of discipline to employ in any particular circumstance:

1. The severity of the offense
2. The employee's past performance record
3. The individual's length of service with your organization
4. Your company's past practice in dealing with similar infractions.

Follow the traditional disciplinary paradigm of:

1. Verbal warning
2. Written warning
3. Final written warning

unless starting with anything less than a final written warning could make you appear irresponsible.

Courts have ruled that employers are obligated to fit the discipline to the offense. A slap on the hand isn't appropriate, for example, when egregious conduct occurs. That's why sexual harassment or discrimination findings typically start at the written or final written stages of discipline—even for a first offense.

Tell Me More

Conduct-related infractions typically provide employers with the most latitude in composing a company response. Take the case of employee theft or embezzlement. Such misconduct warrants immediate termination. A summary dismissal is appropriate because you can't send a message that says, We'll forgive you this time, but if you do it again, you'll be fired. On the other hand, performance- or attendance-related infractions typically require employers to provide full workplace due process in the form of written and final written warnings.

Remember, you're responsible for treating like cases alike; that doesn't mean you'll necessarily treat everyone the same way. Employee transgressions don't exist in a vacuum. Sleeping on the job, for example, may warrant a written warning for a first offense when committed by an attorney or financial analyst. That same infraction might warrant a final written warning for a head nurse in charge of a hospital's intensive care unit, because such behavior could jeopardize patient care. If committed by an anesthesiologist in the operating room during a procedure, sleeping on the job might justify a summary discharge.

As you can see, sleeping on the job isn't the only issue: The circumstances surrounding the act of sleeping on the job play a crucial role when determining available remedies to ensure that a particular behavior is not repeated. In addition, a first-time offense committed by a twenty-year employee most likely won't be treated as harshly as an offense committed by a new hire during his introductory period.

Finally, from a standpoint of fairness, realize that employees who are disciplined for inappropriate conduct or poor performance often share their concerns with their peers. It isn't uncommon for "war stories" to be shared, and disciplined employees learn how the company has treated others in the past who engaged in similar conduct. If your response differs greatly from and is more aggressive than your organization's past actions, realize that you'll not only have a morale problem on your hands, you may also be legally challenged to justify the apparent inconsistency of your actions. Inconsistent employment actions in and of themselves are not unlawful; however, if such perceived unfairness occurs against a member of a protected class, it could be interpreted as discrimination. Be careful to review your past practices before doling out discipline or termination. This should become a routine part of your performance management system.

78. What is an appropriate disciplinary time window?

First, realize that "stay clean" time windows are a matter of company preference and past practice. Progressive discipline shouldn't be looked at as a "formality" that companies have to go through before they're free to terminate someone for cause. On the other hand, it would be naïve to think that all situations will improve once managers provide dedicated attention to their underperforming employees via the progressive discipline process. Therefore, documenting the expected time frames for performance improvement becomes a critical part of all written warnings.

Be reasonable. Certain consequences should have no time limits. An employee who engages in behavior that could be construed as harassing or discriminating, for example, may not be ready for termination in your opinion. However, you'll want to send a strong

message that such behavior will not be tolerated in the future and
that any additional incidents could result in termination:

> John, if you *ever again* engage in conduct with a coworker, supervisor, or customer that could be considered hostile, offensive, or antagonistic, you may be immediately discharged.

> Mary, if you *ever again* loudly and publicly reprimand your secretary or other subordinates, if you use profane language in the workplace, or if you demonstrate behavior that could be construed as condescending or stripping individuals of their dignity, you will be immediately terminated.

Remember that open-ended consequences typically allow you
to retain maximum flexibility. Rather than placing time windows
around an employee's "stay clean" period, simply document the
expected consequences this way:

> Jim, failure to demonstrate immediate and sustained improvement may result in further disciplinary action up to and including dismissal.

Such language is recommended at the conclusion of all documented
warnings because it provides you with the most discretion on a go-
forward basis.

Many companies still adhere to the "calendar" approach to
progressive discipline. There's certainly nothing wrong with this
style; however, many employers fear that workers will stay clean
only long enough to get through the probation period—only to
commit the same errors once the probationary window has expired.

Tell Me More

Since this calendar approach is so common, let's look at how it
works. Employers who use disciplinary time windows typically
dole out "stay clean" periods in thirty-, sixty-, and ninety-day increments. Ninety days is normally the maximum for most performance
and attendance related problems; most courts would consider "stay
clean" periods for longer than that to be onerous.

Thirty days: To closely monitor a poor performer's work, use a
short window such as thirty days. If the individual is having diffi-

culty performing the essential functions of the job, that should be enough time to observe results. Shop floor workers, administrative support staff, and customer service representatives typically fall under this category.

Sixty days: Salespeople in many professions who aren't meeting benchmark performance standards typically get sixty-day windows. It takes about that long to make a sale, close the deal, and wait for the receivables to cash in.

Ninety days: To keep employees clean for the longest period of time (for example, with absenteeism and tardiness problems), use a ninety-day window. Remember, you're not married to the employee for a guaranteed ninety days; if anything goes wrong *within* those ninety days, you can automatically move to the next step of discipline (or termination). It's just easier for employees to be on time for thirty days than it is for ninety days, so why not hold them to a higher standard?

Here's how to couch these "calendar" warnings to buy yourself the most discretion possible:

> Janet, you are now being placed on a final ninety-day warning for tardiness. If *at any time* during this ninety-day period you incur two more incidents of unscheduled tardiness, you may be immediately dismissed.

By the way, if Janet survives the ninety-day window and then has two consecutive tardies a week later, you'll still retain the discretion to terminate her. Most courts and arbitrators would recognize that you're not obligated to start the entire process over again just because your employee passed some "magic" time limit. However, if two months go by and then Janet has two consecutive tardies, you very well might have to issue another final written warning. As with all cases of progressive discipline and termination, individual cases must be determined on their own merits. When in doubt, confer with appropriate legal counsel to review the specifics of your case.

79. Is it a good idea to remove disciplinary warnings from an employee's file?

Dick Grote recommended in his best-selling book *Discipline Without Punishment* (AMACOM, 1995) that removing discipline from an employee's file after a year has positive, motivational effect on employee morale. After all, he reasons, all employees make mistakes and errors in judgment. If disciplinary warnings are the appropriate company response to such indiscretions, then companies can also minimize the sting of disciplinary intervention by removing those documents after some predetermined time (such as a year), provided the employee has remained free of any infractions.

Such an action is purely voluntary on your company's part. There's no law that mandates that employers in any state must remove such records. You'll typically see this concept of record removal in the collective bargaining process as unions argue that their members are entitled to such a benefit. Nonunion employers are under no obligation to provide this benefit.

You've got to balance the motivational benefit of allowing employees to "clean" their records with the downside of liability should that behavior repeat itself. Certain workplace issues have a tendency to repeat themselves over time and to become "systemic." For example, sexual harassment, discrimination, and incidents of workplace violence should never be removed from an employee's personnel file. The law has a long memory, and your deliberate erasure of historical records that codify prejudice or intolerance could later be interpreted as irresponsible or incriminating. Therefore, in order to wipe out institutional discrimination and to protect the safety of all your workers, discard this one-year removal clause for infractions related to harassment, discrimination, or violence.

Tell Me More

What about other kinds of infractions? Would the removal of written warnings after one year free from job performance problems benefit your company? Ultimately, that's up to you to decide. Think of it this way, however. If one of your employees received a glowing letter of recommendation from a customer, and that letter was placed in the individual's personnel file, you probably wouldn't remove it after a year. In essence, it becomes a historical record of what occurred at some point in time. If you were later to discipline that individual for substandard customer service, the progressive disciplinary document would supersede that historical letter of recommendation.

Similarly, if one of your employees is written up for substandard customer service but then really turns her performance around, you have the right to add another document to the file recognizing this new achievement. An example of this kind of recognition can be found in Appendix N.

Is there a legal downside to such positive follow-up letters? There could be. By formally documenting improvement and then shortly thereafter terminating the employee for substandard job performance, you may run the risk of losing a wrongful termination claim. For example, a plaintiff attorney representing the ex-employee might argue that your documents were inconsistent and ambiguous. "After all, the follow-up letter neutralized the prior disciplinary warning, and then you terminated my client anyway" goes the typical line of reasoning.

Still, good management is all about risk management—not about risk avoidance. You can't manage by fear of lawsuits. Instead, you have to find that fine balance between protecting the company and motivating your staff. Before you implement such a policy, discuss your options with outside counsel. Your decision's motivational impact may help withstand union organizing campaigns and lower turnover. However, depending on the state in which your company sits, such a policy may have more limitations from a liability standpoint than you're willing to assume.

80. How do I document my concerns on an annual performance review if I haven't discussed those issues with the employee in the past?

The primary rule of performance management is that there should be no surprises. When an employee feels ambushed by stored-up complaints that his manager has been withholding over long periods of time, that manager has failed to communicate properly. Since communication is the bedrock of business, that manager needs to be trained more effectively in dealing with adversity, delivering bad news, and managing conflict.

That being said, remember that the path of least resistance is avoidance. Even the best managers will attempt at times to avoid broaching uncomfortable topics if they feel that bringing them up will only make matters worse. Maybe avoidance allows the work to get done with minimal friction. But when it's time for the annual performance review, that manager will be hard pressed to articulate on paper the subordinate's multiple shortcomings. Many managers deny the problem even further by doling out "satisfactory" scores (much to their later chagrin when they wish to terminate the employee for cause). On the other hand, there is a way to gently communicate the ongoing problems at review time while still aggressively dealing with the problem. Let's look at how it's done.

Tell Me More

First, the manager in question should assume responsibility for failing to communicate properly when speaking with the employee about the review. Second, the manager should qualify written comments with statements like, "Although Laura and I didn't discuss this issue during the review period . . ." or "This was not formally brought to Laura's attention at the time it occurred." Yes, your statements diminish the impact of the message you're making when you include such disclaimers. Still, it's only fair to do so, and your employee will have an easier time accepting your criticism if it's not perceived as an ambush.

Here's how your verbal conversation might sound:

> Laura, it's time for the annual review, and I've been meaning to have this meeting with you for quite some time. I apologize to you, and I assume responsibility for not having shared my concerns with you earlier. However, I don't feel that your performance or conduct are up to par relative to your performance in the past. This year has been a difficult one for you: We've had multiple complaints about your tone of voice with customers—issues that I've smoothed over with customers myself rather than bringing them to your attention. Also, your loan-to-value ratios have contained errors that the desk appraisers have caught in their audits of your work. As a result, several have shared with me that they don't trust your work to be top quality, especially when you appear to be under pressure.

> Your overall performance score on this evaluation will be "does not meet expectations." I want you to know that I'll qualify that by saying that these issues were not brought to your attention immediately as they occurred. I can't hold you fully accountable for fixing problems that you're not aware of. On the other hand, tone of voice with customers and simple loan-to-value calculations are the basics of your job. Just because I haven't taken the opportunity to sit with you to discuss others' concerns doesn't justify your behavior or lack of attention to detail.

I've written my review of your performance. I'd like to review it with you now. If you have any immediate questions, just let me know. Otherwise, I'll ask you to take this home and study it. I'm sure you'll have other questions tomorrow, and I'd like to be able to answer them for you as concretely as possible. I also want you to know that I'll bring any performance or conduct issues to your immediate attention from now on so that you won't feel surprised or anxious about how I'm evaluating you.

Oh, there is one other thing: I'd like to have another formal performance review with you in ninety days. Although you won't receive a merit increase now because of the current review, there is a possibility that you'll receive a merit increase in ninety days if your performance and conduct show significant improvement.

Similar language should be used in the "Comments" section of the written review. An example can be found in Appendix O.

81. Can I dock a worker's pay for substandard job performance or unacceptable conduct?

The short answer is Yes, but how you apply the docking of pay will depend on workers' exemption status. First, remember that docking workers' pay has a shaming element to it. It's not enough that the worker received a written warning for substandard job performance or inappropriate workplace conduct; on top of that, he'll have to explain to his wife and children why there's less money in this week's paycheck than there was in last week's.

The idea of docking pay and suspending employees without pay harkens back to the days of poor management-labor relations, when mistrust guided the workplace. It is far more effective today to build trust and confidence by treating adults with dignity and respect and by holding them accountable for their actions by gaining their buy-in. However, certain employers still maintain policies and practices in which unpaid suspensions are part of the progressive discipline process. If your company still adheres to these practices, be sure that you're implementing them correctly and not violating wage and hour laws.*

*See *Federal Wage and Hour Laws,* by R. Brian Dixon (SHRM Foundation, 1994).

Tell Me More

Nonexempt employees (i.e., those who are eligible for overtime pay) may have their wages withheld in hourly or daily increments as a punishment for poor performance or conduct. As a result, nonexempt workers may be sent home for a day or a half-day without pay. Their wages are measured in hourly increments, and you need not pay them for any time not worked.

On the other hand, exempt employees (e.g., managers) have restrictions placed on how their pay may be docked. Exempt workers need not be paid for any *"workweek"* in which they perform no work. That means that exempt employees must have *at least one week's pay* docked for a disciplinary infraction. (The one and only time that an exempt employee may have less than a full week's pay docked is when that employee violates a safety regulation that puts the safety of the plant or coworkers at risk. This is a specific, carved-out exception to the rule.)

Furthermore, if you're going to place an exempt worker on an unpaid suspension, you must make the unpaid period last (a) at least five business days (b) in the same calendar week (i.e., Monday–Friday). Those five days, in contrast, should not straddle two workweeks (for example, Thursday and Friday of one workweek and then Monday, Tuesday, and Wednesday of a second workweek). The reason? Exempt employees must be paid a full week's wages for any workweek in which they perform any work at all.

I know this sounds confusing. That's because it is. Here's what could happen to you, though, if you administer this incorrectly: If you were to place one of your managers on a three-day unpaid suspension (which is less than a full week and therefore violates this rule), that could result in the manager's exempt status being violated. In other words, the exempt manager could be considered a nonexempt employee who is entitled to overtime pay. Consequently, the Department of Labor's Wage and Hour Division could end up sticking you with a massive "back wages" assessment for overtime due your manager!

There's an easy way around the quirky wage and hour rules that govern exempt and nonexempt workers' wages: Avoid unpaid disciplinary suspensions. First, they're simply too hard to administer and consequently not worth the trouble. Second, they rarely turn around underperforming employees because they generate feelings of anger and distrust. Third, there's a much better alternative.

A *paid* disciplinary leave, known as a "decision-making leave" or "day of contemplation," is a once-in-a-career benefit where companies pay for an employee's time-out period. As a result, the paid leave eliminates the embarrassment so often associated with disciplinary suspensions. In addition, when you place an employee on a one-day paid leave, you have the right to ask him to complete a homework assignment on his day off. A sample homework assignment is presented in Appendix P.

Is there ever a time for unpaid disciplinary suspensions? Possibly. When an employee engages in willful misconduct or egregious behavior that smacks of retaliation or harassment, a traditional unpaid suspension may be warranted. That's up to you in your discretion as management. Even so, consider the one-day paid suspension as an alternative: Guilt works better than anger, even in extreme cases.

When you're considering docking an exempt employee's pay, contact the appropriate legal counsel to ensure that you're administering this payroll issue within both federal and state guidelines.

82. What's the most effective way to deal with excessive absenteeism problems?

Commerce Clearing House (CCH) Inc.'s *1999 Unscheduled Absence Survey* estimates that excessive absenteeism costs corporate America somewhere in the neighborhood of $600 per employee annually—a hefty toll, considering that not all absenteeism stems from legitimate illnesses. The first place to look when addressing excessive unauthorized absenteeism is your company policy. Many companies place caps on annual sick leave allowances; others refuse to write a policy for fear that the written document will limit their discretion in dealing with employees on a case-by-case basis. Your decision to implement a policy should depend on the frequency of worker absenteeism relative to industry and geographic standards.

In addition, setting policy can be challenging because employers need to determine the parameters of the program:

- Will they measure actual days or "incidents" (i.e., an uninterrupted series of days off from the same sickness or injury)?

- Do they believe that a no-fault or an excuse-based system will be more effective?
- Will a rolling year or a calendar year serve as the optimal performance measurement time period?

Beyond the nuts and bolts of your written policy, your past practice must also be closely examined. If you're inconsistent in the application of your organization's rules, a judge or arbitrator may determine that your fickle actions could justify a claim of discrimination or retaliation from a terminated worker.

Tell Me More

How much time off is considered excessive? There's no easy answer, but juries typically consider one sick day per month, or twelve days a year, as a threshold. More than that and it's likely that the discharge will be sustained; less than that and a plaintiff attorney may convince a jury that your decision to terminate was premature and possibly just a pretext.

Fixing the problem can be accomplished in three steps:

1. Review your organization's written policy with the help of legal counsel in order to ensure that you'll be able to retain the most discretion in managing this thorny issue.
2. Review your organization's past practices (for example, all of the disciplinary actions and terminations related to unauthorized absence in the past two years) across departments, divisions, and locations. Account for inconsistencies in prior decisions. Remember that you retain the discretion to change a policy or practice by notifying employees in advance and in writing: You're not obliged to perpetuate a problem once you discover that changing the rule or practice could make things better. Simply follow a rule of reason: If employees are given advance notice of the organization's changed expectations, they should be held accountable for meeting the new standard on a go-forward basis.
3. Document substandard performance consistently.

A sample documentation letter appears in Appendix Q.
List the dates and days of the week of the actual incidents. In

addition, document the negative organizational impact that resulted from the individual's unauthorized absenteeism.

Finally, if your policy does not spell out the specific number of incidents that could lead to termination, include general consequential language. On the other hand, if your company policy spells out the number of incidents of unscheduled absenteeism that will result in dismissal, include that specific information instead.

83. How do I handle employees who pattern their unauthorized absences around their regularly scheduled weekends?

The definition of a "pattern" is a frequent, predictable, and observable employee action that repeats itself over time. When employees take more than 50 percent of their time off around weekends or holidays, then a pattern may be established. (In the example in Appendix Q, the employee took four of five days off on a Monday or a Friday; thus, 80 percent of his unscheduled absences occurred around the weekend.) Just remember that this 50 percent rule isn't a legal definition; it is, instead, a reasonable company rule that you may wish to establish.

Tell Me More

"Patterning," in this author's opinion, is a separate infraction from unscheduled absenteeism. Consequently, it should be handled separately in the written warning. Simply create two headings in the written warning:

> Issue 1: Excessive, unauthorized absenteeism
> Issue 2: "Patterning" incidents of unscheduled absenteeism around regularly scheduled time off

Sample wording for this separate section is included in Appendix Q. With these progressive discipline tools in hand, you should be successful in minimizing further incidents of "patterning," because most employees will avoid this perception problem once it's been brought formally to their attention.

84. How does FMLA limit my right to discipline employees with excessive absenteeism problems?

The Family and Medical Leave Act (FMLA), a labor standard and leave law, makes you liable for punitive damages should you violate job protection rules. It's no surprise, therefore, that many employers avoid confronting excessive absenteeism for fear of facing a lawsuit somewhere down the road.

Tell Me More

Does a doctor's note legitimize excessive absenteeism? More important, does it mean "hands off" any employee who relies on a doctor's note to substantiate his own or a family member's illness? These are difficult questions, and the correct answer will depend on the laws of your state. Still, a little knowledge will go a long way in shedding some light on the mysterious shadows surrounding FMLA.

What's important to remember when looking at the FMLA's reach over your company's performance management program is that FMLA-related leaves apply only when an employee or family member has a "serious health condition" as follows:

1. An episodic or chronic condition that requires inpatient hospital stays
2. Continuing treatment by a healthcare provider
3. A period of incapacity of more than three calendar days

More often than not, employees who take off for sick time don't necessarily meet the threshold of having a "serious health condition." As such, the FMLA may have little impact on your decision to document excessive absenteeism in the form of progressive discipline or to ultimately terminate an employee who violates your company's absenteeism control policy.

On the other hand, doctors' notes may preclude your taking any adverse action (including progressive discipline or termination) against an employee for one key reason: in certain states, medical certifications need not identify the condition being treated unless the employee consents. Therefore, a doctor's note will usually only tell you the date of the condition's onset and its estimated duration—no more. As a result, determining whether an FMLA-qualified "serious medical condition" is at hand may be difficult. When in doubt, speak with legal counsel about your rights when doctors allow the individual to take what appears to be excessive time off. Cases like this need to be handled on a case-by-case basis.

85. How can an EAP (employee assistance program) help?

Employee assistance programs (EAPs) can play a very important role in your company's performance management system. EAPs are highly recommended because they are one of the most cost-effective benefits available to employees and employers alike. The concept is simple: Personal issues in workers' lives will ultimately impact their work. When employers provide their workers with a confidential service to help them work out their personal issues, the workers' performance on the job won't suffer.

What kinds of personal problems do EAPs deal with? Among the most common issues are:

- Alcoholism
- Drug addiction
- Depression
- Anxiety
- Family crisis (divorce, illness, death)
- Family issues (raising teenagers, marital discord, blended-family issues)
- Bereavement
- Suicide prevention

Intake counselors at the EAP refer confidential callers to the appropriate providers in their neighborhoods. Callers benefit from the confidential services available to them, and companies should benefit from reduced absenteeism and workplace injuries, as well as from increased company morale.

Since you don't want your managing supervisors to ask employees about their personal lives, this benefit can go a long way in helping managers help their workers without imposing or crossing a line. Managers can simply say, "Sam, you're giving me too much personal information. I care, but I'm not your best resource. Remember, we have an EAP to help you at times just like this. I'm sure they'll be able to help you better than I could."

Tell Me More

The costs of EAP programs are typically based on the number of employees who will have access to the program. As a general rule, figure that premiums range from $2 to $3 per employee per month for a basic program. (If you choose a higher benefit level, those amounts may increase.) So if you have 500 employees, the cost could be somewhere between $1,000 and $1,500 per month.

When you document substandard job performance in a written warning, you may want to include an EAP referral as part of the performance improvement plan. After all, referring an employee to an EAP is a very proactive, responsible step that you might take as an employer to help your staff members. Be careful, however, not to make the EAP mandatory. The beauty of the benefit lies in its voluntary nature. The confidential nature of an EAP is compromised if you make it an extension of your disciplinary authority. Here's how to document an informal EAP referral in a written warning:

> Nina, our employee assistance provider, Prime Behavioral Health Group, can be confidentially reached to assist you at (800) 555-5555. This is strictly voluntary. A booklet regarding the EAP's services is attached to this document.

In addition to informal, voluntary self-referrals, there are also "formal" referrals where you, the employer, become involved in the process. For example, if an employee exhibits flagging performance and also appears mentally depressed, suicidal, or potentially hostile, you may then formally refer the individual to the EAP. In the case of formal referrals, you would discuss your perceptions of the work performance problems with the intake counselor on the front end and, with a signed release from the employee, receive limited feedback about the individual's attendance, compliance, and prognosis.

In certain cases (for example, with potential workplace violence issues), you have the option of not permitting the individual to return to work without a "return to work release" from a licensed healthcare practitioner. Note that such leaves are typically paid through the period of initial evaluation. Beyond that, the employee must use accrued time off to be compensated while receiving further treatment.

Still, be sure to discuss "formal" EAP referrals with legal counsel before initiating the process. Recent case law shows that plaintiff attorneys have argued that formal EAP referrals have created burdens for employers under the Americans with Disabilities Act (ADA). Specifically, these attorneys have argued, on the basis of a mandatory EAP referral, that the employers did indeed *perceive* that their clients were disabled. (The ADA protects individuals who are perceived as having a disability.)

Furthermore, you may strongly suggest that an individual contact the EAP, but you shouldn't mandate that he attend by threatening termination. After all, the employer-employee relationship blurs when you mandate that a worker see a mental healthcare professional outside the workplace. As a matter of fact, such a requirement can even give rise to claims of invasion of privacy in certain states. You'll probably be better off making a note in your log that the worker refused your invitation to speak with the EAP counselor and leaving it at that.

86. What are the three biggest mistakes that employers make when documenting discipline?

Employers commit three basic errors when documenting discipline. They:

- Fail to document their affirmative efforts at helping to rehabilitate their workers.
- Document "state of mind" offenses.
- Codify the damage done to the organization.

Let's look at each of these categories briefly. First, remember that employees and juries expect companies to do more than simply point out problems. Companies must act responsibly by reaching out to disenfranchised employees and welcoming them back into the fold. Such a goodwill outreach may take on the form of one-on-one training or outside seminars or workshops, or it may simply mean providing an employee with a copy of a policy so that the individual clearly understands what's expected. Be sure to document whatever steps you take to help the employee improve the situation at hand.

Second, be sure to avoid what are known as "state of mind" offenses. Sometimes managers try to really impress upon employees in writing how bad their actions were. Consequently, they include terms in the written warning such as "willfully," "purposely," "deliberately," "intentionally," or "maliciously." Such mental element qualifiers certainly appear to strengthen the point that the manager is trying to make, but they escalate the written warning so that it may appear to become a personal attack.

In addition, plaintiff attorneys suing for wrongful termination may now hold you to a higher standard when they ask you questions like, "How did you know my client did that purposely? Would it have made a difference in your decision to terminate her had she not acted purposely?" Therefore, avoid these words whenever possible when documenting discipline.

Third, always bear in mind that disciplinary documents are discoverable. That means that a plaintiff attorney can subpoena your written warnings and use them against your company. Therefore, avoid stating that an employee "sexually harassed" a coworker. Sexual harassment, as a term of the trade, is a legal conclusion. Instead, describe the behavior so that a court can compare the documented behavior to the company's definition of sexual harassment. Otherwise it will be a matter of determining damages owed, not whether sexual harassment took place.

Similarly, don't state: "Your failure to follow standard operating procedure has jeopardized an entire pool of loans." Should a class-action lawsuit later unfold down the road, that one disciplinary document may be used as evidence that it was an employee's fault that a pool of loans was not sold in the secondary mortgage market.

Tell Me More

How should you document incidents of inappropriate conduct or substandard performance without codifying the damage done to your company? Simply use language that is less concrete and more fluid in tone. Sample language of a written warning for sexual harassment cases can be found in Appendix L.

In the case of the improperly pooled mortgage loans, you might write: "Your failure to follow standard operating procedure *may have* jeopardized an entire pool of loans." Again, avoid absolutes and codifying specific damage done to your company.

87. What are letters of clarification?

Many employers make the mistake of looking at corrective action as a black-and-white choice. They either do nothing at all, or they prepare very formal disciplinary documents that may leave an employee feeling alienated and threatened. However, there is a middle ground.

A letter of clarification is an alternative response that allows the supervisor to formally acknowledge her concerns in writing without inflicting the shame associated with formal warnings (e.g., "failure to provide immediate and sustained improvement may result in further disciplinary action up to and including termination").

On one hand, letters of clarification are presented to the employee in written format and require the employee's signature. Logically, when things are written down, they are perceived more seriously. In addition, when employees sign their names to documents related to their performance or conduct, they develop a healthy sense of paranoia that those documents may be used later down the line to establish some pattern in their actions.

On the other hand, letters of clarification specifically state that the document isn't a disciplinary warning. As such, employees don't walk away from your meeting feeling beaten up for having been written up. Instead, they sense that they've had a private meeting with management to discuss management's perceptions about how they can improve their performance. That sense of respect and dignity helps employees assume responsibility for the situation.

Tell Me More

Your opening should express your concerns about the individual's performance, conduct, or excessive absenteeism. It also clarifies that the letter is not a disciplinary document, merely a formal acknowledgment that the individual's performance has suffered. A sample clarification letter can be found in Appendix R.

A final caveat: Letters of clarification work best for long-term employees who should be accorded ample workplace due process because of their tenure in your organization. The clarification letter could later be portrayed as management's attempt to solve the performance problem without having to resort to formal discipline. On the other hand, you shouldn't always hand out clarification letters as precursors to formal discipline. Union representatives may argue that you'll have created a precedent and past practice if you use such documents for certain employees but not for all. Therefore, use these tools carefully, and reserve them primarily for your longer-term employees.

88. What if an employee refuses to sign a written warning?

Many managers mistakenly believe that employees must sign written warnings in order for those warnings to be valid. That's not really the case. The purpose of progressive discipline is to communicate problematic performance issues in an effort to raise employees' awareness so that performance improves.

When an employee is given a written warning (or letter of clarification, for that matter), several things may occur:

- The employee may sign the document on the spot.
- The individual may ask for several days' time to review the document before signing it in order to write a rebuttal.
- The worker may simply refuse to sign the document without further discussion.

All of these options are acceptable. What is important, however, is the documentation of the events. Even with goodwill efforts and suggestions that you put forth, employees may still simply refuse to sign. When that's the case, it's time to call in a witness. The witness's role is simply to verify that the document was given to the employee. This way, if an employee later denies having been given the warning, the witness can refute that claim.

Tell Me More

Let's briefly look at the three circumstances. When employees sign a written warning, they formally recognize that they received it. Therefore, they can't deny later in court that they were given ample notification of the problem and a chance to provide their own side of the story via a rebuttal.

When employees ask for time to review the document and compose a rebuttal, provide them with up to seventy-two hours (or whatever period of time you deem reasonable) to return the warning to you. That seventy-two-hour window doesn't provide them with any special job guarantees or protection periods. In other words, if you give an employee a written warning on Monday and ask her to return it to you by Wednesday, she could still be terminated on Tuesday if she commits an egregious act. What's critical is that you, the employer, can state that the employee received the document on Monday, discussed it with management, and understood management's expectations from that point forward.

On the other hand, if the employee refuses outright to sign anything, you should understand that anger and a feeling of victimization are probably driving the person's emotions. Explain that signing the document is important to show that he received it. Likewise, the manager should sign it to show that he is committed to both helping the individual succeed while holding him accountable for measurable performance improvement.

If the employee still refuses, encourage him to write a rebuttal. The employee gets the last word when it comes to progressive discipline: Your assuring him that his rebuttal will not be rebutted makes for a more even playing field. Giving the employee a few days to provide his side of the story on paper is a good business practice because, from an evidentiary standpoint, a written rebuttal is as good as a signature.

If you need to call in a witness, the witness should be another member of management, not a peer or coworker. After all, management has an obligation of confidentiality regarding delicate matters like progressive discipline. Peers, on the other hand, may share inappropriate information with others and consequently breach privacy.

It's recommended that you hand-write the following on the signature page of the warning:

The employee refused to sign. Notified employee that these are our findings of what occurred and that he would be expected to meet these standards of performance/conduct.

At that point, the manager should sign the document, and the witness should sign the document as well. The witness may then leave the room. Remember, the witness isn't there to be brought into the situation or otherwise pass judgment. However, the witness must be in the room with the employee present and must also receive verbal instruction to sign the warning in the employee's place. Witness acknowledgment is then complete. You should give a copy of the signed document to the employee and keep the original for your own records.

89. Should I rebut a rebuttal or allow the employee to have the last word?

This is a very common question among line managers. In general, we all have a need to justify our opinions. If we write that a staff member displays disrespectful conduct toward clients, commits excessive errors when performing routine tasks, or takes too many sick days off, our perceptions shouldn't be challenged, right? Well, there are two sides to every story. It's not uncommon for employees to attempt to re-create your version of history by providing their own version of events that led up to the written warning or substandard annual review.

So, should managers generally respond in writing to employee rebuttals? The short answer is No. Unless new information surfaces from the employee's rebuttal, there is little need to justify your statements by chasing paper. Simply stated, you don't want to keep going back and forth on paper as to who's right and who's wrong. The original document stands; the employee writes a rebuttal. Then both documents are placed into the employee's personnel file. Period.

Tell Me More

In general, allowing employees to write rebuttals is a healthy employment practice. First, it creates a more even playing field. Both sides have the opportunity to create a written record that they feel more accurately reflects events, and that type of communication should always be encouraged. Second, an employee rebuttal may surface new information that you didn't know about. If it does, you'll have the discretion to rewrite or destroy the warning you gave the employee originally. Third, if an employee is invited to write a rebuttal but fails to, it may be harder for the individual to challenge that warning some time in the future while sitting in front of a judge or arbitrator.

Here's how to avoid the problem from the outset: Before you meet with an employee to give her a written warning, discuss your intentions and your concerns. Tell your subordinate, "Anne, I'm conducting this meeting because it appears to me that a written warning will be necessary. Before I sit down to write it, I want to learn your side of the story. There may be extenuating circumstances that I'm not aware of."

Assuming that there aren't extenuating circumstances to change your course of action, write the warning *after* your meeting with the employee. By doing so, you'll show that you're a fair arbiter of workplace disputes. You'll demonstrate that you listen to both sides of a story before reaching a conclusion. Also, you'll have the opportunity to share the message that a written warning is in the works, thereby alleviating the stress that comes when these kinds of workplace documents are suddenly brought to someone's attention as "signed, sealed, and delivered."

One more thing: As much as possible, include the employee's side of the story in your disciplinary narrative. Construct statements like this: "When I asked you why . . . you said. . . ." Such statements show on paper that you've listened to the employee's side before resorting to discipline. That's the best management practice of all.

90. Can a union employee demand that a steward be present at a progressive disciplinary meeting with management?

Yes. The Supreme Court ruled in the 1975 case *National Labor Relations Board v. Weingarten, Inc.* that employees in a unionized organization have the right to union representation during an investigation interview if the employee reasonably believes that the meeting may result in disciplinary action. Although you're not required by law to tell unionized employees that they have the right to the presence of a union representative, you may still wish to do so. If that is the case, you should tell your subordinate that the meeting may result in discipline and that she has the right to have a union steward present.

If a union steward isn't available at the time you're planning on having the meeting, you should reschedule. You might even send the employee home with pay pending the meeting if the employee's actions were egregious. Forcing a meeting when a steward is unavailable may only give the union a separate cause of action against you.

Tell Me More

That being said, it may be a wise management practice to inform unionized employees about their *Weingarten* rights even if they don't voluntarily request a steward's presence. First, it's a fair and open way to manage your employees. Second, understand that managers often have fairly defined views of unions: They either feel that management should cooperate with unions in the employees' best interests or believe that management's responsibility is to minimize the union's influence over the organization.

As a result, corporate cultures may develop that are either cooperative or hostile vis-à-vis union intervention. The pros and cons of union involvement in companies' management practices go far beyond the scope and purpose of this book. Regardless of your feelings, it's important to recognize that failing to recognize *Weingarten* rights or relying on formalities may only aggravate the situation.

Therefore, in this author's opinion, reminding an employee of her right to have a steward present at a disciplinary meeting, even if she doesn't ask, demonstrates to your workers and to the union that you're fair and objective in your management practices. That's an important perception to preserve regardless of your feelings regarding union activities. In addition, such open communication in the workplace may minimize employees' needs for union membership in the first place.

91. Can a nonunion employee demand that a coworker be present at a progressive disciplinary meeting with management?

Possibly. The *Weingarten* case in 1975 confirmed that unionized employees have the right to act in concert for their mutual aid and protection as set forth in section 7 of the National Labor Relations Act (NLRA) and to ensure evenhanded treatment of employees. At that time, the National Labor Relations Board (NLRB) didn't expand the *Weingarten* interpretation to include nonunion employees.

However, on July 10, 2000, that changed. The NLRB abandoned its long-standing limitation on *Weingarten* rights and extended those rights to nonunion employees in *Epilepsy Foundation of Northeast Ohio*, 331 NLRB No. 92. In that case, the NLRB overruled its prior decisions and extended the *Weingarten* benefits to union and non-union employees alike.

In short, employees, even in nonunion jobs, have the right to request the presence of a coworker at an investigatory interview that the employee reasonably believes could result in disciplinary action.

Tell Me More

There appear to be limitations on employees' rights in this new interpretation. First, nonunion employees must request the presence of a coworker representative. Your company doesn't have any obligation to provide a representative if one hasn't been requested. Second, the employee has the right only to the presence of a *coworker*—not a union steward or attorney. Requests for attorney participation in internal company matters should especially be denied.

In addition, I believe it is not in your company's best interests to voluntarily share with employees that they have the right to coworker participation. Whereas *Weingarten* rights have been around for union employees for twenty-five years, this new interpretation for nonunion employees is untested.

In addition, *coworkers* in general—unlike union stewards, who are trained in basic employee relation principles and practices—may not understand the fundamental rules of management intervention. As a result, unqualified "coworker" involvement may create problems in sensitive investigations. By expanding the "need to know" circle, the coworker's presence creates a greater chance of loss of confidentiality or breach of privacy.

This new interpretation of *Weingarten* constitutes a substantial change in the law and imposes additional duties on nonunion employers. The case is on further appeal as of this writing, so it's best to check with qualified legal counsel whenever a nonunion employee requests the presence of a coworker at an investigatory meeting that could result in discipline.

Chapter 8

Terminations for Cause and Summary Offenses

92. How long do I have to terminate an employee after a final incident occurs that violates prior warnings?

The simple answer is, The sooner the better. Companies' termination decisions should occur as soon as possible after management has completed its internal fact-finding investigation. Final termination decisions are necessary after a summary offense such as gross insubordination, theft, or fraud occurs or after a worker violates a final written warning in the progressive discipline process.

Your failure to terminate an employee very soon after the event may be interpreted by a court as an acceptance of the employee's conduct. A plaintiff's attorney may argue that you condoned the behavior by failing to act on it within a reasonable amount of time and that you should consequently be precluded from changing your mind at a later, more convenient date.

Since delay of more than a few days could imply an acceptance of the misconduct or substandard job performance, your subsequent discharge of the employee could be challenged. Remember that you can be held to have violated the implied promise of good faith and fair dealing if your decision to summarily discharge the worker appears to be just a pretext, capricious, or unrelated to business needs.

Tell Me More

On the other hand, it is sometimes difficult to conduct an investigation and reach a conclusion within a day or two after a precipitating event. If you meet with an employee regarding a manager's complaint and more witnesses will need to be polled and additional evidence will need to be gathered, place the employee on a paid investigatory leave. Tell the employee that the investigation may result in a termination. Inform the individual that you will call him at home with any questions that surface and keep him abreast of the pending investigation. Finally, let the person know that you will ask him to return to your office once a decision is made so that it can be discussed face-to-face.

In addition, you may plan to terminate an individual on a Tuesday morning, and that person may call in sick that day. In such cases, keep the employee on the payroll until she returns to work. The day she arrives should be the ultimate termination date.

Finally, understand that not all companies are able to cut final checks on the same day that they're requested. If your organization requires twenty-four hours to process final checks, you should still meet with the employee on the day she returns to work in order to terminate her. However, depending on payroll rules in your state, you may need to ask her to leave the company premises but keep her on the payroll for an additional day.

For example, in California, if the employee calls in sick on Tuesday and Wednesday but returns to work on Thursday, you should meet with her on Thursday to conduct the termination meeting. Inform her, however, that payroll will need twenty-four hours to cut the check, so she'll actually be paid through the end of business on Friday. This way you'll meet California's wage and hour regulations that stipulate that employees are to receive their final wages on the day of termination.

Other states do not require that workers receive final wages on their termination date. Instead, they provide employers with more flexibility by allowing companies to pay employees' final wages at other intervals—for example, by the next due date in the pay cycle. Learn your state's, county's, or city's regulations regarding final payment of wages. The lesson here, however, is to be sure to keep people on the payroll for additional time so that you avoid violating any wage and hour regulations. After all, you may be challenged for wrongful termination: You don't want to add to your liability or potentially show a jury that you were sloppy in such basic matters as getting people their final check on time.

93. Should letters of termination be specific or generic?

It's up to you. Some companies don't provide any written information to employees upon their termination for fear that the documentation may be used against the organization. They simply provide employees with final checks and COBRA paperwork. Other companies provide a very basic written statement declaring, "Today will be your last day of employment with the company." No cause of termination is mentioned.

Still other companies provide very detailed information in a written letter explaining all the reasons why termination is occurring. Remember, a well-constructed termination letter could go a long way toward fending off potential litigation claims because contingency plaintiff attorneys are less likely to take a case that appears to be airtight in favor of the employer. On the other hand, a termination letter with inaccurate information could be the very documentation a plaintiff attorney needs to prove that the company was less than responsible in the fact-finding that led up to the decision to terminate.

Tell Me More

If you're going to write a specific letter of termination, include the following information in the body of the letter:

- Written warnings
- Performance reviews that show the employee was not meeting expectations
- Merit reviews that show the employee received no increase in pay
- Any decision-making leaves or suspensions that the employee received prior to termination
- Any other affirmative efforts you made in an attempt to rehabilitate the employee

A sample specific letter of termination is presented in Appendix S.

Note that specific termination letters always describe a "final incident" that has led to the decision to discharge. A clean final incident that breached the terms of prior warnings is the "threshold event" that triggers the termination action. Clean final incidents are easily documented and are consequently often found in documented termination letters.

One final note: Some employers ask that employees sign these termination letters as a matter of practice. In those cases, there is usually a line at the bottom of the page where employees can sign after a statement that reads, "I have received a copy of this document."

Requiring employees to sign their own termination letters, as an evidentiary matter, ensures that there won't be any dispute that the employee received the document. There's no harm in adding it, of course; it's just more of a stylistic issue. Otherwise, there isn't much need for an acknowledgment countersignature. Therefore, add the countersignature requirement only if your company is more comfortable with the added closure it may bring to the employment relationship.

94. If an employee gives two weeks' notice of resignation, are we permitted to let the employee go that same day?

Most resignations are fairly straightforward: Employees give you written notice of their intentions to leave the company, and two weeks later they're gone. However, many companies with salespeople ask account executives to leave the same day that they give notice. The logic there is that salespeople who are leaving to join the competition may bring sensitive client information with them.

It's also the case that managers sometimes feel that certain non-sales employees are better off leaving that same day that notice is given. The reason? If those employees are perceived to be troublemakers, if they have access to sensitive company information (especially information systems or finance employees), or if they appear to have mentally checked out, then having them around may be a morale or security problem.

In such cases, it is certainly acceptable to ask employees to leave the day they give notice. After all, they've already given notice of their intention to leave your company, haven't they? Wait—there's a catch here. If this is done incorrectly, you could be exposing your company to unnecessary liability.

Tell Me More

When employees give notice of resignation, they are technically seen as the "moving party" in the termination. They have the right to give two weeks' notice and work through those two weeks, especially if your company states in its handbook that it expects employees to give two weeks' notice upon resignation.

If you ask employees to leave that day, however, then you set the final date of termination. Technically speaking, you become the "moving party," and you'll have changed their resignation to a termination. What does that mean? First, from an unemployment insurance standpoint, the employee may be eligible for unemployment. If the company is the moving party, states will typically award a claim of unemployment insurance to a petitioner employee.

Second, there is a possibility that an employee who leaves under adverse circumstances may pursue legal action against you in the form of a wrongful termination lawsuit. Remember that in wrongful termination challenges, the burden may be on you to prove that you had cause to terminate. Since you were the moving party but the employee may have had no performance problems during his tenure, you wouldn't necessarily be able to demonstrate that you had cause to terminate. And lo and behold—you'd have to settle out of court because you'd have no defense.

There's a combination solution to avoid this unemployment claim and wrongful termination liability exposure: First, ensure that you have a clearly defined employment-at-will working relationship by documenting the at-will policy on employment applications, in company handbooks, in offer letters, and in free-standing employment-at-will confirmation statements. Second, simply pay employees for their two weeks' notice if you require them to leave the same day that they give notice. In essence, that two-week payout serves as a simple insurance policy. The employee is paid through the end of the notice period, that individual remains the "moving party," and claims for unemployment insurance or wrongful termination liability should be minimized. Make this a standard employment practice whenever you relieve people of their duties before their resignation date.

What if the employee verbally resigns but won't give you written confirmation via a letter of resignation? If you suspect that a substandard job performer who gives notice may change her mind in the interim, you should confirm her verbal resignation in writing by presenting her with a confirmation of resignation (see sample in Appendix T).

Such a written confirmation will make it more difficult for the individual to change her mind one week later and attempt to keep her job—despite her earlier notification of resignation.

Finally, what if an employee rescinds her resignation during the two-week notice period and demands to have her job back? Be careful here—she may indeed have the right to keep her job! The key question that a court would look at in a situation like this is, Did you as the employer *act in reliance* on the worker's notice? In other words, did the company post the job opening, interview other candidates, reassign work within the unit, or offer the position to another candidate? If the answer to most of these questions is Yes, you will have a better chance of successfully defending a charge of wrongful termination.

If, on the other hand, you've done nothing in the two-week notice period, a court might argue that the employee was indeed free to rescind her resignation and get her job back. In that case, a court might interpret your refusal to reinstate the individual as an error in judgment on your part. The lesson here is simply this: When problematic and underperforming employees give you two weeks' notice, don't start dancing in the aisles too quickly. You're better off taking immediate action to fill the position being vacated by posting it internally, running an ad, and reassigning work to remaining staff members.

Of course, in certain instances, you may choose to retain a well-performing employee who rescinds her resignation, but you have to be careful about setting an unwanted precedent. In the future, it could be argued that if you allowed one employee to rescind a resignation, you'll have to allow others to do so. Therefore, you shouldn't develop an active practice of allowing such changes of heart at the eleventh hour.

95. How do I handle job abandonment?

Job abandonment occurs whenever an employee simply disappears from work without gaining advanced permission. Put simply, the person goes AWOL (i.e., "absent without leave"), and you're left wondering what to do. Can you terminate the person outright? Do you have to give written notice and time for the employee to respond?

Understand that there is no law that requires you to act a certain way in response to an employee's abandonment of his job. What you do is a matter of company policy and past practice. Although you have a fair amount of discretion in handling such matters, you should err on the side of caution: Pulling the plug on workers who act irresponsibly may feel good, but it's not necessarily the optimal way to respond. After all, your reputation as a fair employer may be at stake.

Tell Me More

It's best to provide AWOL employees with written notification that they will be terminated if they don't respond by a specific date. Here's how it works: Many companies have policies that define job abandonment as unapproved time away from work for three consecutive days. Let's assume you don't hear from an employee on Monday—a simple no-call, no-show. You'd probably call that employee at home and leave a message on the home answering machine stating your concern. (Of course, when enforcing policies of this sort, you must be sensitive to human health concerns. There is always a possibility that the employee was in an accident or may be hospitalized and unable to communicate with you.)

By Tuesday afternoon, you'll make a second phone call. In this message, inform the employee that you'll be sending an overnight FedEx or Airborne letter to the individual's home (see Appendix U for a sample letter) for a Wednesday arrival. Your voice mail message should state that if she doesn't report to work or at least call by Wednesday afternoon, you'll assume that she's abandoned her job. You'll process her termination accordingly.

What if the employee's home phone number is no longer in order? Send the letter anyway. Ditto if the letter comes back undeliverable. It's the employee's responsibility to keep you informed of address and phone number changes. If an employee fails to do that, it further demonstrates the employee's irresponsibility. Process the termination on Wednesday. The termination date should be Wednesday; most states will permit you to pay the employee only through the last day worked. In this case, you would pay the individual only through the previous Friday.

96. Can we terminate an employee for egregious behavior at a company party?

Absolutely! Company-sponsored functions are an extension of the company itself. Employees are responsible for holding themselves accountable for all aspects of their conduct and behavior as if they were back in the office. Unfortunately, many employees forget their manners at company picnics and holiday parties by overdrinking or otherwise making fools of themselves. They then sit back and wonder why they're being disciplined or terminated the next day because things got out of hand at a party.

Let's look at an example. A female employee at a company holiday party had way too much to drink. She then became "overly friendly" with some of her male supervisors, and her tongue made its way into a few of the gentlemen's ears. She hung all over these people, and, to their dismay and shock, anyone who tried to stop her was yelled at and groped. In short, she was out of control in public, and her behavior repulsed those who witnessed it. When the nice people from human resources came to escort her to the women's restroom, she became belligerent and pushed people away from her.

The result? She was terminated the next day for inappropriate workplace conduct. Unfortunately, she couldn't remember what happened, but the human resources folks were able to recount enough of the details that she got a pretty accurate picture before too long. Her response, interestingly enough, was defensive: "Why should I be terminated for my behavior at a company-sponsored event? After all, I would've never acted that way in the office. Besides, you provided the alcohol! When there's an open bar, I sometimes get carried away. I'll apologize to the appropriate people for my behavior, but I want my job back!"

Tell Me More

Does she have a point? Will an apology suffice, seeing that the company provided the alcohol? Or can an otherwise stellar employee be terminated for a one-time indiscretion, even if it occurred off company premises?

Unfortunately for her, the answer is that employees may be terminated for one-time indiscretions that occur off company premises. First, remember that sexual harassment may exist when workers are exposed to unwanted and offensive behavior of a sexual nature or with sexual overtones. This employee's behavior may be considered serious enough to cross the threshold of harassment in the company's interpretation. At the very least, such behavior could be considered a breach of company policy or of the organization's standards of performance and conduct.

Second, remember that your treatment of an egregious situation like this may create a precedent in terms of how you handle future actions. People tend to remember incidents like this for years to come; if the employee was not discharged, it may be more difficult to discharge workers in the future for similar egregious misconduct.

Finally, remember that at any type of company-sponsored party, your organization can be held liable for employees' actions during the party as well as for any injuries incurred (yes, that could even mean a workers' compensation claim in certain states). As a result, you might want to incorporate the following suggestions into your holiday party or picnic plans:

- Distribute a memo before the party reminding employees that appropriate workplace conduct standards will be maintained at all times. Employees are to act responsibly, and excessive drinking or other inappropriate behavior could result in disciplinary action or dismissal. In addition, confirm that attendance at the social event is voluntary.

- Use professional bartenders when serving alcohol. Instead of having an open bar, provide "ticket bars" where employees are given coupons, and establish a drink limit per individual. Instruct managers and supervisors that they are not to buy drinks for their employees under any circumstances.

- Collect employees' car keys at the beginning of the party, and stop serving alcohol early. Distribute car keys at the end of the party after you've ensured that employees or their family members are sober. (This could be seen as draconian, so discuss this as part of your celebration planning.)

- Offer a wide variety of nonalcoholic beverages, and offer protein-rich foods that slow the body's absorption of alcohol.

- Instruct volunteer spotters and designated drivers to monitor the party and, if necessary, to drive intoxicated employees home.

- Arrange for taxis or other public transportation, or book a block of rooms in a convenient hotel for anyone whose functioning may be impaired by alcohol.

97. What is the best way to conduct an employee termination meeting?

Employee termination meetings are exceptionally difficult. Any time that you unilaterally remove someone from the workplace, anxiety increases. Fear of not finding the right words, feelings of guilt, or fear of being physically threatened make even the most self-confident managers nervous. Companies handle the logistics of the termination meeting differently; what's got to be consistent, however, is the compassion for the individual.

Following are general guidelines for conducting such meetings:

- Treat the soon-to-be-fired employee with respect and dignity.
- Invite a management witness (usually someone from human resources) to the meeting.
- Give the employee as much freedom as possible to exit on his own terms.
- With information-sensitive positions like those in IS or finance, arrange in advance to have the individual's computer systems shut down at the same time the termination meeting is occurring; also determine whether the individual will need to be escorted from the premises under supervision. (This is extreme and doesn't preserve dignity; it is, however, necessary at times.)

Tell Me More

Many managers make the common mistake of shaming employees at the time of termination. To deal with their own nervousness, they assume a militant and aggressive approach while defending their actions. Some even state, "If you're planning on suing us, be my guest: We've got the best legal representation in town." Such aggressiveness adds little value to any meeting. Instead, it makes the terminated employee feel angry and belittled.

Instead, be empathic. It's okay to say you're sorry that the circumstances have come to this. Here's a sample close for such a meeting:

> Jim, it's never personal; it's all about business decisions that companies are forced to make after they've made reasonable attempts to help an employee improve. I realize that sometimes it's just not a match. Call it poor timing or the right person matched with the wrong job. I want to thank you for all your efforts. I know you've tried to make this work. I hope you can understand what led us to this decision, and I hope that you find in your heart of hearts that it's fair. These things happen to all of us at one point or another in our careers. I just want to make sure that you feel we handled this matter professionally and respectfully, because it's not a decision that we've made without a lot of consideration. We wish you well.

A management witness should attend all termination meetings. First, both managers will feel more at ease having someone to share the burden with. Second, a witness will be able to testify on behalf of the company at a later date should the employee claim that management made discriminatory remarks or other inappropriate comments at the termination meeting. Third, there is an element of safety in numbers. Although workplace violence is rare, having a second adult in the room minimizes the chances that a worker will react physically to the discharge.

Regarding logistics, some companies escort terminated employees off the premises with the help of armed security; other companies ask human resource representatives to accompany employees back to their desks to oversee the packing of their belongings. Each circumstance has to be reviewed on its own merits.

In general, you should be able to allow employees to gather their personal belongings as they see fit. Some employees require assistance with boxing; others prefer to return to work on a Saturday or after hours so that they don't feel humiliated in front of their peers. Still others will simply want to walk back to their desks on their own, clear things out, and say goodbye to their coworkers. The important point is this: Ten minutes before the termination meeting, they were free to roam about the office as they saw fit. They weren't criminals then, and they shouldn't be treated like criminals now.

In cases where information systems (IS) or finance employees have computer access to critical company information and where you have an active practice of shutting down computer systems of those people during termination meetings, continue your practice. However, be sure to explain to the employee that when she returns to her desk after your meeting, access to her computer will be denied if she tries to log on. Confirm that this is how all IS separation meetings are handled and that this case is no exception. That should allay any concerns that the employee is being treated more harshly than others who have been asked to leave the company.

98. What if I suspect that an employee may react violently to being terminated?

Despite your best efforts to treat employees with dignity and respect at the termination meeting, some employees, albeit a statistical minority, may react physically to being terminated. We all hear about cases of employees pulling out weapons at termination meetings or returning to work the following Monday morning to exact revenge on their supervisors and coworkers.

Bearing that in mind, let's address some tips for avoiding violence during or after dismissal, a common "triggering event" of workplace violence:

- Conduct termination meetings as early in the day and as early in the week as possible.
- Physically seat yourself between the employee and the door. In other words, you should have access to the door and not be blocked by the employee should an emergency exit become necessary.
- When necessary, employ the services of a security firm to attend the termination meeting in plainclothes, to wait outside your office door, or at least to be standing by a phone in the lobby.

Tell Me More

Many companies terminate employees as late in the day on Friday afternoons as possible. This is a mistake. The traditional logic was simply this: The dismissal should occur as late in the day as possible so that coworkers were not impacted. Friday afternoons made sense so that a "clean break" could be made with the workplace and, more important, so that the whole matter could be swept under the rug by keeping it out of sight.

Unfortunately, many workplace violence incidents occur on Monday mornings because distressed, terminated employees have no one to talk or appeal to. They spend the weekend brooding over the wrong that was done to them and, in a void of communication, determine to wreak havoc on the perceived wrongdoers.

Dismissal meetings that occur early in the day and early in the week, on the other hand, allow employees the opportunity to question what went wrong. They can discuss their perceptions of what led up to the termination and have their questions answered regarding unemployment insurance, reference checks, and company records.

Seating arrangements are important in termination meetings. If an employee is armed and standing between you and the door, you'll have no way out. Whenever possible, seat the employee away from the door at the far end of the room. This should allow you a means of quick escape should that become necessary.

Finally, if you reasonably suspect that the employee may react violently, it will be a good investment on your part to invite armed security to your meeting. For example, a mortgage banking firm planned to terminate an employee on a Tuesday. When that employee appeared at work that day, he was wearing a full-length black leather coat and dark sunglasses, and he carried a gym bag that appeared heavy. The employer reasoned that this was cause for concern, since it was a hot summer day, and this employee never came to work dressed like that before.

The company called a security firm and arranged to have an armed officer attend the termination meeting. The officer kept a revolver in his briefcase on the desk. He was introduced to the employee as a member of the human resources department visiting from the home office. The meeting went without incident. The cost to the company for the armed security officer's presence was $140 ($35 an hour at a four-hour minimum charge). That's a very reasonable fee for such important work.

99. How can I allay some of the anxiety and depression that come with termination?

With early-in-the-day, early-in-the-week terminations, the company also has the advantage of explaining—several times if necessary—its need to terminate the individual's employment. Managers can explain that employees who are terminated for cause typically receive unemployment insurance (or that, at least, the company won't contest the unemployment insurance claim). They can also confirm that no specifics regarding references will be released to prospective employers other than the individual's title and dates of employment. All this will usually go a long way toward allaying the terminated employee's fears about his immediate future and his ability to receive income while in career transition. In addition, employee assistance programs and outplacement services may help.

Tell Me More

Employee assistance programs can be helpful in providing the employee with counseling and psychological support at the time of termination. This benefit, when available, is typically extended for three months after layoffs occur and employees are let go for no fault of their own; there's no reason why the benefit couldn't be extended for those terminated for cause. If you choose to continue EAP coverage, call the EAP to work out the additional premiums. (Coverage typically ends upon termination of employment.) More important, use this opportunity to ask the EAP to notify you if any threats or aggressive actions surface in the counseling session.

Outplacement programs are likewise an excellent benefit for terminated workers because they help those employees immediately focus on the future, rather than lament the present. Statistically speaking, few employees who get outplacement sue the companies that fired them. More important, this benefit can go a long way toward aiding an otherwise unbalanced individual who is trying to come to terms with the reasons he was given for his termination and who is attempting to find fault with supervisors or coworkers.

100. How do I announce that an employee has been terminated?

After an employee is terminated and leaves the premises, it becomes necessary to tend to those left behind. Even when coworkers believe that the termination is justified, it's difficult to carry on. Some people feel awkward mentioning the individual's name; others want more information regarding the incidents that led up to the termination; still others will stir the proverbial pot and want to gossip about the matter.

As the employer, it's important that you allay staff members' fears about a termination for cause. Yes, sometimes firing employees becomes a necessary business decision and rightfully reminds people that their jobs aren't guaranteed. Still, after an employee separation, it becomes time to heal the wound. It's an important opportunity for you to bring people together to answer their questions and to show that the ex-employee was treated fairly and with dignity. It's also an opportunity to bring closure to a matter that may have been brewing for months or even years.

Tell Me More

Besides its healing effect, announcing an employee's separation properly will help you stave off potential claims of defamation. Wrongful termination claims often come with add-on charges such as discrimination, harassment, and slander (i.e., falsely spoken charges or misrepresentations that defame and damage someone's reputation). Ex-employees' lawyers may claim that former supervisors and coworkers maligned or disparaged the plaintiff after she left the company. In addition, attorneys may claim that inaccurate references were given to prospective employers that precluded the individual from getting a job. And voilà—your company is involved in lost-wages litigation, in addition to facing wrongful discharge and discrimination charges.

Here's how to handle this delicate issue and bring closure to remaining employees' concerns while minimizing potential legal challenges:

> Everyone, I'm calling this staff meeting to let you all know that today was Sarah's last day with the company. She left just before lunch, and I didn't want you all wondering where she was. Out of respect for her privacy, I'm not at liberty to share the reasons for her leaving the company. I want you all to know that we treated her respectfully and handled the matter with dignity.
>
> I also want to remind you all that any reference phone calls from prospective employers or from headhunters have to be forwarded to human resources; this is just a confirmation that you're not permitted to give references as per company policy. I'd also ask that you refrain from any unnecessary speculation regarding her leaving.

Again, out of respect for her privacy, it's better that we leave matters be. I want to take this opportunity to see whether any of you have questions or concerns. If not, we can all head back to work now that I've made the announcement. What are your thoughts, everyone?

In short, this is a professional way of handling separation announcements. You'll have "done right" by the terminated worker. It won't get back to the ex-employee that management disparaged her reputation. If coworkers engage in gossip nonetheless, management can always confirm that it did its best to minimize any discussion of the topic among the rank and file. Short and sweet and done with class, such a communication deals with the employee's separation from the organization and allows the remaining employees to get on with business.

Chapter 9

Reductions-in-Force (RIFs) and Layoffs

101. What do I need to know before laying someone off?

There are certain guidelines that you will need to follow when considering a layoff. Specifically, you'll need to evaluate:

- The appropriate position to be impacted
- The appropriate employee to be laid off
- The legitimate reason for the reduction in force
- How long the position could remain unfilled
- What could happen if you were legally challenged for having improperly laid someone off

Tell Me More

How do you determine which employee should be separated? Remember, you can't arbitrarily select someone for a layoff simply because she is your weakest performer or because she happens to be in the position that's being eliminated. As a rule of thumb, you're obliged first to identify a position that is no longer necessary for some legitimate business reason; second, you must then identify the person in the department or unit who is least qualified to assume the remaining duties.

Once you have identified the position to be eliminated, how do you determine who is the person least qualified to assume the remaining responsibilities in the business unit? First, develop a list of all employees in that group with similar titles or responsibilities. For example, if you're looking to eliminate one of three secretarial positions in your marketing department, list all the secretaries (or people who handle secretarial duties) in that department on a sheet of paper.

Second, review the nature of the remaining work to be done after the position is eliminated. For example, if the secretarial position reporting to the vice president of marketing is being considered for elimination, document the responsibilities that will remain in the unit after the reduction in force. (Job descriptions are very helpful for such comparisons.) In this case, answering high-volume or important phone calls, coordinating travel arrangements, composing written correspondence, and developing PowerPoint graphics presentations may be the key tasks left to be done after the reduction in force.

Third, determine which of the three secretaries in marketing is the least qualified to assume those remaining duties. In essence, you'll be comparing all three employees' essential job responsibilities, skills, knowledge, and abilities. In addition, review the employees' annual performance reviews, tenure, and history of progressive discipline to create the appropriate written record. It would also make sense to review their work experience prior to joining your company so that tenure alone doesn't outweigh other considerations. Once that documented comparison has been made of the three employees who could potentially qualify to perform the remaining work, it's time to determine who is the least qualified individual.

If a company has a legitimate business reason to eliminate a position, it probably shouldn't have a need to re-create that position in the near future. In other words, don't eliminate a position you think might be needed in the future. If a company re-creates or re-opens a position shortly after a layoff, it will be hard pressed to prove that the layoff wasn't a termination in disguise.

102. Can I lay off a substandard job performer rather than terminate for cause?

Managers who want to avoid the confrontation associated with progressive discipline and termination often look to the path of least resistance—a no-fault layoff. But layoffs aren't always the easy-out solution that you may be looking for, and you're typically better off pursuing a legitimate termination for cause via progressive discipline. Why? Because managing employee performance problems via progressive discipline holds employees accountable for their actions, establishes a performance improvement plan that actively involves your company in the employee's rehabilitation, and creates a defensible written record to show that you've accorded the employee with workplace due process.

Still, many managers prefer to pursue a layoff because it lacks the ongoing confrontation associated with progressive discipline and because it appears to provide a quicker solution to ending employment. Make sure, however, that you follow the guidelines for layoffs before pursuing this option.

Tell Me More

First, keep in mind that in a layoff you eliminate *positions*, not people. In other words, your written records must reflect that a position is being eliminated because of a lack of work or other financial constraints, and the *individual* who currently fills that position will now be impacted because there's no longer a job to report to. If removing a problem performer is your goal, eliminating that individual's job may be a big mistake. After all, you'll still need to get the work done.

If, after going through all of the considerations for a layoff, you find that the individual identified for a layoff is the person you originally targeted because of her ongoing performance problems, then you may be safe to sever her employment.

If, on the other hand, the underperforming employee is arguably not the least qualified individual (on the basis of your review of all relevant criteria, including performance evaluations and other written records), then you have to lay off one of the other two secretaries. Of course, that means that a layoff is no longer a viable alternative. Therefore, you have to revert to managing that individual's performance via documented progressive discipline.

But wait. There is another key consideration when determining whether a layoff is the appropriate employer action when dealing with underperforming employees. You've also got to keep in mind that courts and juries have certain expectations about employers' responsibilities when eliminating positions and laying off workers. The logic is simply this: If a company has a legitimate business reason to eliminate a position, it probably shouldn't have a need to re-create that position in the near future. If the company re-creates the position soon after eliminating it, a judge or jury might conclude that the company's original action was only a pretext. In other words, the court could be persuaded that the so-called layoff was really a termination for cause in disguise. This could obviously damage the company's credibility during litigation.

How long does the position need to remain unfilled? That depends on your state's statute of limitations on unlawful employment practices. In many states, an ex-employee may file a complaint up to one year from the date that the unlawful practice occurred. Therefore, it's typically safest to wait at least twelve months before filling a position that was previously eliminated.

What if you are willing to gamble and fill the position after, say, six months? Well, if the ex-employee learns that her previous position has been filled and she engages the services of a plaintiff attorney to pursue the matter, then the damages sought will be similar to those in a wrongful termination or unlawful discrimination claim. If you are held to a for-cause standard of termination, you may be burdened with providing documentation to show that you had reason to terminate the employee because of substandard job performance, inappropriate workplace conduct, or excessive absenteeism.

As is typically the case with layoffs, though, employers aren't prepared to show proof via progressive discipline that performance was a problem. As a result, an out-of-court settlement will probably need to be reached. Damages could include reimbursement for lost wages, compensation for emotional distress, plaintiff attorneys' fees, and, in egregious cases of employer misconduct, punitive damages.

Therefore, layoffs should be implemented only when position eliminations are inevitable because of a lack of work or other financial considerations. Because of their complications and limitations, they should not be used as an alternative to dealing with individual performance problems.

103. How do I select who should be let go?

Let's assume that you've been instructed to reduce your budget via position eliminations. You'll have to create a written record to show that you've evaluated all the employees in a given area in order to identify the worker least qualified to assume the remaining job responsibilities. It makes sense to do this because plaintiff attorneys may argue that, even in a nonunion environment, you have an obligation to accord "bumping" privileges to more senior employees.

In other words, simply arguing that "John Doe had to go" because he filled a particular position that was eliminated may not stand up to legal scrutiny. Instead, you'll be challenged by a higher standard: "Why did you let my client, John Doe, go, even though there were other less qualified employees, with less seniority, on your staff?"

Here's a suggestion for preparing for such a legal challenge: Employ the "comparison template" found in Appendix Y for all the employees in the same classification and document that these records were reviewed *before* any action was taken. This way, should you later be challenged, you'll be able to demonstrate the criteria you used in selecting the employee least qualified to assume the remaining job duties after the position elimination.

Also, when conducting a layoff analysis (but before any layoff decisions are made), you should prepare "before and after" statistical reports on your workforce. This statistical analysis will help you determine whether the selection criteria used might result in a statistically significant impact on a protected group, such as minorities, women, or employees over forty. If the analysis reveals a potential adverse impact, then you will need to use different selection criteria or select different individuals. Once the selection criteria produce an acceptable result, the reports supporting that conclusion should be retained for five years.

Tell Me More

When it comes to selection for downsizing, it's critical that your company be consistent in the application of its own rules and past practices. Most companies apply multiple criteria when looking at job eliminations. These criteria include but are not limited to:

• *Seniority-based selection:* With many union contracts, the employees with the least seniority are the first to lose their positions in a layoff. Using only this selection method may limit your organization's discretion in keeping top performers because "time on payroll" is the only consideration.

• *Employee status-based selection:* An excellent strategy to begin your company's downsizing efforts. Using this methodology, part-time or temporary workers are laid off first to ensure greater security for full-time, regular employees. Unfortunately, this method alone may not suffice to help you reach your downsizing goals.

• *Merit-based selection:* As documented in the template in Appendix Y, the merit-based model provides companies with the most discretion because of its inclusive nature. Employees' performance track records, attendance history, education, progression through the ranks at your company, prior employment experience, and progressive discipline are all considered in addition to seniority when decisions are being made about layoffs.

All in all, merit-based selection is the method of choice for most companies. Applied consistently in all layoff situations, it will provide you with prelayoff written records that demonstrate that you objectively selected those individuals for layoff who were the least qualified to help your company succeed. Should a postlayoff legal challenge ensue, your RIF documentation will help you demonstrate your fairness and consistency in separating employees primarily on the basis of performance criteria.

104. What do I need to consider when there are union contract "bumping" provisions?

Most collective bargaining agreements provide "bumping" privileges for union members. Since unionism rewards seniority equally with individual performance, these bumping rights allow more senior members to displace less tenured members of the bargaining unit.

Let's say, for example, that a Clerical Specialist II position is being eliminated in a hospital's radiation oncology department. If Mary Jones is the Clerical Specialist II in radiation oncology, then Mary's position will be eliminated. However, Mary may not be the individual laid off. Instead, a Clerical Specialist II with less seniority elsewhere in the hospital may be laid off. Here's why: Many collective bargaining agreements include bumping language (see Appendix Z for a sample).

There are obviously a lot of clauses that need due consideration when determining which union employees should be laid off (e.g., inside or outside the department, in the same or lower classification). What's important to remember, though, is to document your systematic efforts at determining which employees should be laid off whenever a position is eliminated.

Tell Me More

Employers attempt to retain the maximum discretion in the layoff and bumping processes by including language regarding performance, attendance, and discipline. The trouble for most companies, though, is that skills, knowledge, and abilities are not easily measured or documented. That's why it's so important, especially in a union environment, to avoid inflating performance evaluation grades and to ensure that disciplinary actions are documented. Without those written records, your company will have a difficult time relying on this kind of contract language to lay off substandard performers and to retain the best talent.

In addition, the most effective way to create a complete written record of who gets to stay and who gets bumped is to list all the names of employees in the particular classification affected (in this example, all Clerical Specialist II's) in terms of seniority. The most recently hired Clerical Specialist II on the list will most likely be the one to get laid off.

However, you have to remember to match apples to apples: If the person with the least seniority has specific skills that the "bumping" employee does not possess, or if he or she works the graveyard shift and the "bumping" employee doesn't want such a shift, then you shouldn't lay off the person with the least seniority. Instead, you'll scratch that person's name off the list with a note stating why he won't be the one chosen for layoff. You'll then go up the list to the next individual with the least seniority and evaluate that person for layoff.

You'll continue going up the list until an individual in the particular classification is selected. If there is no individual with less seniority in that classification, then you may look at a lower classification inside or outside the department (depending on the instructions in the contract). If there still isn't an individual with less seniority, then you may lay off Mary Jones in radiation oncology.

Collective bargaining agreements attempt to create a systematic process for providing tenured members with job security by displacing employees with less seniority according to a preset formula. However, it's usually not that easy, because management has the discretion to decide who is most suitable for layoff, and sometimes the union disagrees, resulting in a grievance.

In any case, your best strategy is to apply the collective bargaining agreement bumping rules fairly and consistently. In all cases, be sure to document why you've selected or passed someone over for layoff. Such written records can be your best defense in fighting union grievances or rebutting unfair labor practice charges. Of course, you should discuss projected layoffs with counsel before implementing them. And by all means make sure that the affected employees' personnel files are in order, as they are often subpoenaed.

105. Will our union contract prevent us from outsourcing one of our departments?

When it comes to the options you have in outsourcing various departments within your company, you need look no further than the management's rights clause in the collective bargaining agreement. That clause is probably the most important part of any union contract. A weak clause may be written as follows:

> Except as specifically limited by provisions in this agreement, the Employer retains all rights and authority to manage, direct, and control its operations to the full extent of the law. Such rights and authority retained by the Employer include, but are not limited to, the right to hire and promote, to maintain discipline and efficiency, to assign personnel, specify or assign work requirements and overtime.

Why is this poorly written? Because it does very little to describe specific company rights vis-à-vis managing the workforce and controlling operations. If your union contract has a short, one-paragraph management's rights clause like this one, you'll probably be unsuccessful in arguing that you have the right to outsource any positions covered by the collective bargaining agreement.

Tell Me More

There is an example of a well-defined management's rights clause in Appendix AA. Don't expect unions to give in easily to your demands to include language like this. Done as part of successful union negotiations, however, such language can buy you the flexibility you need to outsource one or more of your departments.

If the language in your company's contract with the union is not as specific as our sample, you may be precluded from outsourcing now. Instead, you'll have to wait until open negotiations at the expiration of the current contract. Be sure to make revision of the management's rights clause one of your next negotiating items.

106. How much notice am I obligated to give employees who are about to be laid off under the WARN Act?

The federal Worker Adjustment and Retraining Notification (WARN) Act may govern the notification requirements and obligations of a layoff when you plan to close an entire plant or to lay off workers en masse. The WARN Act is extremely technical and should be reviewed with legal counsel before any action is taken. Following are some its key terms:

Jurisdiction: WARN applies to businesses that employ (a) 100 or more employees, excluding part-time workers, or (b) 100 or more employees who in the aggregate work at least 4,000 hours per week, excluding overtime hours

Plant closing: The permanent or temporary shutdown of a single employment site or one or more facilities/operating units within a single site, if the shutdown results in an employment loss during any thirty-day period for fifty or more employees (excluding part-time workers)

Mass layoff: A reduction in force resulting in an employment loss at a single work site during a thirty-day period for the lesser of (a) at least 33 percent of the employees and at least fifty employees (excluding part-time workers) or (b) at least 500 employees (again excluding part-time workers)

Employment loss: This is (a) a termination other than a termination for cause, resignation, or retirement, (b) a layoff exceeding six months, or (c) reduction in work hours of more than 50 percent during each month of any six-month period

Notices: The employer must give sixty days' advance written notice of a plant closing or mass layoff to (a) each affected employee or, in the case of unionized employees, to their union representatives, (b) to the state dislocated worker unit, and (c) to the chief elected official of the local government.

Tell Me More

Determining whether your company should be governed by the WARN Act can be a complex issue. In the event of a mass layoff, if 500 full-time employees are to be laid off at a single site, then WARN applies. In the same situation, if 33 percent of your full-time workforce (and at least fifty employees) are going to be laid off at a single site, then WARN applies. But what if the layoffs are planned over six months, rather than thirty days? What if employees at different work sites or employees of separate and identifiable business units within the same physical site are being laid off? You can see where the WARN application gets tricky.

More important, can your company structure the layoffs to avoid meeting the WARN thresholds? For example, if you lay off fewer than fifty employees now and wait thirty days before laying off additional workers, can you avoid WARN's provisions? This is a question for legal counsel and goes well beyond the scope of this book.

Finally, understand what WARN *isn't* meant to be. Layoffs that affect fewer than fifty workers at any given time are not governed by the Act. Plant closings or mass layoffs caused by events that are not reasonably foreseeable (e.g., natural disasters or union strikes and lockouts) may be implemented on less than sixty days' advance written notice. The sixty-day rule also does not have to be strictly followed if the company is, at the time notice would be required, actively seeking capital to continue its business operations and in good faith believes that giving notice will hasten the acquisition of capital. In addition, the law wasn't intended to protect workers who lose their jobs less than sixty days after the sale of the business; it is, instead, intended to protect workers only from closings or layoffs prior to a sale.

Penalties for failing to provide appropriate notice to displaced workers may include back pay for up to sixty days, the costs of employees' benefits for that period, and fines not to exceed $500 for each day of the violation. However, the company's liability for back pay and lost benefits is reduced by any wages paid to employees and by the continuation of benefits for any period of the violation.

If the WARN Act does not apply to the layoff you are planning to conduct, then you have no legal obligation to provide employees with advanced notice. Instead, you may lay off employees immediately, and the timing or type of notice and separation payments will depend on company policy and other contractual obligations.

107. What's the best way to handle the actual layoff meeting with the employee?

Layoffs are one of the most difficult management challenges that you'll experience. Although terminating an employee for cause is certainly difficult, there's an element of justification to it: Either the employee engaged in egregious misconduct and was summarily dismissed, or the individual was taken through steps of progressive discipline, in which case, even if the employee doesn't feel the termination is warranted, she'll at least have had advance notice that separation from the company was a possibility.

Layoffs are different. Often the elimination of a job has little to do with the incumbent's performance. If all the food service jobs in your cafeteria are being outsourced to an outside provider, then a whole group of individuals may be let go. If a new executive vice president brings her assistant with her from their prior company, then the current EVP's assistant in your company may need to be let go. The guilt and anxiety you'll feel in such cases can be overwhelming. It's not uncommon for managers to feel that they've personally let people down because those managers weren't somehow able to "save their jobs." This is just one of a number of normal reactions to stress.

Tell Me More

When conducting a layoff meeting with an employee, tactfully get right to the point:

> Hi, Richard. Michael from the human resources department is here with us today because we've got difficult news to share with you. As you know, our company just completed next year's fiscal plan, and it's called for the elimination of three positions in our department. Yours is one of the three that will be eliminated. I want you to know that this action is not based on your performance; we've always been very happy with your work, and I want you to know how much I appreciate how much you've done for our department.
>
> I'm so sorry to have to tell you this. I want you to know that if anything opens up here at the company that you're interested in and that you're qualified for, we'd love to consider you for that position. We're in a hiring freeze currently, but once that freeze is lifted, I'd encourage you to check to see if there are any positions you'd be interested in pursuing.
>
> Today will be your last day with us. Michael will talk to you about your final paycheck, your accrued but unused vacation, and the severance that you'll be eligible for. As much of a shock as this is right now, tell me what questions I could answer for you or how I could help.

> As far as the logistics, tell me what you'd prefer: Would you like us to help you pack up your desk, or would you prefer to come back tomorrow to do that? Would you like to say goodbye to everyone, or would you prefer to just let that be for now? Okay. Thank you again for all your hard work and dedication over the past few years. It's been a pleasure working with you, and I'll miss seeing you in the office every day.

This may sound like an overly friendly approach to letting employees go. However, remember the importance of the human element at times like these. No one wants to be or should be treated like a criminal because his or her position was eliminated. Whenever possible, avoid escorting people off the premises with the help of security. If they weren't criminals this morning, there's no reason they should be treated so this afternoon.

In addition, remember the importance of saying "I'm sorry." Many employment experts recommend avoiding any demonstrations of emotion at times like these. After all, they argue, this is a business decision, and you, the manager, have nothing to be sorry about.

Oh, nonsense! If I were being laid off, I'd hope that my boss were holding back tears. I'd feel so sad to think I wasn't coming back to the office tomorrow. In short, be human and humane—loss of a job is a serious event in someone's life. As with all traumatic experiences, sincere concern and empathy will go a long way in helping people come to terms with their loss.

108. Should a release or separation agreement be prepared for terminating employees?

Companies sometimes opt for releases when separating an employee for cause or because of a reduction in force. When weighing the pros and cons of a release, consider the following issues:

- Is the employee a member of a protected class?
- If so, could that protected employee argue that he was treated differently or held to a different performance standard than other similarly situated, nonminority workers?
- Could a plaintiff attorney see any merit in pursuing a discrimination, harassment, or retaliation (for example, whistle-blowing) lawsuit against your company?

- In a layoff situation, does your company have any plans to fill that position within the upcoming year?
- In a layoff situation, do your company's demographics (age, gender, and ethnicity) poorly reflect the demographics of those about to be laid off? In other words, could a plaintiff attorney argue that your actions might appear to negatively impact a disproportionate number of minority employees?

If your answer to any of these questions is Yes, then a separation agreement may be in order.

Tell Me More

First, remember that one of the key elements of any separation package is "consideration." Consideration is the money or other element of value that you provide employees in exchange for their signing a release. From a legal standpoint, it is the inducement to a contract that validates the transaction. Therefore, you must determine first what appropriate consideration should be offered to the employee in exchange for the release.

Second, remember that if the impacted employee is forty years of age or older, special considerations must given to that individual. Specifically, the Age Discrimination in Employment Act provides that individuals have twenty-one days from the date of notice to review and consider the agreement. Further, it must specifically advise employees of their right to seek legal counsel. In addition, employees must be given seven days to revoke the agreement after they sign it. These "forty-and-over" rights are incorporated right into the release.

Third, when a group layoff is at issue, it is best to offer *all* impacted employees the right to a separation package in exchange for a release (above and beyond company severance). The reason is that, in addition to caring for your soon-to-be laid-off workers, you'll want to ensure that the surviving employees feel that you've handled matters fairly. After all, company layoffs occur when organizations are vulnerable. That means that employees feel vulnerable as well. Retaining talent is critical when companies are shedding staff, so do everything in your power to assure the remaining staff of your commitment to strengthening your business and treating people equitably.

Appendix V is a sample separation letter including an Age Discrimination in Employment Act disclaimer. Note that this is specifically written for a financial services company in California. The purpose of the letter is to demonstrate what a typical release might look like. It should not, however, be copied word for word by your company for use in a layoff situation. Legal counsel should review your final document to conform to the rules and laws of your state.

109. Should I offer to provide displaced workers with letters of recommendation?

Tough question. The short answer is No, but there may be exceptions or ways around this somewhat thorny issue. The reason for the initial No answer is simple: There is little benefit to your company in providing references about prior workers to prospective employers or headhunters. Yes, it would be the nice thing to do, especially after a layoff. After all, there's nothing you'd rather do than hasten employment for your ex-workers who will soon be in career transition. Even in cases where employees weren't very happy, helping them find productive work elsewhere could save you potential headaches from wrongful termination lawsuits.

However, the downsides are obvious. Claims of defamation await you should you provide false or injurious information that precludes an ex-worker's gaining employment. Other similar types of claims that could be brought by a former employee include:

- Invasion of privacy (for the disclosure of private information)
- Statutory violations (e.g., the California Labor Code makes it unlawful for any person by way of misrepresentation to prevent a former employee from securing other employment)
- Unlawful discrimination (e.g., a former employee could allege that a negative reference was given because of her pretermination objections to her former employer's unlawful and discriminatory employment practices)
- Negligence (e.g., a recent California court ruled that, once a former employer elects to provide a job reference, the company must provide *all* relevant information regarding the former employee, both favorable and unfavorable)

Of course, the truth may be an absolute defense to defamation claims related to alleged "false and injurious statements" but not necessarily to discrimination, negligence, or invasion of privacy claims. You won't want to face months of litigation in order to determine whose version of the truth—yours or the ex-employee's—is actually correct.

Without a well-defined policy prohibiting your line managers from granting reference information about ex-employees, you'll have a loose cannon on the deck of your ship. After all, you'll never know who's saying what about whom until that lawsuit crosses your desk. Therefore, create a policy requiring supervisors to refer all references to human resources for handling. You'll sleep better at night knowing that all the supervisors in your company are consistently protecting your organization from unnecessary liability every time their telephones ring with someone asking for information about the performance of ex-employees.

Tell Me More

If your company provides its employees with annual performance reviews, then those reviews (as long as they are signed by the employees) should serve as written proof of any ex-employee's strengths, weaknesses, and areas for future development. Simply provide exiting employees with copies of their historical performance reviews so that they can share those evaluations with prospective employers if they wish. Do not, however, forward ex-employees' performance reviews to prospective employers without the workers' permission. That would be inappropriate and could expose your company to liability.

If you give your employees copies of their reviews, it will take you out of the middle. Performance reviews serve the purpose of evaluating a worker's performance, and that's all that prospective companies are interested in during the reference-checking process. Managers need to simply tell prospective employers, "We typically give employees performance reviews once a year. You might want to check with John to see if he's received any reviews during his stay here. If so, he's free to share them with you if he wishes. Other than that, we're not permitted to engage in verbal performance references and have to refer all calls to our human resources department." Problem solved.

What if your company doesn't provide its employees with annual reviews? Then the whole thing becomes a little trickier. You do, of course, have the right to compose letters of recommendation for your employees. However, if such letters are to be written, they should be brief and based on factually documented information in the employee's personnel file, not on subjective claims related to performance. (Even so, there is some risk with this approach because the former employee may disagree with your characterization of his performance. As a result, the former employee may allege that statements in the letter of recommendation are false and injurious.) A sample letter is in Appendix W.

Of course, you can simply refuse to provide any subjective reference information whatsoever and limit your responses to (a) dates of employment and (b) last title held. However, if you feel that such a stringent "no references" policy will hurt your ex-employees' chances of reemployment, you may wish to rely on a legal doctrine called "qualified privilege" to protect your firm against claims of defamation. (Defamation comes in two forms: "slander" if the information shared is spoken; "libel" if the information shared is written.)

The principle of qualified privilege offers limited protection to employers in most states in defamation cases. To receive the benefit of this protection, you must show that:

- You made reference statements in good faith and based on credible evidence
- You and the person to whom you disclosed the information (i.e., the prospective employer or headhunter) shared a common interest
- You limited your statement to this common interest

The law recognizes that a former employer (that's you) and a prospective employer share a common interest in the attributes of a job candidate (i.e., your former employee). To gain the protection of the qualified privilege, your main task will be to stick with the objective and verifiable facts regarding the ex-worker's performance or reasons for leaving your company and to avoid half-truths, subjective opinions, or conclusions about that individual. If you can establish that you're protected by the qualified privilege doctrine, then the only way that a former employee can succeed in a defamation lawsuit against you is to prove that (a) you knew that the information was false but that you passed it on anyway or (b) that you acted recklessly in sorting out the facts.

Remember, however, that qualified privilege generally pertains only to defamation claims. As stated earlier, reference checks raise other legal issues beyond defamation that could cause problems for you. Still, if you choose to engage in providing reference information, you should require the former employee to sign a request for a detailed reference letter, as well as a release for your company.

How do you prepare for releasing reference information about your ex-employees? At the time of the layoff, create a form for employees to sign that acknowledges permission for you to provide references. A sample form can be found in Appendix X. The form may look like this but should be reviewed by legal counsel to conform to the laws of your state.

Of course, such a release may not protect you from claims of defamation, invasion of privacy, discrimination, or negligence. It will, however, help to open the lines of communication with your soon-to-be ex-employees, clarify that you will treat them objectively, and stipulate that you will limit your comments to work performance matters only.

In addition, share with your employees up front that only specific people in the company will be authorized to provide verbal references or respond to reference requests, and identify who those people are. This way, your company may have a defense should a former worker direct a prospective employer to contact an unauthorized company representative who provides negative references that damage the individual's employment prospects.

One final note regarding sharing references with prospective employers: Should you provide references if you've terminated an employee for discrimination, sexual harassment, or violence in the workplace? The answer that most employment lawyers will give you is that it depends on the laws of the applicable jurisdiction. You may indeed have an affirmative responsibility to share information with prospective employers about an ex-worker's conduct if it involved an unreasonable risk of harm to others.

Check with outside counsel regarding the specific facts of the case before sharing any reference information whatsoever with prospective employers. After all, the balance between an individual's privacy rights and a prospective employer's need to know can sometimes be difficult to determine, especially when dealing with matters like discrimination, sexual harassment, or violence in the workplace.

110. How valuable is outplacement as a tool to help my laid-off employees find new jobs?

Outplacement is an exceptionally valuable tool for aiding employees who have been laid off and who are looking to find new work as quickly as possible. Outplacement is a $1 billion industry that has grown over the past few decades because of the unprecedented number of corporate mergers and acquisitions, usually accompanied by outsourcing, restructuring, and downsizing, which has impacted the lives of many American workers. Companies have recognized the key benefits of employing outplacement firms, including:

- Promoting a favorable, caring image of the company despite its need to lay off workers
- Helping to maintain the loyalty and productivity of the remaining employees
- Reducing the amount of time necessary for displaced employees to find new work
- Minimizing a company's exposure to litigation resulting from company downsizing

What exactly do outplacement firms do for your displaced workers? That will vary depending on the type of package you buy for impacted workers, but *executive* career transition consulting services and re-employment strategies include:

- One-on-one career consulting
- Entrepreneurial development
- Resume preparation
- Mock interview role-playing and video feedback
- Secretarial/PC/Internet/fax support
- Office space/telephone coverage
- Distribution of resumes to executive search firms

If one-on-one executive career transition support appears to be too expensive (see Question 111), then *group* outplacement services may make sense. Group programs include one- to three-day career retraining workshops that cover many of the same topics, just at a more generic level and in more of a lecture format. Still, individualized resume preparation and mock role-plays are usually a part of group services as well.

Tell Me More

Some companies provide their employees with a choice between electing outplacement services or accepting cash instead. It is highly recommended that you avoid this option. Although it appears beneficial to employees at first glance, many workers will, for fear of the unknown, select the cash. That's a big mistake: Even if a large severance is part of employees' separation agreements, it won't diminish the importance of getting their career searches off on the right foot. Therefore, help your employees focus on their future career endeavors, rather than on the short-sighted benefits of cash in hand.

There's another benefit to employees who elect outplacement services over cash: Cash is taxable to the employee; outplacement services normally aren't. Companies can structure outplacement services in a way that minimizes the chances that the IRS will construe those services as taxable benefits by simply showing that the outplacement services primarily benefit the employer, not the employee. Here's how: It's common for companies to require terminated employees to sign a waiver of rights to sue in return for additional severance consideration. Since outplacement is a benefit above and beyond the severance benefits provided by companies in their employee handbooks and policy and procedure manuals, a clause can be added to a standard release that describes the exact nature of the benefit (see Appendix V). In this way, two goals are achieved: First, the company will have demonstrated that outplacement was a primary benefit to the organization, not to the individual, minimizing the chance that the employee will be taxed for the value of the outplacement services received. Second, because the outplacement serves as consideration in exchange for a full release of all claims as part of a separation package, liability associated with wrongful termination, age discrimination, and the like is eliminated.

111. How do I choose an outplacement firm?

Choosing an outplacement firm is as easy as researching your choices in Kennedy Information's *Directory of Outplacement and Career Management Firms.** The book provides profiles of more than 350 firms, including fee schedules and contact information. Kennedy's *Directory* recommends the following guidelines in selecting an outplacement firm for your soon-to-be-separated employees:

1. Ensure that the firm belongs to the prestigious International Association of Career Management Professionals.
2. Tour the firm's offices in person, paying special attention to office layout and technology offerings.
3. Check corporate references with longer-term clients who

The Directory of Outplacement and Career Management Firms, Kennedy Information, (800) 531-0007, www.kennedyinfo.com.

have been using that firm for outplacement services for several years.

4. Ask the following specific questions:

- Are your consultants full-time employees of the outplacement firm, or are they independent contractors? (Ask about consultants' education and experiential qualifications.)
- How many candidates is each consultant responsible for at any given time?
- In general, what is the firm's average time-to-start for candidates in transition?
- How is networking taught?
- Is "trailing spouse" consulting included in executive outplacement programs?
- If candidate testing is part of the organization's standard process for aiding candidates in career transition, what kinds of tests are used, and in what way does testing actually help the firm's candidates in planning their job search?
- Is outplacement a leading or trailing product for the firm? (Remember, the outplacement business contracted in the late 1990s because of improved market conditions, and many companies downsized their outplacement operations and diversified their businesses by engaging in other kinds of management consulting activities, including retained search.)

Tell Me More

As a rule of thumb, executive level outplacement is reserved primarily for key employees at the vice presidential level and above. Outplacement fees at the executive level typically range from 15 to 20 percent of terminated employees' total cash compensation (salary plus bonus). There are usually no time limits on such programs; they last until the executive finds a new position. Therefore, outplacement services for a $150,000 vice president of marketing would cost approximately $25,000.

In addition, there are several time-limited programs for lower fees that are offered on a monthly basis (typically one month to twelve months). Such programs' costs are structured on a flat-fee basis and may range from $3,000 to $12,000 per employee, depending on program length.

On the other hand, group workshops may be more appropriate for employees at the staff level (managers and below). One- to three-day programs cost approximately $1,500 per *session* (regardless of the number of participants). Consequently, outplacement services' fees vary widely at the group level.

112. Will my displaced workers have any trouble getting unemployment insurance?

Unemployment insurance is the only tax that is under your control as an employer. It's important to remember, however, that your company doesn't determine whether an employee wins an unemployment claim; the state does. Of course, you can contest an unemployment claim, but you probably don't want to do that after a layoff. After all, the purpose of unemployment insurance is to help employees who have lost their jobs or suffered some form of wage loss through no fault of their own.

Unemployment insurance is meant to be a very generous and liberally construed benefit for American workers. According to the system's logic, if unemployed workers are denied interim benefits, the United States may revert to a nation of soup kitchens and shantytowns. As a result, administrative law judges award benefits fairly liberally.

Understand that each state legislature has discretion in determining how to implement federal unemployment guidelines. As a result, certain states have very liberal interpretations of the application of unemployment "wage replacement" insurance, while others have stricter guidelines. Still, there are some twists and turns in the unemployment insurance game, so let's take a brief look at the basics regarding layoffs and terminations for cause:

- It's important to understand what it means to be the "moving party."
- You must be able to differentiate between a "voluntary quit" and a "discharge."
- Finally, understand that you can generally challenge an ex-employee's claim for unemployment if you can prove "misconduct" or a "quit without good cause."

Tell Me More

The "moving party" concept is critical to understanding how to manage unemployment taxes. Generally, the party that picks the last day that the employee works or receives wages is the moving party. If employees pick the last day that they work (via resignation), then they are the moving party; if the company dictates the last day that an employee works (via layoff or termination), then the company is the moving party.

Therefore, in order for ex-employees to receive unemployment insurance, they must demonstrate that the company was the moving party and that they are actively engaged in the job-finding process. Let's look at some examples:

- If you lay off an employee on May 30 and give her same-day notice, then your company is the moving party. Ex-employee claimants should be able to successfully collect unemployment because they lost their jobs through no fault of their own.

- If an employee gives you two weeks' notice of her resignation because she's found another job and she works through the notice period, then she's the moving party. Any claim that she files for unemployment will probably be denied.

- If that same employee gives you two weeks' notice of her resignation because she's found another job and you send her home that day without paying her through the notice period, then you're the moving party. In other words, she was willing to work the additional two weeks through her notice period, but you caused her to lose wages prematurely by sending her home. Therefore, she'll probably be awarded a claim for unemployment.

- If an employee gives you two weeks' notice of her resignation and you immediately place her on vacation and charge the balance of the two weeks' vacation against her accrued vacation, then you're the moving party. The reason is that you'll have accelerated the separation date in that an actual wage loss will have been suffered. (The employee would have otherwise been entitled to accrued vacation pay up through the two-week notice period.) Again, a claim for unemployment would probably be awarded.

- If an employee gives you two weeks' notice of her resignation because she's found another job and you send her home that day but continue to pay her through the notice period, she remains the moving party. After all, no actual premature wage loss will have been suffered.

The lesson? The best advice to be gained is that when an employee gives notice to leave on a specific date, you should always get a resignation statement indicating the *real, substantial,* and *compelling* reason that the individual is resigning. You should then continue to pay wages as normal through the notice period.

A "voluntary quit" occurs when an ex-employee is the moving party. However, if an employee quits for "good cause" (good cause is subject to legal interpretation by the various states, of course), he'll most likely collect unemployment insurance benefits. For example, a quit due to intolerable working conditions or due to relocation from Boston to New Jersey may be deemed a "constructive quit," and the individual will most likely receive an unemployment insurance award.

A "discharge" (for reasons other than misconduct), on the other hand, occurs when you, the employer, terminate the individual. In such cases, you'll be the moving party. Therefore, the claimant will most likely receive an unemployment insurance award. If, for example, you terminate a worker for mere inefficiency, unsatisfactory conduct, good faith errors in judgment, or ordinary negligence in isolated instances, then courts will construe your termination decision as a straight "discharge" and award benefits.

On the other hand, in the case of "gross misconduct" or recurring negligence after prior written warnings, you may be able to successfully challenge the individual's claim for unemployment insurance and get relief of charges. What constitutes gross misconduct differs from state to state. Rarely is a single isolated incident enough to establish misconduct. As a general rule, at least one written warning should have been given to the employee for the same or a related violation within the six months immediately prior to the discharge.

One final thought about unemployment insurance: Claimants are responsible for conducting their own job searches and for demonstrating that they continue to look for work. If they fail in this regard, their claims may be denied. This is certainly not in your control, so be careful not to imply that a worker who leaves your company "will certainly be able to get unemployment insurance." That's not your call— it's the state's—and, even if you don't contest the claim, that individual may still be denied benefits if she doesn't meet the responsibilities of a job-seeking claimant.

Appendixes: Sample Policies, Agreements, and Letters

Z. Sample Bumping Provisions for Layoffs
AA. Sample Management Rights Clause in the Bargaining Agreement
    (with a Union)

A. Sample Nondiscrimination and Equal Opportunity Policies

A policy of nondiscrimination and equal opportunity employment may be structured this way:

> It is the policy of XYZ Company to provide and ensure equal opportunity for all persons employed or seeking employment with XYZ Company, in accordance with all applicable requirements of federal and state law.
>
> Therefore, all matters relating to recruiting, hiring, training, compensation, benefits, promotion, transfer, company-sponsored education, social and recreational programs, and treatment in the job will be free of practices that discriminate unlawfully on the basis of race, color, creed, sex, marital status, national origin, age, disability, medical condition, Vietnam-era veteran status, or other characteristics protected by law.

A corporate diversity mission statement might look like this:

> We at XYZ Corporation recognize that diversity is a business issue. As a leader in _____, we appreciate the need to attract and retain a diverse workforce in order to meet our public mission and our corporate goals. To compete for scarce human resources talent and to better meet the needs of an increasingly diverse customer and vendor population, XYZ is committed to hiring, promoting, transferring, and training employees on the basis of merit, ability, and performance.

The corporate diversity policy might continue this way:

> I. Definition
>
> Although "diversity" can be defined narrowly in terms of race, age, gender, or other protected characteristics, we choose to recognize diversity in its broadest sense encompassing personal differences such as lifestyles, education, personality characteristics, and length of time with the company. We acknowledge that diversity is not a program but an ongoing cultural imperative that recognizes the

need for a continuing dialog among employees in order to change perceptions and stereotypes that lessen the value of individuals' differences and uniqueness.

"Diversity" at XYZ is therefore defined as a heightened level of awareness regarding or sensitivity to the need to foster a sense of inclusion and acceptance of others. Our philosophy on diversity is based on respect for one another and recognition that all individuals bring their own unique attributes and experiences to the corporation. Diversity is not about individuals feeling the need to fit into the mainstream; it is, instead, about acceptance of others' differences and appreciation of others' talents.

II. Role of Management

All managers are expected to foster a sense of inclusion among staff members by welcoming new ideas and fostering a sense of collaboration and joint problem solving. Managers will make sure that their employees understand that hiring and promotional policies are based on individual merit. Furthermore, managers will be expected to hire qualified employment candidates with an eye toward enhancing XYZ's diversity initiatives.

III. Role of Staff

All employees are charged with the responsibility of encouraging and participating in open communications regarding an appreciation of our differences. Employees are therefore welcome to form caucus groups of, for example, women, Hispanics, African Americans, or people with disabilities to share their experiences and suggest ways to improve our diversity initiative. These groups will be encouraged to advance mentoring opportunities among peers and managers in order to foster members' leadership skills and career development opportunities.

IV. Role of Human Resources

XYZ's divisional HR teams will act to ensure that XYZ diversity initiatives remain an organizational priority. As such, the various divisions of XYZ may engage in activities such as:

- Creating a diversity library to broaden employees' knowledge of diversity issues
- Advertising Internet Web sites on the company's Intranet site to broaden employees' knowledge of diversity issues
- Integrating diversity training into management workshops re-

lated to employee performance, hiring, and compensation/ benefits
- Establishing a code of conduct that ensures that a policy of equal opportunity employment is affirmatively implemented for all persons, without regard to race, religion, color, sex, age, national origin, veterans' status, or physical or mental disability
- Establishing a complaint resolution procedure, free from retaliation, should any employee wish to complain about perceptions of discrimination or harassment
- Voluntarily advertising in all recruitment ads that we are an equal opportunity employer

Also see Question 8.

B. Sample Arbitration Agreements

Offer Letter Language

> By signing this letter, you agree that any dispute or controversy between you and XYZ Corporation, including without limitation any claims for breach of contract, statute or public policy, personal injury (tort), employment discrimination, or any other claim of any type arising out of or in connection with the termination of your employment, will be submitted to and determined by final binding arbitration in [city, state], in accordance with the provisions of XYZ Corporation's personnel policy manual in effect at the time the demand for arbitration is filed.

Employee Handbook Language (found on the Acknowledgment of Receipt page)

> I agree that any controversy or claim arising out of termination of my employment (other than those arising from a collective bargaining agreement), whether occurring under contract or common law, will be settled by arbitration in the county of my employment by an arbitrator in accordance with the procedure set forth in the commercial rules of the American Arbitration Association.

Employment Application Language

> I agree as a condition of employment that any controversy or claim arising out of the termination of my employment whether arising

under contract, statute, or common law, shall be settled by arbitration in accordance with the procedures set forth in the applicable employment agreement, or, if none, the commercial rules of the American Arbitration Association.

Also see Question 9.

C. Sample Recruitment Brochure

Part I: Our History

Use this opportunity to sell what makes your organization unique. That's easy enough to do if you're IBM, GE, or Microsoft. But what if you're a small dental office that's just getting off the ground? Then you should sell the reasons why you're opening your practice, the kind of service you hope to provide that will allow you to stand out from your competition, and how you envision a corporate culture based on open communication, customer service, and personal accountability. Simply asked, Why should someone want to work for your company? That's your introductory paragraph.

Part II: The Hiring Process

Our hiring process is very thorough. In addition to interviews with human resources staff and departmental management, we will check your business references as thoroughly and with as many sources as possible. This will include a criminal background investigation and drug test at our expense before any offer of employment is extended. We may also require that you provide us with copies of recent performance evaluations to demonstrate your skills, knowledge, and abilities. If hired, you must complete an I-9 form and bring documents on your first day of employment to prove your legal right to work in the United States. You must also attend new-hire orientation within one month of your hire date.

Part III: Starting Salaries and Performance Reviews

We offer very competitive salaries and benefits. Initial salary offers are typically based on pre-established salary ranges and internal equity—the notion that new employees' years of experience and technical abilities should be matched or "slotted" to the years of experience and skills of our existing staff. Salaries are typically determined at the final round of interviews and shared with you at the time of offer.

All employees will be hired "at will" unless a collective bargaining agreement or employment contract dictates otherwise. That means that your employment is not for a specified period of time and may be ended by you or the company at any time with or without cause or notice. In addition, your first ninety days with our company will be considered an "introductory" or "probationary" period. Interim performance evaluations may occur at the conclusion of your introductory period. However, financial reviews occur for all employees only after one year of employment.

Part IV: Benefits

We offer benefit-eligible employees flexible benefit programs that will provide you with significant opportunities and advantages. You may choose from a wide menu of options including medical (traditional indemnity, HMO, point of service, and catastrophic care), dental, vision, life, AD&D, short- and long-term disability, 50 percent tuition assistance for work-related courses at accredited institutions, and healthcare and dependent care reimbursement accounts. Medical and dental benefits become effective on the first day of the month after ninety days of employment. Insurance premiums and benefits are subject to change at any time throughout the year.

After one year of continuous service, you may be eligible to participate in our 401(k) plan; the plan includes a 5 percent or 6 percent match (depending on your salary) at $.25 on the dollar and permits rollovers, loans, and withdrawals. The investment plan vests at 20 percent per year with full vesting after five years of service.

Part V: For More Information

We realize that selecting your next employer is important to you and your career development. We hope this addresses some of your questions. For more information, please visit our company Web site at www._____.com. Our stock is traded on the AMEX under the symbol "xxx." And of course, please keep abreast of our changing job opportunities by calling our job line at (555) 555-5555. We are an equal opportunity employer. Thanks for your interest!

Also see Question 27.

D. Sample Internet Ad

Director of Staffing and Employee Relations

Reporting to the vice president of human resources in a thirty-person HR department, you'll be responsible for employee relations, recruitment, and immigration. In terms of employee relations, you'll structure progressive disciplinary actions, terminations for cause, and layoffs for nonunion employees. You'll investigate claims of sexual harassment and discrimination in a timely manner. You'll also be responsible for working with outside legal counsel when necessary. Employee relations will constitute 40 percent of this job.

You'll personally recruit for forty job openings on average, primarily in the administrative support, technical, and managerial areas. This will include conducting initial interviews and reference and background checks, as well as coordinating pre-employment drug screenings and extending employment offers. You'll also be responsible for tracking monthly cost-per-hire figures, turnover, time-to-start, and "source cost analysis" data. Recruitment will constitute 40 percent of this job.

You'll serve as the responsible officer for all H1, L1, and TN nonimmigrant visas as well as green card/permanent resident applications. Immigration-related work is sporadic; there are approximately fifteen employees currently completing their green cards. You'll rely heavily on outside immigration counsel in all matters related to visa and green card processing. Immigration and special projects will constitute approximately 20 percent of this job.

Also see Question 31.

E. Candidate Prescreening Interview Matrix

Candidate's Name: _____
Today's Date: _____
Position/Location: _____
Resume Attached? Yes _____ No _____

Company and Job Specifics

- Company demographics (size in terms of revenues or employee population, publicly traded/privately held, for-profit/nonprofit)

- Company niche (primary product markets, specialty areas, key competitors)
- Career progression history ("Describe how you've progressed through the ranks at your current company leading me up to what you do now on a day-to-day basis")
- Compensation package (base salary vs. bonus, commission, overtime pay, or deferred compensation)
- Date of next merit review: _____
- Expected increase percentage: _____ percent
- Direct supervisor(s) (number and titles): _____
- Direct report(s) (number and titles): _____
- Extended reports (your subordinates' direct reports): _____
- Software systems currently used: _____

Success Profile

- What is your greatest accomplishment at your current company? (linked to increased revenues, decreased costs, streamlined systems, or saved time)
- What did your last performance review look like in terms of strengths and weaknesses? Would you be willing to share a copy of it with us in advance if we were seriously considering you for a position?
- What would your most respected critic say of your overall performance, and what suggestions would that individual have for managing you most effectively?

Assessment of Candidate's Needs

- What are the two or three criteria you're using in selecting your next company?
- What's your next logical move in progression at your current company? When would you expect to receive that promotion? Have you discussed the opportunity with your supervisor?
- What's your motivation for changing jobs? What would have to change at your current position for you stay there?
- Not to limit you, but please share with me what salary range you're looking for at this point in your career. Also, please distinguish between a minimum and an ideal salary target, just so I know if I'm in the ballpark.

Also see Question 38.

F. Interview Matrix

Current Position

Company (size in terms of revenues or number of employees):	Industry:
Position title: Supervisor(s) (number and titles): Direct report(s) (number and titles):	Dates of employment:
Key achievement(s):	Compensation (base salary vs. bonus vs. commission vs. overtime vs. deferred compensation):
Reason for leaving: 3 criteria in selecting your next company: ■ ■ ■	Salary expectations, availability to begin work: Possibility of counteroffer acceptance:

Prior Position #2

Company (size in terms of revenues or number of employees):	Industry:
Position title: Supervisor(s) (number and titles): Direct report(s) (number and titles):	Dates of employment:
Key achievement(s):	Compensation (base salary vs. bonus vs. commission vs. overtime vs. deferred compensation):
Reason for leaving:	

Prior Position #3

Company (size in terms of revenues or number of employees):	Industry:
Position title:	Dates of employment:
Supervisor(s) (number and titles): Direct report(s) (number and titles):	
Key achievement(s):	Compensation (base salary vs. bonus vs. commission vs. overtime vs. deferred compensation):
Reason for leaving:	

Also see Question 39.

G. Sample Drug Testing Policy

It is the policy of XYZ Company to meet its obligation to provide a drug-free, healthful, safe, and secure work environment. Therefore, it shall:

- Prohibit the unlawful manufacture, distribution, dispensation, possession, or use of a controlled substance on company premises or while conducting company business off XYZ premises.
- Applicants offered a position at XYZ may be required to pass a drug screening test as part of the pre-employment physical examination as a condition of employment. The test shall be administered in accordance with established standards designed to protect the accuracy of the test and the privacy of the applicant. Failure to pass the test will result in the withdrawal of the employment offer.

Violations of this policy shall be considered grounds for "discharge for cause" with possible legal consequences.

Also see Question 54.

H. Ben Franklin Close to Eliminate Candidates

	Candidate #1	Candidate #2	Candidate #3
1. Number of years of related experience			
2. Relative job stability at prior companies			
3. History of progression through the ranks at prior companies			
4. Performance evaluation scores (if available)			
5. Strength of references' recommendations			
6. Technical skills match			
7. Career progression: Is this a good move from a career development standpoint?			
8. Desire factor: Who wants this job the most?			
9. Personality match: Which individual's style best matches your corporate culture?			
10. Highest education level			
11. Minority/affirmative action recruitment goals			
12. Salary expectations			

Also see Question 55.

I. Sample Offer Letter

I am happy to confirm our offer for you to join XYZ Company on May 13, 2001, as the marketing manager. You will report to Heather Hand, vice president of marketing. This letter will confirm the terms of our offer.

Your initial compensation consists of a salary equal to $1,000.00 per month plus two weeks of vacation that begin to accrue from your date of hire. In addition, a benefit package, including medical, dental, life, disability options, and a qualified pension plan, will be made available to you effective the first of the month following thirty days of employment. Your compensation package is subject to modification during your employment in accordance with company policies and procedures. According to the terms of our current policy, this position is subject to a six-month introductory period, at the conclusion of which your performance will be reviewed.

Your employment with XYZ Company is not for a specified period of time and can be terminated by you or XYZ at any time, during or after the introductory period, with or without cause or advance notice. No promises, assurances, or other conduct, whether written or oral, can modify this paragraph unless set forth in a written employment agreement signed by you and by the chief executive officer or his designee.

By signing this letter, you agree that any dispute or controversy between you and XYZ Company, including without limitation any claims for breach of contract, statute or public policy, personal injury (tort), employment discrimination, or any other claim of any type arising out of or in connection with the termination of your employment, will be submitted to and determined by final binding arbitration in [city, state] in accordance with the provisions of the XYZ Company personnel policy manual in effect at the time the demand for arbitration is filed.

An orientation of new employees will be held in the Human Resources department on the second floor on Monday, May 13, at 8:00 A.M. The orientation will last until 1:00 P.M., and lunch will be served. Parking will be validated for your first day only at the Wilshire lot. Permit parking arrangements will be discussed during orientation.

Please bring to orientation documents that establish both your identity and employment eligibility. Enclosed for your review is a handout entitled "List of Acceptable Documents: Approved by the U.S. Department of Justice as Establishing Identity and Employment Eligibility." Failure to provide these documents may postpone your start date.

We look forward to your joining us at XYZ. Please acknowledge your acceptance of this job offer on the terms indicated by signing the enclosed copy of this letter and returning it to me as soon as possible.

Sincerely,

Heather Hand
Vice President, Marketing

I accept the position of marketing manager on the terms described above.

_____	_____
Signature	Date

Also see Question 60.

J. Sample Employment-at-Will Policies

Employment Application Language

In consideration of my employment, I agree to conform to the rules and standards of the Company and agree that my employment and compensation can be terminated at will, with or without cause, and with or without notice, at any time, either at my option or at the option of the Company. I understand that no employee or representative of the Company, other than its president, has the authority to enter into any agreement for employment for any specified period of time, or to make any express or implied agreement contrary to the foregoing. Further, the president of the Company may not alter the at-will nature of the employment relationship or enter into any employment agreement for a specified time unless the president and I both sign a written agreement that clearly and expressly specifies the intent to do so. I agree that this shall constitute a final and fully binding integrated agreement with respect to the at-will nature of my employment relationship and that there are not oral or collateral agreements regarding this issue.

Offer Letter Language

Your employment with XYZ Corporation is not for a specified period of time and can be terminated by you or the Company at any time, during or after the probationary period, with or without cause or advance notice. No promises, assurances, or other conduct, whether written or oral, can modify this paragraph unless set forth in a written employment agreement signed by you and the chief executive officer or his/her designee of XYZ Corporation.

Employee Handbook Language

In addition, I understand that no provision of this handbook is to be construed as a guarantee of employment. I understand and agree that my employment with XYZ Corporation is terminable at will, that I or XYZ Corporation can terminate the employment relationship at any time for any reason with or without notice, unless the terms of any applicable collective bargaining agreement provide otherwise.

I will return any previous employee handbooks to the human resources department and acknowledge this version as the one that describes my employment. I understand that this handbook is not a contract. *Other than the at-will policy,* XYZ Corporation reserves the right to make changes, additions, and deletions in these policies at any time and without notice, at its sole and absolute discretion. I agree to abide by the policies described in this handbook as they may be revised or interpreted by XYZ Corporation in the future and any new policies.

Also see Question 63.

K. Harassment Investigation Template

---

1. What is the nature of the perceived harassment? Specifically, was it a one-time occurrence of offensive behavior, or were there multiple occurrences? (Provide specific details.)

2. Is the perceived activity either sexual or gender-based in nature?   ☐ Yes   ☐ No

3. Is the harassment   ☐ physical,   ☐ verbal,   ☐ visual, or   ☐ auditory?

4. Does the conduct appear to be unwelcome?   ☐ Yes   ☐ No

5. Did the victim confront the alleged harasser and state that the behavior was inappropriate and needed to stop?   ☐ Yes   ☐ No
If so, when?

6. When was the immediate supervisor (or other responsible officer) made aware of the offensive behavior?

7. What, if anything, did the immediate supervisor tell this employee after notification in terms of an appropriate course of action to remedy the situation?

8. When was HR made aware of this issue (relative to the onset of the problem)?

9. Were there any prior accusations (or is there any corroborating evidence from other sources) made against the alleged harasser?   ☐ Yes   ☐ No

10. Are there additional witnesses for the investigation?   ☐ Yes   ☐ No
If yes, contact:

Follow-Up/Conclusion

Has the complainant been informed of the investigation's results? ☐ Yes ☐ No

Has the alleged harasser been informed of the investigation's results? ☐ Yes ☐ No

Recommended Course of Action:

_____

_____

_____

_____

Also see Question 66.

L. Sample Written Warnings

Written Warning: Inappropriate Workplace Conduct

This morning you engaged in insubordinate conduct when you responded to my request to complete the Jones file by the end of business. Your initial response was to *roll your eyes, sigh, and turn to me with your hands on your hips and state loudly*, "If you want that file completed by the end of the day, you can't ask me any other questions between now and then. I need to be left alone!" *Such sarcastic comments are unacceptable because they violate company standards of performance and conduct.*

First, you were aware of today's deadline for the Jones file over a week ago. Second, your concerns were shared loudly in front of three of your coworkers, and I perceived your tone of voice to be upset and uncooperative. Third, you do not have the discretion to insist that all other job responsibilities be removed while you work on a particular project.

In the future, I expect that you will never again voice your frustration in a rude and unprofessional manner. I expect that any future concerns that you have regarding the assignments on your desk will be shared with me privately in my office and not voiced publicly in front of others. Finally, I expect you to inform me anytime that you are falling behind on any of your work so that I can provide you with additional support to meet any pre-planned deadlines.

Also see Question 68.

Written Warning: Substandard Job Performance

There are multiple, serious performance and conduct transgressions that you have committed over the past thirty days and that have recently come to our attention as a result of examining your desk.

Issue 1: You were instructed to follow up on two special cases that were greater than $10,000 and to make first-level appeals to Medicare. We were already over the ninety-day guideline to file an appeal. You ignored that fact and filed the appeal, anyway. This is a consistent oversight on your part and one of your essential job responsibilities. Because you failed to meet the timeliness requirements, the case may not be considered on its merits. Your lack of judgment in taking the next appropriate step to "save the claim" may have caused our company to lose the right to collect moneys due.

Issue 2: Since our verbal counseling session with you on August 14 regarding excessive personal phone calls, you continue to make calls to your home phone, your husband's work phone, and your husband's cell phone. Telephone records show that you called those three telephone numbers a total of sixty-five times in the last month; in comparison, the Medicare office was called only twenty-two times. This suggests that you did not take your former warning as seriously as you could have.

I expect you to adhere strictly to your job duties from this point forward. I expect you to meet all deadlines and to inform me if, for whatever reason, you are falling behind in your work. You are not to make any more personal telephone calls without my approval; if an emergency call becomes necessary, you are to inform me immediately after the call about the nature of the emergency.

I recognize that you may have your own ideas for improving the situation at hand. Therefore, I encourage you to provide your own personal improvement plan input and suggestions on a separate sheet of paper if you wish.

However, you are now being placed on formal written notice that failure to provide immediate and sustained improvement may result in further disciplinary action up to and including dismissal.

Also see Question 70.

Final Written Warning: Substandard Job Performance

Despite your verbal counseling session on August 14 and your written warning on September 15, another serious claims error occurred that must be brought to your immediate attention. I instructed you three weeks ago to follow up on the post-ninety-day Descanso claim (account #91355) in order to remove it from your books. To date, you have taken no action on this claim. When I asked you why you hadn't followed up with the claim to close it out or why you hadn't informed me of the delay, you told me you simply "didn't have a chance to get to it." As a result, your lack of follow-through may bar our company from collecting $1,578 on that account. This is a violation of the written warning given to you last month.

I remind you that I expect you to adhere strictly to your job duties and follow up with your accounts on a timely and consistent basis. I expect you to meet all deadlines and to inform me if, for whatever reason, you are falling behind in your work. In addition, I expect you to complete all the necessary paperwork on the long-overdue Descanso account in order to remove it from our books. This must be completed within three business days.

I recognize that you may have your own ideas for improving the situation at hand. Therefore, I encourage you to provide your own personal improvement plan input and suggestions on a separate sheet of paper if you wish.

However, this will serve as a final written warning regarding substandard job performance. If you fail to demonstrate immediate and sustained improvement in your job performance or if you fail to meet any company standards of performance and conduct, you may be discharged for cause immediately.

Also see Question 70.

Written Warning Containing Multiple (Bundled) Infractions

Mary, on August 14, you were given a verbal warning regarding your excessive, unscheduled absenteeism. You committed yourself to minimizing any further occurrences of unauthorized absence and meeting all company standards of performance and conduct. However, by September 1, you had incurred an additional two days of unscheduled absence, and you were consequently given a written warning stating that any further incidents could lead to further disciplinary action up to and including dismissal.

Today, September 9, you engaged in inappropriate conduct with a coworker. Specifically, you engaged in a shouting match with a coworker in the lunchroom because you couldn't agree on what TV station to watch during your lunch break. Such conduct violates company standards.

You would normally receive a written warning for such inappropriate workplace conduct. However, because of your ongoing problem with unscheduled absenteeism, it appears that you may not have taken your previous warnings as seriously as you could have. It also appears that you are not accepting full responsibility for your actions and overall performance. As a result, a special probation with more stringent requirements is warranted.

Consequently you are now being placed on final written warning for both your performance and conduct. Any further violations of any company policies, procedures, or standards of performance and conduct will result in your immediate dismissal.

Also see Question 76.

Written Warning: Sexual Harassment

This written warning confirms that our company strongly disapproves of any conduct that *might constitute* sexual harassment. We are committed to guaranteeing all of our employees a friendly work environment. Your actions, however, violate company policy.

Your behavior *suggests* that you *may have created* an offensive environment. We expect that you will create a work environment that treats people with dignity and respect and never again engage in conduct that could *appear to* diminish a person's self-worth or sense of well-being.

I expect that you will never again speak with coworkers in a demeaning tone or make gestures or insinuations that *could be construed as* disrespectful or offensive. If you ever again make inappropriate gestures or comments or attempt to invade a coworker's space, make a coworker feel like "less of a person," demonstrate any offensive behavior, or violate any other standards of performance and conduct, you may be immediately discharged for cause.

Also see Question 86.

M. Sample Exit Interview Questionnaire

Part I: The Nature of Your Work Assignments and Job Responsibilities

1. XYZ Company appreciates the diverse nature of its workforce and encourages individuality and personal differences by providing a respectful work environment.
    (a) I strongly agree

  (b) I agree
  (c) I disagree
  (d) I strongly disagree
2. Most of your work assignments and job responsibilities were:
  (a) Very well defined
  (b) Only partially defined
  (c) Not very well defined
3. The time allowed for you to do most tasks on your job was:
  (a) More than needed
  (b) About right
  (c) Not enough to do a good job

Part II: The Relationship with Your Supervisor and Other Staff Members

4. Overall department morale was:
  (a) High
  (b) Average
  (c) Low
5. The working relationships with your peers within the department were cooperative:
  (a) Most of the time
  (b) Some of the time
  (c) Rarely
  (d) Not applicable
6. Any suggestions, questions, or problems that you brought to your supervisor's attention were:
  (a) Encouraged and resolved to your satisfaction
  (b) Discouraged or not resolved to your satisfaction
  (c) Not applicable
7. During the workday, your supervisor was:
  (a) Always available
  (b) Generally accessible
  (c) Frequently not available
8. Your supervisor's expectations of you were:
  (a) Too high or unrealistic
  (b) Fair under the circumstances
  (c) Too low
  (d) Don't know because of minimal feedback
9. Ongoing (informal) and formal performance feedback (via annual written performance appraisals) was provided to you:
  (a) Regularly and consistently
  (b) Occasionally
  (c) Rarely

Part III: Employee Compensation and Benefits Programs

10. The pay for your job was:
    (a) Too high for the work you were asked to do
    (b) About right for the level of responsibility you held
    (c) Too low for the work you did
11. The quality of employee benefits programs at XYZ Company is:
    (a) Better than at other companies
    (b) About equal to other companies
    (c) Not as good as at other companies
    (d) Not applicable
12. Our health insurance programs' costs are:
    (a) Better than at other companies
    (b) About equal to other companies
    (c) Not as good as at other companies
    (d) Not applicable
13. How would you rate your insurance carrier in terms of claims handling as well as selection of providers:
    (a) Excellent
    (b) Average
    (c) Poor
    (d) Not applicable
14. How would you rate your retirement benefits (including the XYZ Pension Plan and 401(k) Savings Plan) compared to the retirement benefits at other companies:
    (a) Excellent
    (b) Average
    (c) Poor
    (d) Not applicable
15. Our tuition reimbursement plan is:
    (a) Better than at other companies
    (b) About equal to other companies
    (c) Not as good as at other companies
    (d) Not applicable
16. Our sick leave and disability policies are:
    (a) Better than at other companies
    (b) About equal to other companies
    (c) Not as good as at other companies
    (d) Not applicable
17. The amount of vacation time granted is:
    (a) Better than at other companies
    (b) About equal to other companies
    (c) Not as good as at other companies
    (d) Not applicable

Part IV: Career Progression Opportunities and Training

18. Your career progression opportunities at XYZ were:
    (a) Excellent
    (b) Average
    (c) Poor
    (d) Not applicable
19. Throughout your employment, you:
    (a) Received the training that you needed
    (b) Didn't receive the training that you needed
    (c) Not applicable

Part V: The Reason You're Leaving XYZ Company

20. The major reason you are terminating (choose one) is:
    (a) Relocation
    (b) Retirement
    (c) Better job and/or wage opportunity
    (d) Transfer to another XYZ unit
    (e) Job insecurity
    (f) Incompatibility with supervisor
    (g) Layoff/end of assignment
    (h) Other _____
21. If you are leaving to work for another industry-related company, where are you going after you leave XYZ Company:
    (a) Acme Plastics Manufacturing
    (b) Taylor Plastics
    (c) Raleigh Group
    (d) Farragut Die and Molding
22. The best thing about working for XYZ Company (choose one) was:
    (a) Meaningful and challenging work
    (b) Nice people
    (c) Strong management and leadership
    (d) Encouragement and appreciation of diverse ideas and cultures
    (e) Pay and benefits
    (f) Opportunities for promotion and cross-training
    (g) Other _____
23. Which of the following unsatisfactory working conditions most hinders performance in your department (please choose only one):
    (a) Lack of supervisory communication regarding the direction and focus of our unit
    (b) Lack of supervisory appreciation for a job well done
    (c) The commute
    (d) Overly demanding work and long hours

    (e) Working conditions in the office (heat, space, and lighting)
    (f) Negative environment devoid of teamwork and camaraderie
    (g) Not applicable

24. Everything considered, how would you rate XYZ as a place to work:
    (a) Excellent
    (b) Average
    (c) Poor

For Supervisors Only

Part I: The Nature of Your Work Assignments and Job Responsibilities

25. With respect to personnel staffing, you were:
    (a) Adequately staffed most of the time
    (b) Occasionally short-staffed
    (c) Inadequately staffed most of the time
    (d) Not applicable

26. With respect to financial resources to accomplish your mission/function, you:
    (a) Had the dollars necessary to meet your goals
    (b) Occasionally lacked dollars
    (c) Were frequently short of dollars
    (d) Not applicable

27. Generally, candidates referred to you for your job vacancies by the human resources department were:
    (a) Well qualified
    (b) Minimally qualified
    (c) Not qualified
    (d) Not applicable

Part II: The Relationship with Your Supervisor and Other Staff Members

28. As a member of the management team in your department, you were involved in decision-making processes:
    (a) Most of the time
    (b) Some of the time
    (c) Rarely/never
    (d) Not applicable

29. As a member of the management team in your department, you were given the flexibility and responsibility to manage your staff:
    (a) Most of the time
    (b) Some of the time

(c) Rarely/never
(d) Not applicable

Part III: Employee Compensation and Benefits Programs

30. Reward systems that you could use to motivate your employees (including merit pools, bonuses, and/or overtime budget) were:
    (a) Adequate
    (b) Not quite sufficient
    (c) Clearly insufficient
    (d) Not applicable
31. Recruitment compensation salary ranges were competitive enough to attract qualified job candidates:
    (a) Most of the time
    (b) Some of the time
    (c) Rarely/never
    (d) Not applicable

Part IV: Career Progression Opportunities and Training

32. Training (formal or on-the-job) on how to supervise and manage is:
    (a) Adequate
    (b) Not quite sufficient
    (c) Clearly insufficient
    (d) Not applicable
33. When you wanted to get formal, off-site training for your employees, you were:
    (a) usually able to get it
    (b) usually unable to get it
    (c) didn't realize outside training was available
    (d) not applicable

Also see Question 72.

N. Sample Recognition Letter for a Previously Disciplined Employee

Travis, as you are aware, you were given a written warning regarding substandard customer service four months ago. Since management's intervention at that time, you attended two customer service training seminars and have demonstrated a new commitment to your role. As a result, you received two letters of recommendation from clients in the past week. Congratulations on your recent achievements! I will attach this document to the written warning in order to recognize your accomplishment and to thank you for having assumed responsibility for the problems that we experienced four months ago. Keep up the good work!

Also see Question 79.

O. Sample Performance Evaluation "Comments" for an Underperforming Employee

On June 30, 2001, Laura and I discussed my concerns regarding her performance and conduct over the past twelve months. However, I shared with Laura that not all these incidents were brought to her attention at the time they occurred. She understood that she would not meet expectations for the annual review period July 1, 2000–June 30, 2001. However, we will formally review her performance again in ninety days. A new review document will be created, and Janet may be eligible to participate in the company's merit pay plan at that time if her performance and conduct improve significantly.

Also see Question 80.

P. Sample Homework Assignment for a Paid Disciplinary Leave

In addition to placing you on a final written warning for inappropriate workplace conduct, our company will give you a day off with pay to rethink your commitment to the organization. The purpose of this administrative leave is to impress upon you the seriousness of your actions. If you choose not to return to work the day after tomorrow, we will respect your decision. However, if you decide to return to work, you will need to provide us with a one-page, written action plan that outlines the concrete steps that you are going to take to ensure that we never have to discuss this matter again. Without that written document, you will not be admitted back to work.

Understand that this is a once-in-a-career benefit. You will not be granted another day off with pay again for performance-related matters. This signed commitment letter will be placed in your personnel file upon your return to work. Thank you very much.

Also see Question 81.

Q. Sample Documentation for Excessive Absenteeism

Maintenance of good attendance is a condition of employment and an essential function of your job. In order to minimize hardships that may result from illness or injury, our company provides paid sick time. However, periodic sick leave taken on a repeated basis may be viewed as abuse of the system. It is your responsibility to establish legitimate illness or injury in order to receive sick leave pay.

You have incurred five incidents of unscheduled absence in this rolling calendar year:

- Friday, October 8, 2001
- Monday, October 11, 2001
- Friday, November 19, 2001
- Monday, November 22, 2001
- Thursday, December 23, 2001

This number of incidents has disrupted the workflow in our unit and has caused the department to incur unscheduled overtime because others have had to carry the extra workload. In addition, a temporary worker had to be assigned to your area so that the deadline for the Vanguard project could be met.

It is imperative that you minimize any future occurrences of unscheduled, unauthorized absence. Failure to demonstrate immediate and sustained improvement may result in further disciplinary action up to and including termination.

Or, if you have a specific company policy regarding absenteeism, you can include that information in place of the last paragraph:

You are now being placed on notice that, according to company policy, if you reach seven incidents of unauthorized absence in the rolling calendar year, you will be given a written warning. A ninth incident of unauthorized absence in the rolling calendar year will result in a final written warning. A tenth incident will result in your immediate dismissal.

Here is one way to respond to patterns of incidents of unscheduled absenteeism around regularly scheduled time off:

> Four of the five incidents of unscheduled absence occurred on either a Monday or a Friday. You have therefore demonstrated a pattern of taking time off around your regularly scheduled weekends.
>
> If any other patterns appear in the next year in terms of how you take time off—i.e., if you take days off either before or after weekends, holidays, or vacations—you will be subject to further disciplinary action up to and including dismissal.
>
> In addition, human resources will be notified of every additional occurrence of absenteeism from this point forward in order to provide you with additional support. Finally, you are now formally notified that any further occurrences of sick leave must be substantiated by a doctor's note. The doctor's note will not excuse the absence; it will, instead, allow you to access your sick leave accrual bank. The doctor's note will be necessary for you to return to work.

Also see Questions 82 and 83.

R. Sample Letter of Clarification

Letters of clarification first state your concerns with the individual's performance and then continue like this:

> This isn't a disciplinary document, Janet. It will not be placed in your formal personnel file and will not be shared with other members of management at this time. However, I have put my concerns in writing to impress upon you the seriousness of these multiple small errors. My greatest concern lies in the fact that you appear less focused on your work now than at any time in the past five years. You also appear to be apathetic about the outcome of your assignments, and several of your coworkers have asked me if you were feeling okay because they too noticed a change in your work.
>
> I want you to know that I'm here to help you in any way I can. On the other hand, I am holding you fully accountable for meeting all hospital expectations regarding performance and conduct. I recognize that you may have certain ideas to improve your performance. Therefore, I encourage you to provide your own personal improvement plan suggestions.

Please sign this document as evidence not only that you received it but also that you agree to accept full responsibility for fixing these problems and changing the perception problems that exist. I know you can do it, and I'm here to support you. Thank you.

Also see Question 87.

S. Sample Specific Termination Letter

This is to inform you that you are being terminated today for failure to perform your work at an acceptable level. On August 7, 2001, you received a verbal correction for substandard work performance and for an unwillingness to perform properly assigned work duties. On October 4, you received a written warning for substandard work performance and glass breakage. On November 2, you received a final written warning for overall substandard work performance.

In this period of time, you were sent to outside training on dealing with conflict in the workplace. Your immediate supervisor met with you daily for twenty minutes over a two-week period to ensure that you understood how to perform your job and to prioritize your work. You were also placed on a one-day paid decision-making leave to rethink your commitment to the company.

Today you committed an error in the handling of your cage wash duties. Namely, you failed to place the rabbit rack in the rack washer after spraying it down with acid. Because you did not notify your coworkers about this exception to standard operating procedures, a fellow worker handled the acid-covered rack and injured his hand.

Your failure to process equipment properly demonstrates an ongoing inability to perform at an acceptable level and a lack of concern for your job. I consequently have no choice but to sever this employment relationship.

Your final paycheck through the close of business today is attached. Within thirty days, we will issue you a statement of accrued benefits. You may choose to continue your medical insurance at your own expense via COBRA. Please contact Gail Lapins in Benefits at your earliest convenience. She will explain the status of your benefits as well as COBRA and 401(k) options and also arrange for the return of any company property.

Also see Question 93.

T. Confirmation of Resignation Letter

Doris, the purpose of this letter is to confirm that I have accepted your verbal resignation today, March 2, and I realize that March 16 will be your last day with our company. You will be relieved of your duties on that day, and you will become eligible for consideration for rehire in the future. Thank you for your contributions to XYZ Company for the past three years. I wish you well in your future career endeavors.

Also see Question 94.

U. Job Abandonment Letter

The purpose of this letter is to inform you that our company defines job abandonment as "failure to report to work without notice for any period of time longer than three consecutive work days." You did not report to or call work on Monday, May 1, or Tuesday, May 2. If you do not report to work or at least contact the company by the close of business on Wednesday, May 3, we will assume that you have abandoned your job. We will process your termination accordingly.

Also see Question 95.

V. Sample Separation Agreement and Release

Dear Michael:

On October 10, 2001, you were informed that ABC Financial has made the decision to eliminate your position as controller effective October 31, 2001. This letter will set forth in writing the terms and conditions of an agreement for an amicable separation of your employment. This letter will outline the payments and benefits for which you are entitled.

Your separation from employment will be effective October 31, 2001. You will have to turn in by the close of business on October

31 all keys, cards, documents, and other company property or proprietary information. You will be paid your final paycheck at that time, which will include your pay through October 31, 2001, as well as any hours of accrued but unused vacation and any hours of holiday pay. Sick time is not a vested benefit, and, therefore, you will not receive any compensation for unused sick leave.

As additional compensation, you will receive twenty four (24) weeks of severance pay, which will be paid in accordance with our regular biweekly pay cycle.

As part of this separation agreement, you may qualify for unemployment benefits through the California Employment Development Department. ABC Financial will not contest your application for unemployment compensation.

You will receive outplacement assistance through the services of Alexander and Associates. You will participate in their Modified Executive Outplacement Program, which will assist you in finding gainful employment for the next six months. Heidi Clair, your outplacement consultant, will provide further details about this outplacement arrangement.

Your group coverage will continue through the end of this month. You will be offered the opportunity to elect COBRA continuation coverage for the plans that are subject to this provision and in which you are eligible to participate. If you choose to elect COBRA, coverage will be continued effective November 1. We will pay your medical premium as a single participant through your severance period.

You will be entitled to receive pension benefits to the extent that you are vested in the company retirement annuity program, in accordance with the terms of the plan.

All other benefits, compensation, and privileges of your employment not specified above will cease as of October 31, 2001.

In consideration of this agreement, you hereby release ABC Financial and all of its affiliated or related entities, as well as past and present officers, directors, employees, representatives, and agents of ABC Financial and any of its affiliated or related entities, from any and all claims, demands, debts, losses, obligations, liabilities, costs, expenses, attorneys' fees, rights of action, and causes of action of any kind or character whatsoever, whether known or unknown, suspected or unsuspected, arising prior to the date of this agreement, all of which are also referred to below as the "Released Claims."

You understand and agree that the Released Claims include without limitation any rights or claims you may have that arise out of or are related to your employment with ABC Financial or the termination of that employment and any rights or claims under the Age Discrimination and Employment Act, 29 U.S.C. Section 621 et seq., which prohibits age discrimination in employment; Title VII of the Civil Rights Act of 1964, which prohibits discrimination on the basis of race, color, national origin, religion, or sex; and all other federal, state, and local laws and regulations prohibiting employment discrimination or wrongful discharge from employment.

You further agree that you shall not communicate, orally or in writing, generally, specifically, or by implication, to any person except for governmental or law enforcement agencies any facts or opinions that might reflect adversely upon ABC Financial or any of its affiliated or related entities or disparage, degrade, or harm the reputation of ABC Financial or any of its affiliated or related agencies in the conduct of your personal or professional endeavors.

You acknowledge that you may hereafter discover facts different from, or in addition to, those which you know or believe to be true with respect to the Released Claims and agree that this agreement and the releases contained herein shall be and remain effective in all respects, notwithstanding such different or additional facts or the discovery of the facts.

This agreement represents a compromise of claims and shall not be construed as an admission by any party of any liability or any contention or allegation made by any other party or a suggestion that any claims or liabilities exist or would have any basis.

You agree that you will keep this agreement and its terms strictly confidential and will not disclose this information to any third party—other than any counsel, tax return preparer, or spouse, who also agree to keep this matter strictly confidential, or to any other parties as may be required by law—including any past, present, or future employees of ABC Financial or its affiliated or related entities.

You will have a period of twenty-one (21) days from the date of this letter to review and consider this agreement, with the assistance of counsel should you so choose, before signing it. You may take as much of this twenty-one day period of time to consider this agreement as you wish prior to signing it.

You may revoke this agreement within seven (7) days after you sign it. Revocation may be made by delivering a written notice of revocation to me within the seven-day period. If you revoke this agreement in a timely fashion, it shall not become effective or enforceable, and all payments provided in this agreement other than your final paycheck, including without limitation severance payments, will not be made.

This agreement shall be governed by California law. It represents the entire agreement between the parties and supersedes all prior negotiations, representations, or agreements between the parties, either written or oral, on its subject matter. This agreement may be amended only by a document designated as an amendment to agreement and executed by the parties to it.

I regret that this reduction in force is upon us. I thank you for your dedication to our company's financial needs over the past eight years. Please review this offer carefully and with the assistance of counsel if you choose. If you accept the offer, please sign below and return the original of this letter so that I receive it within twenty-one (21) days. Please contact me with any questions you may have.

Sincerely,

John Panico
Chief Financial Officer

I have read and understood the content of this letter, and I accept the offer by ABC Financial and agree to the terms of agreement contained in the letter.

Michael Jaimes	Date

Also see Question 108.

W. Sample Recommendation Letter for a Terminated or Laid-Off Employee

The purpose of this letter is to confirm Janet Faraci's employment with XYZ Corporation as a human resources manager from April 10, 1999, to February 25, 2001. Janet's position was eliminated as part of a companywide reduction in force. She reported to the director of human resources and supervised three human resources generalists.

Janet's performance reviews in January 2000 and January 2001 show that she exceeded performance standards. She was commended for having lowered the cost-per-hire in her recruitment areas by implementing an online recruitment campaign that reduced our company's recruitment advertising costs by 60 percent. Turnover in her client groups was reduced from 26 percent to 21 percent in that same time period as she implemented effective management training programs and leadership workshops. She didn't miss one day of work since she began with us, and the consistent positive feedback from her clients improved the reputation of the human resources department.

She was not subject to any disciplinary actions during her tenure. She is rehirable, and we wish her well in her future career endeavors.

Also see Question 109.

X. Sample Release Form for Providing References After Separation

---

Option 1

I authorize XYZ Company to release only my dates of employment and last title held. I release XYZ from any liability associated with providing prospective employers with this information.

X _____   _____
                    Signature   Date

Option 2

I authorize XYZ Company to release any and all information related to my on-the-job performance, including my strengths, weaknesses, and areas for future development. I recognize that this oral reference will specifically address my achievements as well as shortcomings associated with my employment, including references to my annual performance reviews and any progressive disciplinary measures taken against me.

I release XYZ from any liability associated with providing prospective employers with information related to my employment as indicated above.

X _____   _____
                    Signature   Date

Also see Question 109.

Y. Comparison Template for a Layoff Analysis

Employee name:	Employee name:
Title:	Title:
Supervisor:	Supervisor:
Date of hire:	Date of hire:
Adjusted service date:	Adjusted service date:
☐ At will ☐ Collective bargaining agreement ☐ Employment contract (End date: _____)	☐ At will ☐ Collective bargaining agreement ☐ Employment contract (End date: _____)
Demographic:	Demographic:
Department demographics post-RIF:	Department demographics post-RIF:
Length of time in position:	Length of time in position:
Employment history with company:	Employment history with company:
Employment history prior to joining company:	Employment history prior to joining company:
Highest education level:	Highest education level:
Specific skills, knowledge, and abilities relative to current position:	Specific skills, knowledge, and abilities relative to current position:
Performance evaluation history:	Performance evaluation history:
Progressive discipline history:	Progressive discipline history:
Other considerations:	Other considerations:

Adjusted Service Date is the date of original hire less any leaves of absence or unauthorized breaks in service. For example, an employee originally hired in 1998 who left in 2000 and returned in 2001 may be considered a two-year employee, rather than a three-year employee. Similarly, an employee who took a six-month personal leave of absence may not have that time counted toward tenure. However, that's a matter of company policy regarding bridging service dates.

If a union contract exists, you must follow its detailed guidelines regarding bumping privileges whenever exercising employee layoffs. If an employee is governed by an employment agreement for a set period of time, it probably does not make sense to let that individual go since the company will most likely be obligated to pay out the remainder of the contract. Therefore, those on employment contracts are often the least likely to be separated from the company during a reduction in force.

Ethnicity, gender, and age can play an important role when laying off employees. For example, if you select a Hispanic female over forty for layoff when everyone else in the department is a white male under forty, then your actions may expose you to a discrimination claim. Although many employment defense attorneys argue that it's best to *consider* this particular issue without *documenting* it anywhere in your file, we will retain this "demographic" section of our template so that this important issue gets its just consideration.

Similarly, to fend off legal challenges of discrimination, consider what the department's or company's demographics will look like after the reduction-in-force. Here's an example: If a department with sixty employees is 40 percent white, 60 percent minority, and 40 percent male, 60 percent female, then see how those numbers would change after the planned layoff. If a significant shift away from diversity in terms of ethnicity, age, or gender would result, then your organization could be exposed to a class-action discrimination charge. As always, obtain the appropriate legal advice after considering a demographics review and before exercising a layoff.

One of the most critical factors to consider when identifying the worker least qualified to assume the remaining job duties after a position elimination is employee performance reviews. Few documents provide information as critical as a relevant written record when you are determining a company's course of action at a time of layoff.

Written warnings, suspensions, or demotions, especially if recent, will often dictate which individual is least qualified to assume the remaining job duties after a position elimination. If one employee is on final written warning for unsatisfactory job performance, attendance, or conduct, then that individual's written record may compel you to lay off that particular person—even if she has the most seniority in the group.

Also see Question 103.

Z. Sample Bumping Provisions for Layoffs

An employee without sufficient seniority to remain in his/her classification in the department may exercise seniority rights to displace a less senior employee:

(a) Within the same department in a lower classification, provided that, in the Employer's reasonable judgment, the employee seeking to displace has substantially the same or better work-related skills, qualifications, abilities, performance record, disciplinary history, and attendance record as the potentially displaced employee, or, if no such positions are available,

(b) Outside the department in the same classification, provided that, in the Employer's reasonable judgment, the employee seeking to displace has substantially the same or better work-related skills, qualifications, abilities, performance record, disciplinary history, and attendance record as the potentially displaced employee.

Also see Question 104.

AA. Sample Management Rights Clause in the Bargaining Agreement (with a Union)

Management's Retained Rights

Except as specifically limited by the terms of this Agreement, the Employer retains all rights and authority to direct, manage, and control its business and operations. Such rights and authority retained by the Employer include, but are not limited to, the right to direct the work of its employees, to determine the times and hours of operations, to determine the kinds and levels of services to be provided and the means of providing them, to discontinue work or services, to select the equipment used by employees, to determine staffing patterns, to determine the classifications and number of personnel required, to specify and assign work requirements, work schedules, and overtime, to schedule and change working hours, shifts, and days off, to establish and change work rules and safety rules and penalties for violation thereof, *to create, change, combine, and abolish jobs, departments, or facilities,* in whole or in part, subject to applicable licensing requirements, to modify job descriptions, to build, move, modify, or relocate facilities and the work performed therein, to establish budget procedures and determine budgetary allocations, *to subcontract work, provided the Union is given reasonable notice and an opportunity to discuss the effects of such action on bargaining unit employees,* to assign work and to decide which employees are qualified to perform work, to hire, classify, assign, transfer, evaluate, demote, promote, lay off, and re-call employees, to discipline, suspend, and terminate employees for cause, to maintain the discipline and efficiency of employees, and to take action on any matter in the event of an emergency.

Also see Question 105.

Glossary

absence without leave (AWOL) Absence of an employee from work without having first obtained permission. Also known as job abandonment.

adverse impact The negative effects of employment practices, including, but not restricted to, acts that affect a protected group both significantly and unfavorably.

affirmative action The right of employees to be treated equally in regard to hiring, pay, and promotion regardless of their sex, religion, race, or physical or mental ability.

arbitration agreement An agreement between employer and employees to arbitrate all work-related disputes, including statutory or civil rights claims, guaranteeing fairness and due process.

behavior-based interviewing A technique of interviewing that analyzes candidates' past actions and experiences to try to project how a candidate might react in future situations.

bundling offenses Grouping together violations that are fundamentally unrelated in order to document poor performance.

constructively discharge For the employer to make the workplace conditions so egregious that the employee is compelled to leave.

contingency search firm An organization or consulting firm that searches for qualified candidates usually earning less than $100,000. Its fee is earned only if a client company hires one of its candidates.

de minimis infraction   A minor performance- or conduct-related infraction that normally doesn't rise to the level of immediate termination. A de minimis infraction may instead result in verbal counseling or possibly a written warning.

direct sourcing   An attempt to fill positions by cold-calling or by soliciting from competitor firms.

discharge   Termination of an employee for cause.

Employee Assistance Program (EAP)   A confidential service provided by an employer to help employees work out personal issues, such as substance abuse, depression, family crises, and suicide risks.

employment-at-will   A legal agreement between employer and employee that maintains the right of either party to end the employment relationship at any time for any reason. There are many legal exceptions to these agreements.

Family Medical Leave Act (FMLA)   Federal law that mandates unpaid leave of up to twelve weeks to care for immediate family members with serious health conditions.

"for cause" termination   Termination that results from substandard job performance, inappropriate workplace conduct, procedural violations, or absenteeism or tardiness. Also known as just cause termination.

high-potential hire   A new hire who will maximize an employer's return on investment by staying with the company, progressing through the ranks, and adding to the company's technical skills base.

independent contractors   Workers who do not receive benefits. They are instead paid by the project and offer their services to the general public.

job as property doctrine   A legal theory asserting that the right to work is so intrinsic to American citizens that work should not be denied arbitrarily or capriciously without just cause as accorded under the Fourteenth Amendment.

mass layoff	Defined by the Worker Adjustment and Retraining Notification Act as a loss of at least fifty full-time employees who constitute at least 33 percent of the full-time employees at a single site of employment.
measurable standard	An expectation of work responsibilities that is specific, measurable, and clearly communicated in advance.
moving party	The party in a resignation or termination that picks the last day the employee works or receives wages.
plant closing	As defined by the Worker Adjustment and Retraining Notification Act, a layoff of fifty or more employees over a thirty-day period for a period of at least six months.
probationary period	A specified time period during which the behavior and performance of an employee are closely monitored. If the employee does not meet the company's standards during that time period, the employer can take disciplinary action up to and including termination.
progressive discipline	A series of attempts that employers make to turn around poor-performing employees, using verbal and written performance warnings.
protected class	A group of people who share common characteristics and are protected from discrimination and harassment. Some protections have the backing of federal and/or state laws. Examples of protected classes are persons of a particular race, color, religion, creed, sex, national origin, age, disability, veteran status, and sexual orientation.
qualified privilege	A legal doctrine that protects employers from defamation claims when providing references. Employers must offer reference statements in good faith to someone who

	shares a common interest and must limit their comments to that common interest.
reasonable accommodation	The Americans with Disabilities Act of 1990 requirement that employers must make adjustments for disabled persons, including but not limited to modifying work schedules, restructuring jobs, making physical modifications to the work area, installing special equipment, and providing a translator.
resignation by mutual consent	An alternative to firing for cause. Allows the employee to save face and makes the employee the moving party.
retained search firm	An organization or management consulting firm that searches for qualified candidates who are usually earning $100,000 or more. Its fee is paid in three increments regardless of whether a candidate is hired.
separation agreement	A release form signed by an employee who is being terminated that stipulates any extra compensation the person will receive in exchange for not making any claims against the company.
Worker Adjustment and Retraining Notification Act (WARN)	A federal law requiring that a company give advance notice of a massive layoff or plant closing.
workplace due process	A process for disciplining employees that includes: communicating the problem with the employee, identifying measurable goals for addressing the problem, specifying a time period for improvement, and identifying the consequences of inaction.

Resources

Campus Recruitment

The College Placement Council is the umbrella organization for all campus recruitment. Learn more at the National Association of Colleges and Employers Web site at www.naceweb.org.

Career Management/Outplacement Services

For more information, call the International Association of Career Management Professionals (IACMP) at (650) 359-6911, or connect on the Web at www.iacmp.org.

A useful resource is *The Directory of Outplacement and Career Management Firms* (Kennedy Information, 1999, 531 pages). For more information, call Kennedy Information at (800) 531-0007, or connect on the Web at www.kennedyinfo.com.

Contingency Firms

Consult the *National Directory of Personnel Services*, published annually by the National Association of Personnel Services, 3133 Mt. Vernon Ave., Alexandria, Va., 22305, (703) 684-0180.

Drug Testing

For information, refer to American Management Association's 1996 survey *Workplace Drug Testing and Drug Abuse Policies*. For more information, contact American Management Association at (212) 903-8052.

The Institute for a Drug-Free Workplace in Washington, D.C., can be reached at (202) 842-7400. *A Guide to State Drug Testing Laws and Legislation* (9th ed., 2001) is a 650-page manual describing, state-by-state, what employers can and can't do regarding workplace drug testing. For more information, visit the institute's Web site at www.drugfreeworkplace.org.

Independent Contractors

Refer to IRS Publication 1779, *Employee Independent Contractor Brochure.* You can get a free copy from the IRS Forms Distribution Center by calling (800) 829-3676 (1-800-TAX-FORM).

Internet Recruiting

Consult Ray Schreyer and John McCarter, *The Employer's Guide to Recruiting on the Internet* (Impact Publications, 1998), or visit America's Job Bank, www.ajb.dni.us.com.

For a complete listing of free online resume sources, please see either the Riley Guide or Job Hunt at the following addresses:
www.dbm.com/jobguide
www.job-hunt.org

Resumes

news:us.jobs.resumes	United States focus
news:misc.jobs.resumes	General focus
news:bionet.jobs.wanted	Biotech industry focus
news:nyc.jobs.wanted	New York City geographical focus
news:alt.medical.sales.jobs.resumes	Medical sales focus
news:sci.research.postdoc	Job posting for post-doctorate research fellows in the sciences
news:ba.jobs.contract	Contract jobs in the San Francisco Bay area
news:la.jobs	Los Angeles geographical focus
news:de.markt.jobs	Positions in Germany

General Employment Web sites
(according to total reach)

Site	Location	Features
Monster Board 1-800-MONSTER	www.monster.com	Fee to post: $251–$300 Posting period: 60 days # of unique visitors per month: 4.5 million Fee to mine: $5,000 for 3 months; $9,400/year # of resumes in database: 5.9 million
Headhunter.net (770) 349-2704	www.headhunter.net	Fee to post: $100 or less Posting period: 30 days # of unique visitors per month: 3.2 million Fee to mine: $1,500/3 months; $3,600/year # of resumes in database: 240,000
HotJobs (212) 672-1517	www.hotjobs.com	Fee to post: $195 Posting period: 30 days # of unique visitors per month: 3.4 million Fee to mine: **None** # of resumes in database: 2.4 million
America's Job Bank (518) 457-3488	www.ajb.dni.us.com	Fee to post: **None** Posting period: 45 days # of unique visitors per month: Not reported Fee to mine: **None** # of resumes in database: 900,000
Jobs.com (888) JOBSCOM	www.jobs.com	Fee to post: $100 or less Posting period: 30–60 days # of unique visitors per month: 3 million Fee to mine: $495/month # of resumes in database: Not reported

Career Builder (888) 670-8326	www.careerbuilder.com	Fee to post: $175/single posting Posting period: 30 days # of unique visitors per month: 3 million Fee to mine: Not reported # of resumes in database: 1.5 million
Career Magazine (303) 440-5110	www.careermag.com	Fee to post: $100 or less Posting period: 30 days # of unique visitors per month: 500,000 Fee to mine: $2,500/year # of resumes in database: 100,000

Source: Peter D. Weddle, *Weddle's Recruiter's Guide to Employment Web Sites 2001* (New York: AMACOM, 2001).

Boutique Employment Web sites (in alphabetical order)

Banking Jobs (615) 259-9990	www.bankjobs.com	Fee to post: $100 or less Posting period: 30 days # of unique visitors per month: 60,000 Fee to mine: $895/year # of resumes in database: 7,800
Bilingual Jobs (212) 504-8099	www.bilingual-jobs.com	Fee to post: over $300 Posting period: 30 days # of unique visitors per month: 20,000 Fee to mine: $500/month # of resumes in database: 2,000
Insurance Career Center (212) 633-3603	www.insurance.ce.com	Fee to post: **None** Posting period: 90 days # of unique visitors per month: Not reported Fee to mine: Yes # of resumes in database: Not reported

Nonprofit Career Network (888) 844-4870	www.nonprofitcareers.com	Fee to post: $100 or less Posting period: 90 days # of unique visitors per month: 1 million Fee to mine: **None** # of resumes in database: 300
Overseas Jobs No phone listed	www.overseas.jobs.com	Fee to post: $100 or less Posting period: 60 days # of unique visitors per month: 155,000 Fee to mine: Not available # of resumes in database: Not available
Public Sector (212) 821-1291	www.publicsectorjobs.com	Fee to post: $101–$150 Posting period: 30 days # of unique visitors per month: Not reported Fee to mine: $995/year # of resumes in database: Not reported
Recent College Grads (800) JOB-TRAK	www.jobtrak.com	Fee to post: $100 or less Posting period: 30 days # of unique visitors per month: 1 million Fee to mine: None (fee planned) # of resumes in database: 400,000
Showbizjobs (323) 851-6442	www.showbizjobs.com	Fee to post: $101–$150 Posting period: 30 days # of unique visitors per month: 210,000 Fee to mine: **None** # of resumes in database: 1,500
Teachers (916) 723-0107	www.k12jobs.com	Fee to post: $100 or less Posting period: 35 days # of unique visitors per month: 54,000 Fee to mine: Not available # of resumes in database: Not available

Telecommuting (847) 835-2180	www.tjobs.com	Fee to post: **None** Posting period: 60 days # of unique visitors per month: 71,000 Fee to mine: **None** # of resumes in database: 1,800
Veterans (877) 838-5627	www.vetjobs.com	Fee to post: $100 or less Posting period: 90 days # of unique visitors per month: 20,000 Fee to mine: $2,000–$5,000 # of resumes in database: 15,000

Legal References for Hiring and Firing

Sources include Diane Arthur, *The Employee Recruitment and Retention Handbook* (New York: AMACOM, 2001); R. Brian Dixon, *Federal Wage and Hour Laws* (Alexandria, Va.: SHRM Foundation, 1994); and Donald Weiss, *Fair, Square, and Legal: Safe Hiring, Managing, and Firing Practices to Keep You and Your Company Out of Court*, 3d ed. (New York: AMACOM, 1999).

Recruitment and Retention

Consult the newsletter of the National Institute of Business Management, *Success in Recruiting and Retaining*, available monthly from the National Institute of Business Management, McLean, Virginia, (800) 543-2049.

Retained Search Firms

Resources include the *Directory of Executive Recruiters* from Kennedy Information, (800) 531-0007, www.kennedyinfo.com, and *The Euro Directory: Executive Search and Selection Firms in Europe*, from The Recruiting and Search Report, (800) 634-4548.

Sexual Harassment

D. Orlov and M. Roumell, *What Every Manager Needs to Know About Sexual Harassment* (New York: AMACOM, 1999).

Temp Agencies

Refer to *The Directory of Temporary Placement Firms for Executives, Managers, and Professionals* (9th ed., 1999, 504 pages), published by Kennedy Information. For more information, call Kennedy at (800) 531-0007, or contact them on the Web at www.kennedyinfo.com.

Violence in the Workplace

For information, contact the National Institute for the Prevention of Workplace Violence in Lake Forest, California, at (949) 770-5264.

Workplace Absenteeism

Refer to the Commerce Clearing House (CCH) Inc.'s *1999 Unscheduled Absence Survey*, available from CCH at (800) 835-5224, Dept. 7004.

Index